It Happened to Me

Series Editor: Arlene Hirschfelder

Books in the It Happened to Me series are designed for inquisitive teens digging for answers about certain illnesses, social issues, or lifestyle interests. Whether you are deep into your teen years or just entering them, these books are gold mines of up-to-date information, riveting teen views, and great visuals to help you figure out stuff. Besides special boxes highlighting singular facts, each book is enhanced with the latest reading list, websites, and an index. Perfect for browsing, there's loads of expert information by acclaimed writers to help parents, guardians, and librarians understand teen illness, tough situations, and lifestyle choices.

1. *Learning Disabilities: The Ultimate Teen Guide,* by Penny Hutchins Paquette and Cheryl Gerson Tuttle, 2003.
2. *Epilepsy: The Ultimate Teen Guide,* by Kathlyn Gay and Sean McGarrahan, 2002.
3. *Stress Relief: The Ultimate Teen Guide,* by Mark Powell, 2002.
4. *Making Sexual Decisions: The Ultimate Teen Guide,* by L. Kris Gowen, PhD, 2003.
5. *Asthma: The Ultimate Teen Guide,* by Penny Hutchins Paquette, 2003.
6. *Cultural Diversity: Conflicts and Challenges: The Ultimate Teen Guide,* by Kathlyn Gay, 2003.
7. *Diabetes: The Ultimate Teen Guide,* by Katherine J. Moran, 2004.
8. *When Will I Stop Hurting? Teens, Loss, and Grief: The Ultimate Teen Guide,* by Edward Myers, 2004.
9. *Volunteering: The Ultimate Teen Guide,* by Kathlyn Gay, 2004.
10. *Organ Transplants: A Survival Guide for Recipients and Their Families: The Ultimate Teen Guide,* by Tina P. Schwartz, 2005.
11. *Medications: The Ultimate Teen Guide,* by Cheryl Gerson Tuttle, 2005.
12. *Image and Identity: Becoming the Person You Are,* by L. Kris Gowen and Molly McKenna, 2005.

Image and Identity

Becoming the Person You Are

L. KRIS GOWEN, PhD
MOLLY McKENNA, PhD

It Happened to Me, No. 12

The Scarecrow Press, Inc.
Lanham, Maryland • Toronto • Oxford
2005

SCARECROW PRESS, INC.

Published in the United States of America
by Scarecrow Press, Inc.
A wholly owned subsidiary of
The Rowman & Littlefield Publishing Group, Inc.
4501 Forbes Boulevard, Suite 200, Lanham, Maryland 20706
www.scarecrowpress.com

PO Box 317
Oxford
OX2 9RU, UK

British Library Cataloguing in Publication Information Available

Library of Congress Cataloging-in-Publication Data

Gowen, L. Kris, 1968–
  Image and identity : becoming the person you are / L. Kris Gowen, Molly McKenna.
    p. cm. — (It happened to me ; no. 12)
  Includes bibliographical references and index.
  ISBN 0-8108-4909-7 (hardcover : alk. paper) ISBN 978-0-8108-4909-9
  1. Identity (Psychology) in adolescence. I. McKenna, Molly. II. Title. III. Series.
  BF724.3.I3G69 2005
  155.5'182—dc22

                                                                    2005000088

∞™ The paper used in this publication meets the minimum requirements of
American National Standard for Information Sciences—Permanence of Paper
for Printed Library Materials, ANSI/NISO Z39.48-1992.
Manufactured in the United States of America.

Contents

Introduction:
Image and
Identity

So, who are you anyway? What makes you tick? What do you love to do? Whom do you hang with? Where are you from? Where are you going? And why are we asking all these questions? And what the heck does all this have to do with this book?

Welcome to our book on image and identity. We wanted to write this because psychologists and educators (which we are) believe that the primary task of adolescence is forming one's identity. But what does that mean, anyhow? What is an "identity"? And how does one get formed in the first place? One way to start thinking about this is to imagine that you are going to write an online profile, looking to meet other people. What would you include? Sure, most profiles start with something like "Male, 17, I love NASCAR, classical music, and traveling . . . " But, if you look more closely, people seem to be using words like these as abbreviations to communicate who they are.

What would you include in your profile? Would you include your race or ethnicity? Why? Would activities that you enjoy come to mind? How about where you are from? Your role in your family? How far you got in school? Personality traits, like being shy or adventurous? And what are you hoping people will think if they read your profile? In general, what do you want people to know about you and why?

We think of identity as the sum of all the different pieces that come to mind when you try to answer the question "Who are you?" Identity is a sense of self—a huge and sometimes messy concept made up of your personality, your experiences, your traits, your hopes, your preferences, and more. It is who you are. However, we aren't really born as the person we're going to be for the rest of our lives. If you think about what you were like at the age of five, you'll probably realize that you spent your time doing very different things than you do now. You liked different things; you hung out with different people. Your identity is always changing as you go through different experiences and learn new things, about yourself and about the larger world. Most of this development seems to happen during your teen years—adolescence. During this time, we learn more about how to be in the world, and we choose to commit to various aspects of ourselves and our experiences. We decide things like how strongly we value education and learning, how close we want to be to our families, what is worth spending our time on, whether we are passionate or laid back or something in between, which skills we most want to learn, and what we might want to do for a living. We think about and start to decide a lot of things in our teen years.

How the process of becoming ourselves occurs has been studied a lot by social science researchers. To geek out on you a little bit, there are some important factors in identity development that come up regularly as a way to think about it. One model suggests that the important parts of identity development are *crisis* and *commitment*. Crisis is the process of questioning who you are—really devoting energy to thinking about and evaluating who you are and what is important to you. Commitment is the conscious decision to have a certain characteristic or trait be a part of yourself. Generally, teen identity is characterized by being in crisis but not yet committing—you're figuring things out, but you haven't decided anything yet. However, there are some things that you might be committed to that you haven't really gone through a crisis about. For example, if your family has raised you in a certain religion and you follow its tenets and customs without having thought through your personal attitudes toward it very much, that is something you have committed to without a crisis.

As part of the process of figuring out who you are, you may try on certain ways of being, like costumes almost, to see if they fit or feel good. You may try new activities or adopt some different values or beliefs. And you will almost certainly examine the people around you as part of finding role models, evaluating them, and then sometimes choosing not to be like them. You may embrace or discard family traditions and relationships. During this period, some days you will feel that you know it all and are comfortable with the decisions that you have made. On other days, however, you will be uncertain and confused; you may feel adrift or lost. And it is totally okay to feel both ways—it is completely normal to change your mind a lot during this time.

It is worth noting that different parts of yourself become more important at different times, usually just after certain traits or roles become most obvious to you. Most children realize at the age of about two that they are a particular gender—girl or boy. This then can become a part of how they see themselves. Prior to that they were probably just Billy or Susie. Other portions of our identity become more critical as we mature. For example, most teenagers don't feel that their career is a big part of how they define themselves. This is probably because your career isn't even really established yet—you might have a hunch about what you want to do for a living, but it hasn't really become a burning issue. Later in your life, however, your job or career will likely be a very important factor that defines how you see yourself. So the pieces of your identity are still falling together as your life goes on and you add new experiences and roles to your life.

So that's the identity part. However, you've probably noticed that the title of this book is *Image and Identity*. We think that considering what your identity is made up of is incredibly important, and something that probably takes up a huge portion of your mental time and energy. But we also spend time thinking about what other people think of us—of who we are. It is impossible not to worry about how we are seen by others. We consider how other people will see us if we make certain choices. For example, if you really love playing a certain sport, you will probably be very aware of what others think of that sport and what assumptions they may make about you as someone who plays it. We get concerned with our *image*—the way that other people see us. While *identity* is a more internal idea, about what *you* think about yourself and the parts that you're made up of, *image* is more about what the *world* sees—what you put out there. It's about both what you want other people to see and what other people might end up seeing on their own.

Despite the fact that you're constantly told to "be yourself," you can't help but be aware of how who you are affects the way that you're treated. In our world, different kinds of people elicit different reactions. Being tall, short, a smoker, a non-smoker, religious, political, having different hobbies—these all have a profound effect on how other people relate to you. And we take the reactions that other people have to us into account as we figure out who we are—they influence the things that we're comfortable emphasizing or making public about our identity. In writing this book, we have to acknowledge that. As we talk about various things that might be important to you, we will also spend some time considering what it means to *publicly* commit to certain pieces of your identity—the parts that become your image.

One of the struggles of adolescence is working toward independence at a time when you still might live at home and rely on your parents for things you need. Sometimes you may find yourself thinking about how to be your own person, separate and independent from your parents, freely making choices about how you want to spend your time and who you want to be. These are all ways to demonstrate your individuality. At the same time, however, you may just want to be ordinary, like everybody else. It can be difficult to stand out and be different, and sometimes blending into the crowd feels more comfortable. We may want to just do what other people do or be like other folks, because it can be easier. In the end, however, you will probably have to face up to being both an individual and part of a crowd. You are unlike anyone else in the world—no one else has the same combination of traits, experiences, and preferences that you do. But you are also just another human being, living life like everybody else. This realization can make thinking about your identity a little bit easier—to know that no matter what you do, you will be both unique and ordinary.

One of the sad things about American society is that we have very few rituals to mark the transition from adolescent to adult. Sure, there is getting your driver's license, or being able to vote, or going on a first date, or having a first kiss—but our society as a whole doesn't seem to really celebrate becoming more of a grown-up. That is probably, in part, because it's not like you wake up one morning and are an adult. Instead, the process is a lot slower and more gradual. The Amish people (a religious group found in various

RITUALS

What is a ritual anyway? As defined by the Merriam-Webster dictionary, a ritual is "the established form for a ceremony" or "a customarily repeated often formal act or series of acts." A ceremony is defined as "a formal act or series of acts prescribed by ritual, protocol, or convention." It means the way of doing things as accepted by tradition—a regular pattern of actions that mark something. Rituals can be performed regularly, again and again, or only once, to designate a particular occasion or change. The way some religions pray—saying the Hail Mary or counting rosary beads, for example—are religious rituals. The pattern of events that make up a wedding ceremony is a ritual. Organizations sometimes have rituals; in Girl Scouts, when younger girls become full scouts, the ceremony ("flying up") is a ritual. High school graduation is a ritual.

small communities throughout the United States that believes strongly in maintaining separation from the outside world, avoiding modern conventions, and maintaining very conservative traditions of dress and education) have a period that teenagers pass through called *rumspringa*. The word literally means "running around," but what typically happens is that, for a period of time, teens are encouraged to explore— to examine the world outside of the Amish faith and lifestyle to see what it's like. They get to try different activities, experience different settings, meet and spend time with different people, and generally learn more about the choices available to them other than being Amish. The Amish believe that only an adult can fully commit to the church and only when it is a free choice; so rather than baptize children when they are very young and consider them part of the church, they support young adults in examining other ways of life and, hopefully, voluntarily choosing to become full members of the Amish church. It is interesting to note that after this period, 90 percent of Amish teenagers do choose to join the church.

IN THE MOVIES

Devil's Playground (2002)—Lucy Walker, a documentary filmmaker, put together this film about Amish teenagers in the traditional period of *rumspringa*. To ensure that the choice of the Amish lifestyle is not just voluntary, but informed, teenagers are encouraged to explore the non-Amish world for anywhere from a few months to several years, until they can decide to join the church. One teen describes this as "like a vaccination—a little dose of the outside world, just enough so you aren't tempted later." During this period, Amish teens get cell phones, go to the mall, have boyfriends or girlfriends, and even hold huge parties with available drugs and alcohol—all of which are typically forbidden within the Amish culture and at odds with the group's lifestyle. This film follows several teenagers during this period to see how they explore the world and decide whether to commit to the church.

There is something about *rumspringa* that is pretty cool. The idea that it is supported and that teens are encouraged to explore other ways of being, other choices, is great. So is the idea that you get to voluntarily and freely decide who you want to be. We want to encourage you to think about how you might do that in your own life. This book is hopefully about your own quest for the pieces of self that are most important to you.

However, we want to emphasize that just because you make certain choices now doesn't mean that these choices are fixed for all eternity (well, most of them, anyway). Instead, your identity is something that you are constantly reevaluating and changing. Molly, for example, didn't like asparagus when she was younger, but now she thinks it's great. Kris never used to wear skirts and now she loves them. And we have no doubt that tomorrow or the next day, or some time after that, we'll find something that we think is just the most amazing thing ever, and it will become a huge part of who we are and what we think is important. So identity keeps on evolving over our lifetime.

We also want to emphasize that no one single piece of you is who you are. You are not completely defined by being Hispanic, or male, or heterosexual, or Jewish, or class clown, or any other characteristic. To think that you can be summed up with a single word is silly. There are many choices and pieces that make up your identity—some are more important than others, but they are all part of who you are. And we also want to point out that identity doesn't come in packages—just because you have one characteristic doesn't mean that a whole bunch of other things come along with it. If you're female, it doesn't automatically mean that you like the color pink. If you're a football player, it doesn't automatically mean you are physically imposing and mean. Each characteristic that is part of you comes on its own— and you get to decide what other traits go along with it.

But since identity is such a huge part of what we think about and work on and pay attention to while we're teens, we thought it was worth writing about. We wanted to spend some time talking to you about some of the different aspects of self you might be struggling with. This book is only a start, really—a guide to some of the possible answers to the questions of who you are and how you have become (and will continue to become) that person. Through describing a huge range of things many people think of as key to their identity, we hope to help you develop a broad and non-judgmental understanding of who you may be or may choose to be. Some of these things may be so familiar to you that they bore you. Others you may never have thought of. By the end of this book, however, we hope that you will have learned more about yourself and other teens who are both like you and different from you. Even if you don't know the whole answer to the question of who you are, perhaps you will have a better understanding of all the things that might make up that answer and feel more comfortable becoming who you are going to be.

By the way, what are the identities behind the people who wrote this book? Allow us to introduce ourselves:

Hello! I'm Dr. L. Kris Gowen. The "L" stands for Laura, even though everyone calls me by my middle name. I am a teacher and researcher who loves to think about anything related to teen health, especially sexual health. (I already wrote a book in this series called *Making Sexual Decisions*. You should check it out!) I am an avid hockey fan—I play in leagues and also watch the National Hockey League enthusiastically. I am a dog person who has an adorable mutt that I rescued through the Humane Society.

Hey—I'm Dr. Molly McKenna. I'm a psychologist who lives in Portland, Oregon. I have my own private practice where I see older adolescents and adults for psychotherapy and psychological evaluations. I work with people who have problems of all kinds—from depression to career problems to relationship issues. But when I'm not working, I hang out with my husband and two awfully cute cats. I read more books than just about everyone I know, and I love hiking and camping when the rain out here stops. I'm also a huge sports fan and drop everything on Sunday mornings to go watch the Minnesota Vikings at my favorite sports bar, where I knit blankets. Seriously.

But we are not the only people who contributed to this book. In putting this book together, the two of us talked to several teens to find out more about how they felt about who they were and what others thought of them. You'll meet some of them in profiles throughout the book. And you, too, can contribute to this book. At the end of each chapter, we have given you some questions to get you started thinking about your own identity. Hopefully these extra tools can provide even more help as you read this book and consider who you are and who you are becoming.

FINDING YOURSELF: IT'S NOT AS EASY AS IT SEEMS[1]

Teenage life is supposed to be easy, isn't it? That's what our parents tell us (you know, the dreaded "when I was your age . . . " story and how we have it great now), that's what the movies tell us, that's what the media and advertisements tell us. Teenagers should be romping around streets having fun, hanging out with friends, when in reality, this doesn't even begin to portray the feelings a normal teenager has: frustration, confusion, annoyance at not being understood. It's the quest of every teen to find his or her self, and this process is not an easy one.

I know that a lot of us put on different masks. I do it all the time. You know what I'm talking about. You act differently around other people, not only accentuating certain parts of your personality, but when something comes up that you don't know about, you pretend you do to save yourself from humiliation. I think we all do it at one point or another. My freshman year of high school, I had so many friends, but I was different with every single one of the groups I was in. My friends from one group would complain that when I was with a certain other group, I would snub them. When I realized what I was doing, and how much I was hurting people, I really had to take a good look at myself. That's when I asked myself the big question I'm sure you all have at one point or another: Who am I? Before thinking about it, I had unknowingly just picked up the likes and dislikes of the people I happened to be around. But now, I was asking myself questions, like: Do I really like to dress this way? Do I really like this type of music? Why am I always jealous of my friends? The answer to most of the questions was clear: I didn't like to dress that way, I didn't like that music, and I was jealous of my friends because they knew the way they were was what made them popular. And no matter how hard I tried, I couldn't be them; I was stuck with myself.

This isn't to say that finding yourself is by any means simple. After I figured this out, my self-esteem plummeted. I'd dug myself a hole and as hard as I tried to get out, it just seemed to get deeper. The process of beginning to find out who I really was took months . . . and if you haven't figured this out, it's a very hard one. As a society like this, we are constantly bombarded with what we should be like, and it's hard to find oneself while one is being smashed with images, clothes, music, and the lifestyle one should have, but in reality doesn't really exist.

So, how do you start? I would say, just start with asking yourself a few simple questions: Am I really doing what I like, or do I follow the lead of my friends? Am I happy with who I am right now, or do I feel like there's more to me that I haven't discovered yet? If you're not doing what you like, and you feel that there's more to you that has yet to be known, you just have to start by distancing yourself from the negative and focus on the positive aspects of yourself. Don't dig yourself into a hole. Keep your self-esteem up, but slowly and gradually realize what it is you truly love to do. Is it dance? Music? Art? Writing? Computers? Talk to people? Everyone has a talent that's waiting to be shared, and through that talent, a good self-concept, and encouraging, supportive people, you can find who you are, and be happy with it. However, keep in mind that the process of growing is a never ending one, and you'll constantly be learning about yourself as life goes on. Just don't be a follower; take the initiative and find out who you really are, and take the first step in being satisfied. Don't do it for anyone else; do it for you. We all know it's not as easy as they want us to think it is.

NOTE

1. By Joyce Sutedja, writer for Popzineonline.com. She is currently attending University of Southern California. First published on www.popzineonline.com. Accessed online August 27, 2004. Reprinted here with permission.

Who Are You?

YOUR FAMILY

We are brought into this world by our parents, whoever those folks might be. At the very beginning of life, we were all products of the genetic blending of our biological mother and father. We inherit some traits and potential for certain characteristics from our biological parents; and if we have siblings, we share many of these possibilities with them. So we start out with a big bucket of genetic potential given to us by our parents. After that, however, things get a little fuzzier. But whether you like it or not, whether it's obvious or subtle, our families are a huge influence on who it is that we become.

We don't really choose our family. Families just sort of happen to you. We get born into a certain situation, like it or not, and it affects who we are and how we see the world. Social scientists argue that we learn a great number of things from our families. Without even knowing it, we pick up ways of being in the world that we carry with us for the rest of our lives. First, we inherit genetic material from our biological parents that can have a powerful influence on who we end up being. But even that isn't so simple. With the advent of reproductive technology such as in vitro fertilization and surrogate motherhood, the question of who your parents are can be less than clear. Nonetheless, the sperm and the egg that met, once upon a time those many years ago, carried information that has played a huge role in creating you. Things such as eye color are genetically determined, as are height, shoe size, hair texture, and other stuff. There are physical illnesses that can be passed on from parent to child—sickle-cell anemia, epilepsy, hemophilia, and muscular dystrophy. Certain mental conditions are also considered to be influenced by genetics; among these are bipolar disorder (manic-depression), alcoholism, and attention deficit hyperactivity disorder (ADHD). In addition, if you have biological siblings, you share some of these genetic tendencies with them as well. Obviously, who your *genetic* parents are can have a big impact on who you become.

However, most experts in human development feel that there is a powerful interaction between our genetic inheritance and the environment in which we are raised. One or the other alone can't quite explain how we turn out. Studies of twins are often used in research to demonstrate the impact of genes and environment. Identical twins raised together share both genes and environment; fraternal twins raised together share environment but only some genes; and identical twins raised in different families (yes, this happens in adoption sometimes) share genes but not environment. Although identical twins who are raised together have exactly the same genetic makeup and same environment, there are cases in which one twin develops a disorder and the other doesn't. There are also identical twins raised apart who end up sharing a lot of things, such as the same profession or even marrying people with the same names. So while what you inherit and the circumstances in which you are raised are both very important factors in who you become, neither of them determines it entirely.

We could talk a great deal about what you get from your parents in terms of genetics, but neither of this book's authors is a geneticist or biologist. Therefore we're going to stick to what you are more aware of and involved in—the environment you grow up in, specifically, your family. There are tons of ways that your family might impact your identity: your parental/family structure, brothers and sisters, whether your parents work, being adopted, the style of relationships within your family, or starting your own family.

The Structure of Your Family

In the 1950s, *Leave It to Beaver* was a popular sitcom about what appeared to be a traditional American family—Mom

Family Structure of Children under age 18 (2004)

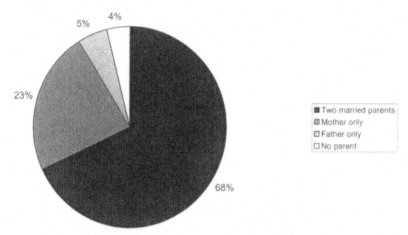

Legend:
- ■ Two married parents
- ▦ Mother only
- ▣ Father only
- ▢ No parent

Census Graph of Percentages of Family Structures[1]

wore pearls, stayed home to raise the kids; Dad went to work, smoked a pipe in the living room when he came home; and the two happy children got in trouble (but not too much), did their homework, were good neighbors, and loved their parents. Once upon a time, this was the "ideal" family in the United States. The expectation was that Mom would stay home and Dad would be the breadwinner and the kids would benefit from this arrangement. However, we're willing to guess that the majority of people reading this book are not likely to have grown up in that sort of environment. The percentage of families with a married man and woman and their own biological children is decreasing—which means that other family formations are more and more common.

Nowadays, mothers usually work. Sometimes there are two moms or two dads. At times the father isn't a major part of the family; sometimes a stepfather is very invested and involved in the family. Some children are raised by Grandma and Grandpa. Sometimes the house includes Mom, Dad, aunt, uncle, cousins, and more. There are more kinds of families than we once ever imagined. We consider all these arrangements still to be families, and no one type is more appropriate or better than any other. After all, what is a family supposed to do? A family provides basics such as food, shelter, financial support—but also love, affection, belonging, a worldview, and feedback for developing appropriate behavior and skills to deal with the world. Whether or not you have a "traditional" family, where you get these things doesn't matter.

However, while all sorts of combinations of people can be families, different family structures can have an impact on your developing identity. Think about the assumptions you make about what is "normal." If you grow up in a family with two married parents, in a community where most teens' parents are still married, then you might think that sort of family is what you should strive for. However, children of single-parent families might feel that it is more acceptable to raise a child on one's own. You get used to what you see and what you see working out, and your own family is just one example of that. What is acceptable to you will probably affect what you look for in your own life. If you feel like you are supposed to get married, you may conduct relationships differently than someone for whom marriage is less of an issue. If your parents are divorced and things go pretty well, you might feel that although divorce isn't a good thing, it doesn't necessarily mean the end of the world and a family can continue to function after a marriage ends. But if your parents are divorced and there is a lot of tension, you might feel more like getting divorced is something to avoid at all costs because of the effect it had on you personally.

Having a close relationship with a parent is a huge influence on identity. If you really care what your mom or dad thinks about you and what you choose to do or be, you will probably make some different choices than you would if you weren't close to them. Some kids who live with only one parent feel like they have a closer relationship with their mom or dad because there is only one parent in the household. Instead of two relationships between which to divide your energy, you can focus on one—which often makes that relationship stronger.

Being raised by one parent can affect you in other ways. An absent father can be a huge influence on identity for teen boys, for example. Some guys say that they don't feel like they ever

really had a chance to learn what a father is supposed to do—
and the absence of male role models impacts what they think is
important to becoming a man in today's society. But having a
father who is present but relatively uninvolved can have the
same effect. Teens might reject a father as a role model or
powerful influence because they feel his only qualification to be
a father is being a genetic donor. So just because your dad is in
your life doesn't mean that he is necessarily a huge force in who
you become. You might consciously reject his role in your life.

Brothers and sisters are a bigger part of our identity
development than you might initially recognize. We can see
how parents impact us, because they have power over things
that happen in our lives. But brothers and sisters teach us
almost as many things. Siblings can help you see how your
parents deal with you—you might find yourself comparing the
way you are treated by them to how they treat your sibling. You
might get jealous if your brother seems to be getting more
privileges than you get. Or, if you see your sister being
disciplined more often than you are, you might feel like you're
the "good kid." How you are viewed within the family can
have a huge effect on your subsequent development.

We also might learn from watching older brothers and sisters
try things first. If your sibling gets away with something or is
punished for a particular action, you will be more or less likely
to try it yourself. We get to practice having relationships and
communicating with siblings. Often our experience with conflict
and how to handle it grows out of having fights with our
brothers and sisters. If you have a lot of brothers and sisters, you
might be used to spending time in large groups and even prefer
it. If you're the only girl in a family of boys, you will probably
have some assumptions and experiences regarding what it is like
to live with men. This could make it easier to adjust to sharing a
home with another guy, or it might make you want to spend
more time with women to learn what that's like. As you can tell,
the structure of your sibling relationships will almost certainly
be a big influence on relationships you have later in your life.

Being an older or younger sibling can also affect who you
become. Some people think that oldest children are more

achievement oriented than younger ones, sometimes being affected by having attention taken away from them when the younger sibling comes along. Middle children, in contrast, are sometimes thought to be less noticeable or neglected in relation to the oldest and youngest kids. The youngest is often considered to be a little spoiled or needing more attention as the baby of the family. However, despite these stereotypes, research generally fails to prove that these patterns exist. So you will have to figure out for yourself—how does your niche or order in the family affect you? Were you asked to take on a lot of responsibility when you were younger because you were the oldest? Were you protected from experiences as the youngest? Your relationship to the others around you probably helped shape the way you relate to others.

Twins have a special experience as siblings. You have someone who is your age, who may be genetically identical to you, with whom you spend an incredible amount of time. The relationship that develops between twins is like none other between people. Some twins say they can sense when the other twin is sick or feeling bad, for example. However, sometimes the struggle to create your own personal identity can be complicated by the fact that there is someone so close to you who shares so much with you. It's hard to feel like you are your own distinct person if someone looks exactly like you, was dressed like you when small, might have a similar name, is always around you, gets all the same gifts, and is treated the same as you. So while you have a relationship that is different from other siblings, you might find yourself fighting against the assumption that you and your twin are exactly alike. (Obviously, fraternal twins have less of this kind of pressure.) Twins may spend more energy trying to distinguish themselves from one another, demonstrating through choices or behavior that they are *not* the same.

What is interesting is that while others may look at twins and see them as alike, twins are generally incredibly aware of the differences between them. Their families are like that too—some twins say the only time their parents get them confused is when they are sleeping. The challenge for twins is getting across

> ## TWINS—SEPARATE, BUT TOGETHER
>
> Courtney and David are fraternal twins who recently graduated from high school in Montana. Courtney describes herself as moody, quiet, and shy, while David thinks he is quiet and introverted, too, but also sarcastic and very motivated. They believe that growing up as a twin had an impact on who they have become.
>
> **Q: How does being a twin influence who you are/help shape the person you are?**
>
> **Courtney:** I am compared with David quite a bit. We were not even two separate people growing up. We were just known as the twins. One single entity.
>
> **David:** Frankly, I think it helped me understand women better (not completely). I care about my sister and I can't stand the thought of her being in any kind of pain, physical or emotional. I think overall it just made me more caring.
>
> **Q: How do you think being a twin influences how others see you?**
>
> **Courtney:** They tend to think that I am just like David, and in a lot of ways I am. In high school half the people just knew me as David's sister. The other half just said "David has a sister?" I actually loved it. I kept a low profile and had my friends and just kept to myself. David and I had a system and it got us through high school. We never really talked to each other and by doing so we got along better than any other siblings at our high school. But then again I don't think I would have made it through high school without him.
>
> **David:** I'm not sure that it does; most people are surprised that I am a twin when I tell them. In high school I think it affected her more than it affected me. She kind of saw me as the smart one, and it frustrated her if she thought that the teachers favored me because of it.

to the outside world how your differences distinguish you from one another. Competition and separation are big issues for twins as well. When you spend so much of your life with another person, making the transition to not sharing as much can be difficult. Going to different colleges or moving to different cities can be a huge adjustment. The balance between connection and independence is important to establish for twins and comes with time.

Not having siblings can also have a powerful influence on your identity. Only children have different relationships with their parents. If you are the only kid, you are probably going to get a different amount of individual attention than a child who has brothers and sisters in the house. Only children tend to learn to talk earlier than kids who have siblings. Only children are not asked to take responsibility for younger brothers and sisters, so they may have to develop the skill of taking care of other people outside of their immediate family.

Being adopted carries with it specific challenges that can affect an individual's identity very strongly. During adolescence, when you question who you are and how you might have gotten that way, it is natural to wonder what was given to you genetically by your parents and what you learned from the environment in which you were raised. Adopted teens may have more questions about themselves than teens who were raised by biological parents—wondering what the people who passed on their genes to them are or were like. You might wonder who you might be or become if you hadn't been adopted. If you are an adopted child with other siblings who are not adopted, you might have questions about the degree to which you belong in your family. You can also struggle with questions about the circumstances of your adoption. Adopted teens sometimes say that they have a particularly hard time making plans for their future when they have so many questions about their history. For some adopted children, the process of figuring out who they are includes a search for their birth parents. While the issues surrounding this type of a quest are much bigger than we can deal with here, answering the question "Where do I come from?" can be a big part of figuring out who you feel you are and where you got those characteristics.

Your Own Family

Another way that family can affect your identity is through the family you may create on your own. While it is not as common as it once was, teens do get married and teens definitely do have children. Getting married might seem particularly odd to you. In all states except one, you cannot legally get married without your parent's consent until you are 18 (though a few states have exceptions in the case of pregnancy). However, it used to be fairly normal to get married before the age of 18. Whether or not pregnancy is an issue, the

idea of marriage could be
appealing—when you
are in love and feel
that you want to be
together forever,
marriage becomes a
possibility you might
consider. People get married
as a way to demonstrate their commitment to one another.

In 2001, 445,944 babies were born to girls age 15 to 19. This is equivalent to the population of the entire city of Fresno, California.[2]

Some teens get married as a way to get out of their parents' house and have a life of their own. If you feel that waiting until after marriage to have sex is important, getting married sooner rather than later may be appealing for you. More recently, some people have argued that allowing or encouraging teen marriage is a way to reduce the problems of unwed motherhood. But people who get married before the age of 19 have much higher divorce rates than those who get married after age 20.[3] Girls who get married are less likely to follow through with higher education than those who do not.

Being a married teen has some particular challenges. Where do you live? On your own? With parents? Will you continue with your education? How will you handle money? Children? Work? Your in-laws? Not to mention that you will probably be one of the only people you know who is married—it's pretty unusual to get hitched before you get out of high school. Taking on the role of spouse or parent can be a really dramatic change from what teens typically do, and it should be considered carefully.

What about having children—creating your own family? Once you reach puberty, you can biologically have children of your own. Needless to say, this can be a huge part of one's identity. For many years, teen pregnancy has been a major concern for the public. Over the late twentieth century, the

Only 1 percent of teens aged 15–17 were or had been married as of 1998.[4]

rates at which girls age 15 to 19 were having children increased surprisingly rapidly. However, recently, teen pregnancy rates have declined. Researchers think this is a result of teens having less sex and using contraception more often and more successfully. But for those young men and women who have chosen to have children while teenagers, life changes pretty dramatically. If you have another being dependent on you for needs such as shelter, food, love, and attention, the way you spend your time is likely to be very different than someone without the same responsibilities. And since teen parents are more likely to be unmarried (79 percent of births to women age 15 to 19 were outside of marriage in 2003[5]), there is usually no spouse to count on to help out with parenting. It can be really hard to raise a child and stay in school; it can be equally hard to hold a job that earns enough money to support a kid while making sure the child is well cared for.

The world's youngest mother gave birth at the age of 5 years 7 months (she suffered from a hormonal disorder called precocious puberty). The world's youngest recorded father was 12 years old.[6]

Becoming a parent adds one more challenging responsibility to what is often an already full plate.

It is important to note, however, that being a parent is one of the most amazing experiences available to us as people. Once you become a parent, you are always one—and most people really enjoy this aspect of their life. For some young women, becoming a mother gives their lives a direction or purpose that they didn't previously have; you have a family of your own, someone to care for and love. The responsibility of parenthood is more than made up for by the joy of watching your own child grow up. Being a teen parent can definitely be done, but it is awfully hard and far more challenging than raising a child later in life.

What Goes On in Your Family

While family structure is one way that our families influence who we become, the way you treat each other and the life you have together is also important. It seems obvious, but just because a family has two still-married parents, two kids, two cars, and a dog doesn't mean that it is the same as another family with the same attributes. The way we learn to relate to one another is a big part of our identity that is given to us from our family. This comes from the way your family chooses to lead their lives—lifestyle choices such as employment, recreation, priorities, values, and other circumstances that aren't necessarily choices. But it also comes from how you actually interact with each other—what you say, how you spend your time, and how you act around your family.

The roles your parents play can affect your beliefs about what you should become as well. If your mom works outside the home, you might feel like it's not only okay but even desirable to work yourself if you're a girl. Or you might decide that when you have children you want to stay home with them. If your dad stayed home to take care of kids, it might be easier for you to see childrearing as a part of masculine identity. You might want that too. Think about the division of labor within your house also. If your mom does all the gardening and yard work while dad handles cooking, you'll have a different attitude about who is responsible for which chores than someone who comes from a family where the women always do the cooking. But again—this is an area in which you might decide to depart from family patterns. Molly's mother was a big gardener—she loved to grow things, and she encouraged Molly and her sister by asking them to help out with the planting and weeding. But Molly hated it. She could have learned that gardening is fun and worthwhile and something she might want to spend time on. Instead, she found herself deciding that she didn't want to and has left the yard work to other people.

Whether our parents work and what kind of jobs they choose is only part of what we learn from our parents. *How* they work is also something we see. If your mom works eighty-hour weeks and seems to love her job, you'll think differently about employment than if she worked part-time and grumbled about it constantly. Your parents model for you a way to think about your role in the workplace. Do you bring work home?

11

Do you talk about what happened during the day or not? Do you ever socialize with folks from your job? Are you supposed to stay at one job as long as possible or switch around? Balancing work, play, and family is a struggle for most people, and seeing how your family handles it teaches you some strategies that you might use later with your own family.

We learn what to expect from primary relationships and how to relate to other people through watching our parents. After all, you spend more time with your family while you are growing up than with anyone else. You get to see how they deal with one another, what happens when you do certain things, and what they expect from you. The way they treat each other and the concepts they have of what marriage or partnership is for affect the way that we later act in relationships ourselves. If your parents stayed happily married, for example, you might think that remaining married is a very important goal. But if your parents were unhappily married, arguing a lot or avoiding one another, you might question whether simply remaining married is a good way to measure the strength of a marriage. From what you see going on in your own family, you will probably develop a sense of things like how much physical affection you are comfortable with, what amount of time a family is supposed to spend together, or how separate a parent's marriage is from family relationships. For example, different families deal with emotions in very different ways. In some families, no one ever gets angry; or you may get angry, but you are not supposed to *do* anything about it. In others, people yell all the time. Some families are talkers, hashing out everything that has happened to them together, while other families are more doers, spending more time being active and less time being analytical. Given that this happens, you will probably grow up being more comfortable with the way your family did things than other ways—not necessarily because it's better, but because it is familiar. You might need to adjust to new or different ways of doing things as you spend more time with people outside of your family.

Family members who have illnesses or need special care can impact what you do and who you are. Helping a parent or sibling who has a disability can cause you to develop a very strong sense of responsibility for others. Learning while you are younger to take on the task of caring for someone else may turn you into the kind of person who feels capable being in charge of and looking out for other people. For example, the National Institutes of Health estimate that 19 million children have some type of substance abuse in their families.[7] Children of substance-abusing parents sometimes grow up earlier than other kids because they find themselves taking over for parents who aren't dealing appropriately with their responsibilities. They can also grow up thinking that a particular level of alcohol or drug use is normal, and they may not be able to judge what behavior is dangerous.

But perhaps the most important way that your family influences your identity is through family culture. In a way, the people among whom you grow up make up a community. And like any community, there are rules, customs, traditions, patterns, and other ways of being that are considered normal. These can be really small—like whether you put the toilet paper roll on so that the paper comes out from the top or from underneath. Or whether you eat hamburgers with ketchup or mustard. Or whether your family spends time looking after pets or not. But they can also be really big. If your parents went to college, they might expect you to go to college too and structure family life to support that decision. A musical family filled with people who play many different instruments will encourage you to make music an important part of your life; you might go to lots of performances or sing holiday songs around the piano or just hear your parents playing music often. If your parents were close to their families, they might expect you to spend a lot of time doing things with the family. Your parents might not notice it, but they often subtly encourage you to do things the way they did. This might be because they think it's the best way to do things, but it can also be because it's the only way they can imagine doing things—after all, they only did it one way, so it's the only experience they have. Families have stories that they tell over and over about their shared experiences also. Only the people who were there while you were growing up know about these things in the same way that you do.

This influence can be really subtle—after all, you probably never thought about whether your family drinks skim milk or not, for example. But some of the things you learn from your family will become more obvious as you get older. It's normal to question whether you want these things to be true of you. You can answer this question by simply adopting your family traditions and culture. Some teens find that they are really comfortable with the things taught to them by their family. You can absorb what your family does and is and decide that you wish to be the same kind of person.

Others find that they want to be as different as possible, or to avoid making the same choices that they feel their parents mistakenly made. Sure, your family can affect you directly—through what they give you, teach you, or show you. But your family can also affect you *reactively*, through leading you to choose to reject things that you learned in your family. You can look at the way your family did things and decide that you want to be very different. For example, everyone in your family might be in education or teaching, and you might decide that it is more important to you to make more money, so teaching is not for you. You may choose to reject some of the things you learn from your family and do something else—and this is because you decide that something your family did or was doesn't feel right to you. Keep this in mind as you think about the influence that your family has on you.

CULTURE AND ETHNICITY

You have probably heard the old saying that America is a melting pot where different cultures mix together to make a new, uniquely American culture. But perhaps America is better described as a fruit salad in which different flavors and objects co-exist, sometimes combining with each other to make new, interesting experiences, but in which each fruit remains distinct and maintains its own characteristics. The United States is made up of people from all kinds of different backgrounds—and your culture is an enormously influential part of that.

But what is culture? It's sometimes confused with ethnicity or race and might be linked to those, but culture is more about the customs, traditions, and ways of life of a group of people. In contrast, race is more about categorizing people by their physical characteristics or genetic similarity, and ethnicity is categorizing people based on their country of origin or religious background. For example, we might refer to someone as being Asian when we think of his or her racial background, but there are *huge* differences between Korean, Chinese, Japanese, Indonesian, Thai, and Vietnamese cultures, just to name a few.

> Most children are aware of their cultural backgrounds and labels by the time they are 7 or 8 years old.

So how does your culture affect your identity? There are lots of things that we pick up from our cultural background that we take for granted. Your culture may affect basic things like what you eat—both for everyday meals and special occasions. For example, Molly's family used to eat oyster stew for Christmas Eve dinner—her grandparents say that this is a tradition passed on from their families who emigrated from Germany. Many people find that certain foods are associated with certain traditions and beliefs that are a part of their cultural history.

QUINCEANERAS

In Hispanic/Latina traditions, it is customary to celebrate a young girl's transition from childhood to maturity. In the Mexican, Puerto Rican, Cuban, and Central American traditions, this passage is marked by a "quinceanera" marking her 15th birthday. A quinceanera is usually a big party that includes a religious ceremony, food, music, and often a choreographed dance. The girl being celebrated will perform a religious ritual and receive lots of presents. The average cost of a quinceanera is estimated to be $15,000. There is even a quinceanera Barbie doll that comes with a traditional gown, tiara of flowers, present, and picture frame.[8]

Your culture may also influence your values, such as how you treat your family and elders, or what qualities you look for in a romantic partner. Your culture may place certain guidelines on whom you can marry and what the ceremony will be like. Your decision to go to college, pursue a particular career, and where you choose to live can all be influenced by your cultural background.

One of the concepts that is key to understanding how culture can be a difficult area of identity is "acculturation." Acculturation is the process through which members of one cultural group adopt the beliefs and behaviors of another group. Usually, acculturation occurs when a minority group adopts the customs of a majority group, changing to fit in with the mainstream. This can happen through speaking the official language of a country instead of one's native language, adapting to a new set of values, joining social groups, or changing customs to more closely match the new group.

Think about what it would be like to move to a foreign country. At first, you'd feel and be very different from most of the people that live there. You would probably speak a different language, prefer to eat different foods, dress in a different style, and behave differently around people. Over time, however, in order to get by, you'd probably learn some of the local language, find a few things that you liked to eat that were part of the local environment, and even take on some of the customs of meeting and greeting people, perhaps bowing or shaking hands differently. Slowly, you would become acculturated. However, the degree to which we become acculturated to a new environment varies from person to person. If you adopt most of the traditions and attitudes of your new country, you're pretty highly acculturated; if you retain many aspects of your old life, you have pretty low acculturation.

Over time, a family's acculturation level might change as well. Imagine you are the first one in your family to leave your country and start over in a new one. Maybe you have already done this; maybe your parents were the first people in your family to move to the United States. You will likely cling to the aspects of home that feel comforting to you—eating the same foods, following the same rituals, spending time with people who are like you. But your children might be more comfortable moving between your old world and their new one, straddling the gap between them. And their children may still follow many of the same traditions but be more identified with the new culture. So as generations pass, acculturation changes—and this transition may mean moving from identifying as Somali to Somali American to African American to American. Or it might not—some people always choose to express strongly their original background out of pride.

These changes in acculturation over time can create some tension, especially if you and your parents differ in terms of your level of acculturation. Children of immigrants who are born in the United States sometimes find themselves living in different worlds from their parents. Teens might speak English all day with their friends, only to come home to parents who still speak only their native language. Teens can find pressure from family members to preserve certain aspects of their original culture, which may sometimes conflict with the way they feel contemporary America is. It can be a struggle to respect your background and heritage while becoming an individual who fits into a new or different world.

Some teens find themselves simply rejecting their cultural background and trying to be only "American," rather than any sort of blend. Kris, a first-generation child of immigrants from Eastern Europe, was so embarrassed about her background and culture that she threw away a lot of valuable jewelry that was traditional in her mother's country. She didn't want to be thought of as "the Latvian girl"; she wanted to be like everyone

As of 2000, there are over 5 million biracial citizens in the United States.[9]

else (she now regrets doing this and is very proud of her ethnic heritage). You can go the other way, too, though. You can immerse yourself in your culture, preferring to spend time only with people from your background, speaking your native language, observing original cultural traditions.

Another interesting situation arises when your identity is multicultural. We live in a society that tries to simplify cultural backgrounds into six basic categories. Think about some of the forms you fill out—the census or college applications, for example. Usually, you can check either white, black (or African American), Asian, Hispanic, Native American, or "other" (whatever that means). However, sometimes those categories don't work. Bicultural (or biracial or biethnic) people don't have a clearly defined category. You might have parents from different cultures who originally speak the same language (e.g., a Mexican mother and a Puerto Rican father who speak Spanish), or completely different cultures (e.g., Japanese and French), or be the child of people who identify with more than one culture. How about someone whose mother is German Japanese and whose father is from Nicaragua? What culture does that person belong to?

GREAT RESOURCES

Association of Multi-Ethnic Americans: www.ameasite.org
Their mission statement says: "We believe that every person who is multiethnic/multiracial has the same right as any other person to assert a personal identity that embraces the fullness and integrity of their actual ancestry."

Biracial Family Network: www.bfnchicago.org
Founded in 1980, its mission statement is: "To establish spaces of comfort and connection among members of multiracial families. To take action against racist and discriminatory practices. To educate people and communities about multiracial experiences."

Many multiracial teens feel as if they get the best of two worlds because of their experiences of being brought up with two different cultures. Others, however, feel like outcasts because they find themselves rejected by people from both cultures. Or they are rejected by one culture and accepted by another, even if they want to acknowledge their whole cultural background. If someone is forced to gain acceptance by denying part of their heritage, they may go through life feeling fake or incomplete. Finding support is important for everyone, but especially so for those who have a multicultural background.

Think about it—even though society tries to put us into a certain category or box ("check one please"), there are as many

STRUGGLING WITH HER CULTURAL IDENTITY

Dora is an 18-year-old who is half Chickasaw. She describes herself as smart, a tomboy, and a "tank," because of her athletic build that she thinks is more masculine than feminine.

Q: How does being Native American influence who you are?
Dora: I'm half Chickasaw, but I really didn't think of myself that way until my mom made me take a college class on it last year. It was hard not to take the course personally. It really opened my mind to how bad my people were treated and still are. It makes me angry and stronger to know what my relatives have been through.

Q: How does being Native American influence how others see you?
Dora: People always think I am Mexican or Asian. They never see me as Native American. They don't even think about that background as a possibility. So I have to correct them to make them more aware that we exist. We were here first.

different types of cultural backgrounds as there are individuals. And you get to personally decide which aspects of your culture you want to be an important part of you. You might prefer certain foods because you grew up eating them but decide that your culture's traditional way of marriage is not something you wish to follow. You may learn a lot of history about where your grandparents came from or travel to their original country.

Even though coming to terms with your cultural identity and how much of a particular culture you choose to adopt is a very personal decision, sometimes people make assumptions about you based on your cultural background. Despite the passage of the Civil Rights Act of 1964, there are many aspects of America in which people of color do not fare as well as the white majority. The sad fact is that people of color are more likely to experience poverty, higher crime rates, lower social status, and racist and discriminatory treatment. In school, history is often taught from a Eurocentric point of view, downplaying or ignoring the accomplishments and experiences of people as well as events from other parts of the world. These external influences make it

---

TEENAGERS OVERSEAS

While this book is primarily concerned with teens in the United States and Canada, it is interesting to make some comparisons to the lives led by adolescents in other countries. Some random facts:

- In China there are 373 million people under the age of 18.[10]
- In India, 43 percent of people over the age of 15 are unable to read or write.[11]
- Fifty percent of Chinese teenagers suffer from nearsightedness.[12]
- The age to receive a driver's license in South Korea is 20.[13]
- In Greenland, 56 percent of 15-year-old girls report that they smoke cigarettes daily.[14]

difficult for people of color to develop a positive view of their culture and can even lead to self-hatred and a distorted view of one's self, one's community, and one's culture.[15]

Sometimes this discrimination can cause people to feel angry or resigned about their cultural status. Sometimes it may lead people to "act white" in hopes of fitting in better. When this happens, the people who try to assimilate might be called names by people from their own background. African Americans are called "Oreos," for example, while Asians are referred to as "bananas"—black or yellow on the outside, but white on the inside. The old sitcom *The Cosby Show* was accused of having the characters acting like a bunch of Oreos, because even though the family looked black, they acted white (i.e., were rich, had an intact family, and a "perfect" home). More recent sitcoms such as *The Bernie Mac Show* are praised

IN THE MOVIES: GANGSTER FILMS
Some black leaders are angry with the way in which gangster films portray black youth. These films, which began in the 1980s with *Boyz in the Hood* and *Menace II Society*, portray black youth as poor, angry, violent, and remorseless. The films glamorize the violence of gang activity while sending the message that trying to get out of this existence is hopeless. Black leaders claim that these messages only serve to perpetuate both whites' stereotypes of black youth as well as the cycle of criminality in black urban youth. Even though most of the people behind these films (the directors and producers) are African American, there are people who see these movies as racist and want this genre to stop.[16]

BEING ADOPTED INTO A TRANSCULTURAL FAMILY

Some children are adopted, which in itself can be a difficult experience as a child tries to understand his or her background. However, this challenge can increase if he or she is adopted by a family whose cultural makeup is different. They (and their parents) may be more likely to face criticism, prejudice, and offensive remarks. Ideally, a transcultural family will learn about the heritages of both the adoptive parents as well as the child. Attending support groups, living in a diverse neighborhood, and studying different cultural backgrounds together are all great ways to help a family become closer while appreciating everyone's differences. Sometimes the child may identify with his or her adoptive parents' background rather than his or her own. Other times, an adopted child may have a strong desire to explore his or her biological culture. No matter the decision, it is important to get support through the process and go through it with others. It makes the journey more enjoyable and meaningful.

for their more accurate portrayal of an African American lifestyle.

Cultural stereotypes can also influence a person's image. Such stereotypes not only apply to people of different backgrounds, but teens from particular cultures have their own stereotypes to manage. African American males are often seen as anti-intellectual and violent, whereas Japanese youth are assumed to be obedient, smart, and interested in math. These stereotypes influence other people's ideas about you when you meet them—they may assume that you are a particular way simply because of what you look like. Hear these assumptions enough and you may even start to believe them yourself.

It's important for everyone to have a safe space to observe, question, and challenge the stereotypes of his or her culture. Having parents, friends, or mentors you can talk to about issues of racism, cultural biases, and growing up in America helps you come to terms with your background and how your particular cultural makeup is viewed by American society. Ideally, you will be able to integrate the best of both worlds—the dominant culture and your traditional culture—to create a balance that makes you feel comfortable and productive in your life and in your own skin. You are independent, an individual expression of your own unique experiences and background, but still connected to your roots.

GENDER

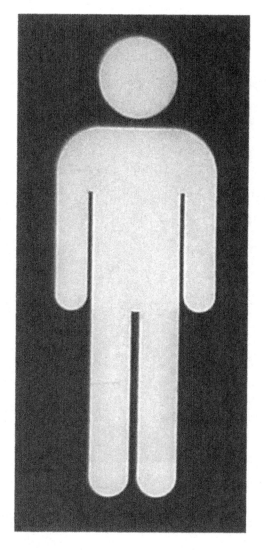

One of the most obvious parts of your identity is whether you are male or female, a boy or girl, man or woman. Think about it—one of the first things that's asked when a baby is born is "Is it a boy or a girl?" Sometimes a person doesn't even ask if the newborn is healthy or if the mom is okay first.

This emphasis on gender continues while you are a baby. Scientists call the way a society believes boys and girls should act, dress, and be treated *gender roles*. The way you are dressed, cuddled, and played with as a child is based on these gender roles. For example, boys are more likely to be dressed in blue shorts and shirts decorated with tugboats or fire engines. Girls, on the other hand, are more likely to be dressed in pink dresses with flowers and bunnies. Dress a boy in an outfit with lace and frills and people will question your sanity, and maybe even accuse you of mistreating your child! Gender roles can be that strong.

Researchers have even shown that people treat babies differently depending on whether they think a baby is one gender or the other. In one study, people looked after a three-month-old baby named Chris (a name used for either a boy or a girl) while the experimenter (who was posing as the mother) excused herself to use the restroom. The experimenters had the baby wear a yellow outfit on purpose, so its gender wasn't

obvious. In different cases, the baby was labeled male or female, or the gender of the baby wasn't mentioned at all. The experimenter found that the toys chosen for the baby to play with depended on what the person thought the gender of the baby was. When the baby was labeled a girl, people gave the baby a doll to play with. When they thought it was a boy, they gave the baby a football. When they didn't know what gender the baby was, many people asked the experimenter before they played with it.[17] They would stare at the baby, hold it, but otherwise not say very much at all. Same baby each time, but depending on whether the person thought it was a boy or a girl, how that baby was treated was very different.

These experiments demonstrate how important knowing someone's gender is. We feel like we need that information to know how to behave toward someone. People even ask about the gender of pets and apologize if they refer to it by the wrong gender. Like the animal can tell the difference in what you call it!

Of course there are real differences between girls and boys. Those differences are, for the most part, biologically based. Boys and girls differ from one another in their anatomy, hormones, and chromosomal makeup. Besides the obvious anatomical differences, boys are usually taller and hairier while girls tend to have broader hips. There are also some minor brain differences between the sexes; girls, on average, tend to have better verbal skills while boys tend to have better spatial abilities. These differences are usually called *sex* differences, because they are based on one's biological sex. *Gender* differences are something else. Gender differences are not determined by nature but by society. How you think you should look, act, feel, and express yourself is based on gender roles or society, not on your biological sex. For example, the

idea that men are born leaders while women are more likely to
be part of a group is created by society and culture, not
biological differences.

Given the strong emphasis
our society gives to gender,
it's important to
understand your own
feelings, opinions, and
attitudes toward your gender
and the other gender. That way
you can recognize how you might make assumptions about
yourself and others or expect certain behaviors from certain
people simply because someone is either male or female. One
way to do this is to think back on your life as far back as you
can remember. Think about your life as a child, and even a baby
if you can. Come up with as many details about all the things
you have done and experienced so far. Then, imagine you had
to live your life over again—as a member of the other gender. In
other words, if you are a boy, relive your life as if you were a
girl, and if you are a girl, relive your life as if you were a boy.
Make a list (either in your head or on paper) of all the ways
your life would be different if you had been born the other sex.

> **Your personal set of gender rules
> is pretty much fixed by the time
> you are only six years old.**

The list you make for yourself is the beginning of your
assumptions about how the two genders are different from one
another. Society also has its own assumptions and expectations
about the two genders. The most basic gender stereotype is that
women are more caring and emotional while men are more
independent and competitive. Trying to fit into your
"appropriate" gender role may create conflict between these
assumptions and your personal goals. For example, as a girl, you
may be hesitant to be aggressive, speak your mind, or aspire to
be a leader; oftentimes, girls like that get called "bitch." As a
boy, you may resist showing your feelings or expressing your
desire to become a caring father in fear of being called a "sissy."
When your personality conflicts with what is considered your
appropriate gender role, it can make you may feel awkward.
What do those phrases imply about what the genders are
supposed to be like?

25

GENDER EXPECTATIONS AND STEREOTYPES

When was the last time you heard:

- "That's not very lady-like."
- "Big boys don't cry."
- "You throw like a girl."
- "You guys are playing like a bunch of girls!"
- "Be a man!"
- "Is that any way to treat a lady?"

Even though many would agree that traditional gender roles are less strict in today's American society than they were during the 1950s, there is still pressure for an individual to conform to his or her appropriate gender role. This pressure can be seen in career choice. Although there are more women doctors and lawyers than ever before, the ratio of female to male computer scientists is still pretty low. And it's rare to see a female construction worker (if you do, she is likely the one holding the traffic sign, not the one operating the crane). Men, too, seem to have career restrictions based on gender roles. How often have you seen a male nurse or secretary? There are also very few male elementary school teachers. In fact, the number of men in more traditionally female positions such as nurses and elementary school teachers has not increased in the same way that the number of women has increased in traditionally male jobs such as doctor and lawyer. Although there are no actual laws or rules dictating which careers are and are not okay for certain genders, we still assume that certain jobs are more suited to a particular gender. Such unofficial restrictions may consciously or unconsciously influence your own decisions when it comes time for you to think about career goals, which courses you are going to take in school, which hobbies you want to pursue, or even what you choose to wear.

So what if there are gender roles? Isn't it good that we have different roles for boys and different roles for girls? Well, maybe yes and maybe no. Although life would not be as interesting if everyone were the same, sometimes gender differences can limit a person. We usually hear about how gender differences limit girls and women. Women in the working world earn less than men; women in other countries

OCCASIONALLY IT MUST BE HARD TO BE EITHER GENDER[18]

About being a woman: Because woman's work is never done and is underpaid or unpaid or boring or repetitious and we're the first to get the sack and what we look like is more important than what we do and if we get raped it's our fault and if we get bashed we must have provoked it and if we raise our voices we're nagging bitches and if we enjoy sex we're nymphos and if we don't we're frigid and if we love women it's because we can't get a "real" man and if we ask our doctor too many questions we're neurotic and/or pushy and if we expect community care for children we're selfish and if we stand up for our rights we're aggressive and "unfeminine" and if we don't we're typical weak females and if we want to get married we're out to trap a man and if we don't we're unnatural.

About being a man: If I chase girls I'm a dog and a pig and if I don't I'm a "faggot" and if I have a decent job it must be because I stole it from a female and not have earned it on my own merit and if I cry I'm a pussy and if I don't I'm callous and insensitive and if I don't play sports I'm a wimp and if I do I'm a hungry jock and if I like romance it must be that I just want her in bed and if I like to talk to her it can't be because I just like to and there has to be something wrong with me if I just want to be close with her instead of having sex and if I have too many female friends or too friendly I'm a womanizer and if I don't I'm not in touch with my "feminine side" and if I take a woman's studies class it can only mean I want to meet girls and God forbid I should actually be in love with someone, because if I am I surely must be whipped.

Source: Unknown

have fewer rights than men; women are more likely to be the victims of sexual crimes and feel less safe than men.

Women also have it tough when it comes to sexual experience and reputation. According to one survey, 90 percent of teens say that a girl can get a bad reputation by having sex, but only 41 percent think that boys can get a bad reputation for having sex. The same behavior—having sex—can give a person a different image based simply on whether he or she is a boy or

GENDER ROLES IN RELATIONSHIPS

In boy-girl relationships, each person takes on different roles and responsibilities based on his or her gender. According to a survey of teens[19]:

- **70 percent say that the boy usually asks someone out on a date.**
- **67 percent say that boys usually make the first move sexually.**
- **63 percent say that girls usually decide whether the relationship will become sexual.**
- **70 percent say it's usually girls that say no to sex.**

a girl. Similarly, 79 percent of teens believe that a girl can lose her boyfriend if she doesn't want to have sex, but only 54 percent believe that a boy will lose his girlfriend if he doesn't want to have sex.[20] Same decision, different consequence—all because of gender. How do you think your gender influences your sexual decision making?

But there are gender differences that show that it isn't always great to be a guy, either. This fact can be shown in the statistics of school performance. Boys earn 70 percent of the D's and F's and represent two-thirds of those teens labeled "learning disabled." Meanwhile, girls are more likely to be members of honor societies, school government, and debate clubs. They also have higher future aspirations, on average, than boys and are more likely to go to college.[21] Boys also get into more serious trouble than girls. Boys are responsible for 80 percent of the crimes tried by juvenile court and make up 90 percent of all drug and alcohol arrests.[22] Still think guys are better off than girls?

Here are some other less extreme examples that show how gender roles can limit both boys and girls. Although nowadays both girls and boys play sports, which sport they choose to play can be influenced by their gender. What happens when a boy decides to take up figure skating as opposed to hockey? What if a girl decides she wants to go out for the football or wrestling team? Or say that you want to join the band; that's something both boys and girls can do. But what happens if a girl wants to play the tuba or bass drum? What about a boy who wants to play the triangle or piccolo or flute? Gender roles and expectations still exist—they are just more subtle than they used to be.

SEXUAL ORIENTATION—A PART OF WHO YOU ARE

Sexual orientation refers to your feelings of romantic and sexual attraction. People can be attracted to members of the same gender (gay, lesbian, homosexual), the other gender (straight, heterosexual), or both genders (bisexual). It is important to point out that sexual orientation is not the same thing as gender and gender roles, even though people often confuse them. People often assume that feminine men are gay and masculine women are lesbians. But that is not necessarily true. Just because a boy is interested in things that are usually considered "feminine activities" such as cooking and ballet does not mean he is gay. And girls who play lots of sports and don't like to wear skirts are not necessarily lesbian. The reverse is also true. There are many gay men who can be described as "macho," and similarly, there are lesbians who wear makeup and dresses. In other words, a person's sexual orientation is separate from whether or not he or she follows traditional gender roles.

So what does it mean to be gay, lesbian, or bisexual? If you depend on the media or stereotypes for the answer, you'd think it meant that you would have certain tastes in music, a particular fashion style, or even a specific set of political beliefs. People tend to assume that there are all sorts of things that come in a package with being gay, lesbian, or bisexual. But that's not true. If you are homosexual, that means that you prefer romantic and/or sexual relationships with people of the same sex. If you are bisexual, you can see yourself having a romantic and/or sexual relationship with people from both sexes. And that's all it means. You can still like whatever things you like and believe whatever you choose to believe. Sexual orientation isn't really about anything other than love and sex, regardless of what others try to tell you.

Trying to figure out your sexual orientation may be easy for you or may prove to be a challenge. It is a totally different experience for everyone. Finding out who you are sexually may not happen right away. Some people know when they are very young whether they are straight or gay or bisexual. Other people need more time to figure it out. Because our society puts pressure on people to follow a heterosexual lifestyle, it is common for people to not recognize their own sexual orientation until much later in life. In the meantime, some people may experiment sexually with members of either or both sexes before they decide on their sexual orientation, while others know right away whom they are attracted to. There is no need to rush, so take your time if you are not sure. Exploration and questioning are normal for everyone, no matter what sexual orientation a person is. Allow yourself to have different feelings and thoughts about your romantic life without putting a label on yourself. Your attitudes and even your actions may change over time. Many gay people have had sexual experiences with the other gender, and many straight people have had sexual experiences with their own gender. And you can still be a virgin and know whether you are straight, gay, or bisexual. So there is no need to rush into anything you are not comfortable with just to prove to yourself or others you are a particular sexual orientation. It takes time to know who you are.

A question many young people ask is "How will I know for sure if I am gay, lesbian, or bisexual?" (Notice how we never ask the question "How will I know for sure if I am straight or heterosexual?") The simple, yet complex answer is "You will know when you know." There is no set time, age, or experience that will guarantee an answer. Instead, it is different for everyone. Some people figure out their orientation by the crushes they get when they are young. Other people begin to feel sexual attractions to friends during puberty and realize that they are not going through some sort of phase. Still others are not sure until they are away from their homes and allowed a little more freedom to develop their romantic and sexual feelings.

Unfortunately, it is not always easy to discover or admit that you are gay, lesbian, or bisexual. Our society can be pretty prejudiced against those who are not heterosexual. Tasteless jokes, name calling, and stereotypes about gay, lesbian, and

GAY AND HAPPY

Alex is 20 and a sophomore in college. She went to high school in New Jersey and is now majoring in sociology at a school in Ohio. She is very involved in theater and is very passionate about acting and directing.

Q: How would you describe yourself?
Alex: I'm a dyke—but I like to think of myself as queer. It's the word I'm most comfortable with.

Q: How does being queer influence who you are?
Alex: I think I am part of a new generation. There was so little support for people like me when I was in high school. But I think being queer is rad because it's a different perspective to see the world in. I see things other people don't and this makes me understand myself and others really well. It also makes me passionate about gay rights and standing up for what I believe in.

Q: How does being queer influence how others see you?
Alex: People didn't know what to do with me. They try to put me in a category, like lesbian, but I don't like that word, so I don't agree with them. They don't know whether to be angry with me or feel sorry for me.

bisexual (GLB) people are everywhere. In fact, a study of students in public high schools in 1993 found that 97 percent of students reported regularly hearing homophobic remarks from their peers.[23] In fact, the typical high school student in 1997 heard antigay slurs 25.5 times a day—that's more than one per hour![24]

The sad thing is that homophobic remarks are so common they may even begin to feel normal, which is not right. Why is homophobia so prevalent in our society? Because people are often afraid of what they do not understand. Sometimes this fear turns into discomfort or even

Homophobia: **The irrational dislike, intolerance, or hate against anyone who is not heterosexual.**

SAD, BUT TRUE

Seventy percent of GLB teens have been called names and made fun of. More than one-third have been threatened with violence. More than 10 percent have been assaulted.[25]

hate. In order to cope with their fear, people will put down those who are different from them. This does not mean that homophobia is okay, but understanding why some people act this way can help you see that it is not your "fault" that you are gay, lesbian, or bisexual and that there is nothing wrong with who you are. It's the people who harm others simply because they don't understand them that have a problem.

The level of homophobia in your community will probably affect how you feel about being gay, lesbian, or bisexual. Your discovery and understanding of your sexual orientation may be a cause for celebration, or it may be something you want to run away from. But no matter what environment you are facing, the first thing you need to do is face yourself. Once you understand and accept your romantic and sexual feelings, you will be better able to tackle the immediate environment and the world around you. If you find yourself ashamed or disapproving of your own sexual orientation, you are not alone. It is not uncommon to feel angered or disappointed in yourself when you realize you

GREAT WEB RESOURCES

Don't know where to turn? The Internet is a great place to find the support and information you need about sexual orientation. Here are some of the better places to turn:

Out Proud: www.outproud.org
The National Coalition for Gay, Lesbian, Bisexual, & Transgender Youth

PFLAG: www.pflag.org
Parents, Families, and Friends of Lesbians and Gays

Youth Resource: www.youthresource.com
Created by and for gay, lesbian, bisexual, transgender, and questioning (GLBTQ) young people

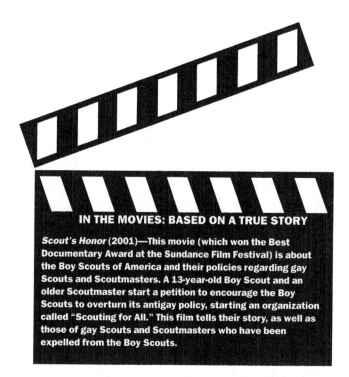

IN THE MOVIES: BASED ON A TRUE STORY

Scout's Honor (2001)—This movie (which won the Best Documentary Award at the Sundance Film Festival) is about the Boy Scouts of America and their policies regarding gay Scouts and Scoutmasters. A 13-year-old Boy Scout and an older Scoutmaster start a petition to encourage the Boy Scouts to overturn its antigay policy, starting an organization called "Scouting for All." This film tells their story, as well as those of gay Scouts and Scoutmasters who have been expelled from the Boy Scouts.

are not heterosexual. This is because homophobia can actually be internalized—in other words, you may fear homosexuality even though it may be a part of you. If you feel any form of self-hatred or find that you do not accept your sexual orientation because it does not fit into the "norm" of our society, it is a good idea to reach out to a trusted friend, or even seek counseling so you can get support as you learn to accept this part of yourself.

Coming Out: Letting Others See You

If you believe that you are not heterosexual, you may be thinking about sharing this news with friends and/or family. This process is called "coming out." Deciding to talk about your sexual orientation with others can be a very scary and/or lonely time. You might not be sure about how those you care about will react to the news. You are putting yourself on the line, making yourself vulnerable, and possibly opening yourself up to rejection from those who simply do not understand your sexual preferences.

A GLB student who has the support of at least one teacher or school staff member is more than twice as likely to apply for college and have higher grade point averages.[26] Having support not only helps sense of self but your accomplishments too!

Before you come out to anyone, make sure you have support. Even if that person is an online buddy, knowing you have someone who will stand by you no matter what happens will help you feel strong and help you make good choices. See the "Great Web Resources" box to help you find someone to talk to online or a support group in your area.

Remember to be picky about whom you come out to. Think about whom you might want to tell, and try to figure out what their reactions might be. When you talk to someone about your sexual orientation, you are sharing a special part of yourself that not everyone deserves to hear. While your sexual orientation is an important part of you, it is also a private thing and you do not have to feel like everyone needs to know. You want to feel safe with that person while you are being very personal and vulnerable. So only talk to those people who you think will understand you, who you respect, and who see you as the wonderful person you are.

Some people will see you differently after you have come out to them. Even though, inside, you are the same person, others will see you from a new perspective, and that may cause them to treat you differently. Hopefully they will understand that you

OUT AND PROUD!

Singer/songwriter Melissa Etheridge
Actress Ellen DeGeneres
Talk show host Rosie O'Donnell
Tennis star Martina Navratilova
Congressman Barney Frank
Michael Stipe of REM
Actor Nathan Lane
David Geffen, cofounder of Dreamworks SKG/Geffen Records

are still the person they have known, but sometimes people will react negatively because of their own ignorance and stereotypes about sexual orientation. They may become sad, angry, confused, or concerned. If you come out to someone and they seem shocked or surprised, give them time to process your news. Let them know that you can answer questions they may have. You may be the first GLB person they realize they know (they may know others who have not come out to them yet). Educating them might help them understand that you are still

THE FIVE STAGES OF SAME-SEX IDENTITY DEVELOPMENT[27]

A researcher and counselor named Eli Colman discovered that many people go through these five stages as they learn to become comfortable with their gay identity:

1. *Pre-Coming Out:* This is when a person first becomes aware that they are attracted to people of the same gender. Sometimes people in this stage are not happy because of society's negative attitudes toward GLB people. They turn this negative attitude onto themselves and wish they were different.
2. *Coming Out:* People at this stage have figured out their sexual orientation and are now more comfortable with it. They begin to accept who they are and start to tell people they trust about their sexual orientation.
3. *Exploration:* Once someone has come out to themselves and others, they start exploring the gay and lesbian community and may start to date. However, people will often feel awkward and confused because everything is so new to them.
4. *First Relationship:* It may take a while, but at some point a person finds someone he or she is attracted to, the feeling is mutual, and they start to date. This is a chance to see that dating someone of the same gender is possible in today's society, even if the relationship does not work out in the end.
5. *Integration:* People who reach this final stage of their sexual identity development see themselves as complete human beings who have a lot to offer society. Their sexual orientation is an important part of who they are, but they understand they are much more than just gay or lesbian. They may or may not be in a relationship, but no matter what, they see that they are good people.

their friend, family member, or co-worker, and that your relationship with them does not need to change as far as you are concerned. Then trust that the people in your life—the ones who will accept you and support you as you are—will come back when they can. In the meantime, form new relationships with people who will stand by you right away so you are never left with the feeling that you are completely alone.

The important thing to realize is that, no matter whom you are attracted to sexually or romantically, your sexual orientation is only a part of who you are. Your sexual orientation is only part of your identity. Your hobbies, sense of style, taste in music, career goals, culture—everything about you put together helps make you the person you are. Whom you happen to date (or not date) is only a small piece of that. Too often, people see sexual orientation as the main way to define a person. And although it can be an important part of who you are, it will never be the only part of who you are.

YOUR TURN

Here are some questions for you to think about:

1. How are you like your mother? Your father?
2. What is your role in your family (entertainer, peacemaker, caretaker, etc.)?
3. How does the structure of your family affect who you are?
4. What role does your extended family (grandparents, cousins, etc.) play in your life?
5. What have you learned about relationships from your parents?
6. What are your family's traditions?
7. What's your ethnic background?
8. What do you think the image of your culture is?
9. How does your culture influence what you eat? Or what you wear?
10. Have you experienced discrimination? How did it affect you?
11. How might your life be different if you were the other gender?
12. How does your gender affect how people treat you?
13. What have you learned about gender roles from your family?

14. What have you learned about gender roles from your culture?

15. Have you ever been told that you couldn't do something because of your gender?

16. How do you define your sexual orientation?

17. What assumption do you see others make about people who are not heterosexual?

18. What resources does your community have for people who are not heterosexual?

NOTES

1. U.S. Bureau of the Census, *Current Population Survey, March 2002* (Washington, D.C.: U.S. Bureau of the Census, 2002).

2. National Center for Health Statistics, *Births: Final Data for 2002*, NVSR Report 52, No. 10 (Hyattsville, Md.: National Center for Health Statistics, 2003).

3. N. Seiler, *Is Teen Marriage a Solution?* Center for Law and Social Policy Pub. No 02-20 (Washington, D.C.: Center for Law and Social Policy, 2002), accessed June 24, 2004, at www.clasp.org/DMS/Documents/1018642957.61/teenmariage02-20.pdf.

4. Seiler, *Is Teen Marriage a Solution?*

5. *Guinness Book of World Records 2004* (New York: Time, 2003).

6. National Center for Health Statistics, *Births: Final Data for 2002.*

7. J. A. Califano, *No Safe Haven: Children of Substance-Abusing Parents* (New York: National Center on Addiction and Substance Abuse at Columbia University, 1999).

8. Quinceanera Boutique, accessed June 24, 2004, at www.quinceanera-boutique.com/quinceaneratradition.htm.

9. R. D. Nash, *Coping as a Biracial/Biethnic Teen* (New York: Rosen Publishing Group, 2000).

10. UNICEF, accessed June 25, 2004, at www.unicef.org/infobycountry/china_statistics.html.

11. UNICEF, *The Official Summary of the State of the World's Children 2004* (London: UNICEF, 2004).

12. China Today, accessed March 18, 2004, at www.chinatoday.com/data/data.htm.

13. J. MacNeil, "South Korea's Teen Beat," accessed March 18, 2004, at www.teenwire.com/views/articles/wv_19991008p018.asp.

14. C. Currie et al., eds. "Health and Health Behavior among Young People," *Health Behavior of School-Aged Children Study* (Copenhagen: World Health Organization, 2000).

15. W. Cross, "The Psychology of Nigrescence: Revisiting the Cross Model," in *Handbook of Multicultural Counseling*, ed. J. Pontero, J. Casas, L. Suzuki, and C. Alexander (Thousand Oaks, Calif.: Sage, 1995), 93–122.

16. B. Kitwana, *The Hip Hop Generation: Young Blacks and the Crisis in African American Culture* (New York: Basic Civitas Books, 2003).

17. C. A. Seavey, P. A. Katz, and S. R. Zalk, "Baby X: The Effects of Gender Labels on Adult Responses to Infants," *Sex Roles* 9 (1975): 103–110.

18. Accessed May 14, 1004, at www.cyberslayer.co.uk/jokes/joke1058.html.

19. Kaiser Family Foundation, *Gender Roles* (2002), part of the Sex Smarts survey series co-sponsored by *Seventeen Magazine*, accessed May 14, 2004, at www.kff.org/entpartnerships/loader.cfm?url=/commonspot/security/getfile.cfm&PageID=28886.

20. Kaiser Family Foundation, *Gender Roles*.

21. M. Gurian, *Boys and Girls Learn Differently: A Guide for Teachers and Parents* (New York: Jossey-Bass, 2002).

22. M. Gurian, *The Wonder of Boys: What Parents, Mentors and Educators Can Do to Shape Boys into Exceptional Men* (New York: Putnam, 1997).

23. *Making Schools Safe for Gay and Lesbian Youth: Report of the Massachusetts Governor's Commission on Gay and Lesbian Youth* (Cambridge, Mass.: Massachusetts Governor's Commission on Gay and Lesbian Youth, 1993).

24. K. Carter, "Gay Slurs Abound," *Des Moines Register*, March 7, 1997, 1.

25. A. R. Augelli, "Victimization History and Mental Health among Lesbian, Gay, and Bisexual Youths," presented at the meeting of the Society for Research on Adolescence, New Orleans, La., 1998.

26. M. Sims, "Largest Ever Study of Anti-LGBT Harassment in Schools Shows the Problem Is Widespread, Dangerous and Preventable," *GLSEN News Release*, accessed June 4, 2004, at www.glsen.org/cgi-bin/iowa/educator/news/record/1444.html.

27. E. Coleman, "Developmental Stages of the Coming-Out Process," in *Homosexuality: Social, Psychological, and Biological Issues*, ed. W. Paul (Thousand Oaks, Calif.: Sage, 1982).

Your Body

Your body can be a means of expressing yourself. What you wear, how you change your body, how you treat your body, and how you feel about your body all contribute to your sense of style and how you feel about yourself. In a sense, your body is one of the few things that you truly own in this world; what you do with it can reveal a lot about who you are as a person and how others see you. After all, your body is the package that you come in, and until you act or speak, it is the only thing people can see or know about you.

Although there is a popular phrase in America, "you can't judge a book by its cover," the fact is that many people do make their first impressions of people based on how they look. So, it is important to be aware of this as you decide on an image or look to present to the world. That is not to say that people will know all about you by simply seeing what you look like, but many people believe they can learn a lot about others simply by what they look like. How do you use your appearance to show people who you are and what you are all about? Can you adapt your sense of style to fit into different situations? These are important things to consider as you express your individuality through your body.

> **Over half of girls (53 percent) and a third of boys (36 percent) worry about how they look.[1]**

WHAT YOU WEAR

Every morning you have to decide what you are going to wear that day. Sometimes the decision is easy, while other times you might struggle trying to figure out what you want to put on. But no matter what your final choice is, what you wear will help determine how people treat you and what people think about you.

Clothing is one of the main ways you can present an image of yourself to the world—this makes your fashion style both an exciting and important thing to consider. Someone wearing all black is going to give off a different impression than someone in khakis, a tucked-in shirt, and a belt. In fact, from those brief descriptions, you may have even labeled these two people. The first might be a goth or alternative, while the second might be a prep or geek. From just the basic idea of an outfit, people can make a lot of assumptions about the person inside.

So, the trick is, what do you want your clothes to say about you? Some people like to dress in the latest trends and styles. It shows that they are current, modern, and involved in the latest version of "cool." Some people like to dress in a similar way as their friends do. This shows that they are part of a particular crowd. People can even dress to reflect their interests; for example, surfers often wear a certain style of shorts and shirts from specific

WHAT IS HIP?

For better or for worse, fashion trends change pretty quickly; high fashion shows occur two times a year, setting the trends for the next few months. This rapid change can be a good thing because it allows a person to try many different styles, but it also can get pretty expensive if you try to wear only the latest "in" looks. The good news is that fashion trends also tend to repeat themselves. For example, the looks that were popular in the 1960s reemerged; bell-bottom jeans and tie-dye shirts could be found in stores everywhere. Then, the 1970s made a comeback—this is where we get the low-rider jeans and peasant blouses for women. Now, the 1980s are coming back. Just take a look at the neon colors and jelly shoes at the mall. Think those are a new idea? Think again, and ask your parents or older relatives what they wore when they were your age. Chances are, you are looking at a newer version of it today. So, how can you afford the latest fashions? By buying used or vintage clothing. Check out a thrift store and get the original stuff for a bargain price.

surf shops. Concert t-shirts reveal what sort of music you are interested in. Sometimes the clothes you wear serve a more practical purpose; wearing a sweater during a New York winter or something waterproof in Seattle is often a good idea. But even with this practicality in mind, what style you choose is up to you.

There are also people who prefer to develop their own unique fashion sense. They may mix and match different styles, or they may stick with a fashion trend that is years out of date. Being comfortable (both physically and psychologically) can be more important than keeping up with the latest fashions. People who develop their own unique style may stand out more; sometimes a person simply wants to be seen as different, and clothing can be a way to convey that uniqueness or rebellion. However, sometimes people wear clothes that stand out because they cannot afford to wear what everyone else does, or their culture dictates what they have to wear in public. Men who follow particular branches of Judaism, for example, are expected to wear a yarmulke; women who belong to certain Islamic faiths are required to cover their faces. Bottom line is, clothes can say a lot about a person, but one outfit does not say everything there is to know about the person inside.

We also might dress differently in different situations. For example, sometimes a person may want to "dress to impress." Whom you are trying to impress will determine what you wear. Dressing to impress a teacher or a potential boss is quite different from trying to impress someone you are attracted to. Or maybe you want to make a good impression when you first meet a long-lost relative or a new neighbor. Different outfits create different impressions. Considering what type of event and the people who will be there can all factor into your decision about what to put on your body. Your decision whether or not to follow the rules about what to wear in certain situations can also say something about your attitudes and values.

There are situations that may limit your choice of what to wear. Your school or place of employment may have a dress code that limits what you can or cannot wear. Some people love dress codes because they can make life so much easier—there's no need to get up early to pick out clothes, no need to worry about whether your sense of style is in or not. Uniforms can also make it seem like everyone is on the same team. When people dress the same as everyone else, they might feel as though they are a part of a group. There's unity and a sense of belonging.

Others hate the idea of uniforms because they feel they rob them of their self-expression. When everyone is dressed the same, they feel like no one can see them for the unique individual that they are. Sometimes, organizations with a dress code or uniform understand this and allow students or employees to wear accessories of their own. You might see interesting socks, shoes, scarves, or jewelry used to make a uniform look unique for an individual. Then there are other people who don't like uniforms because they aren't very comfortable or the style isn't flattering on them. These people end up spending a lot of time wearing something that does not fit them well, which makes them feel self-conscious and awkward and might cause them to be less likely to express themselves. It's hard to be yourself if you aren't comfortable.

A lot of times the latest fashions are determined by celebrities. Famous people tell us what is cool by wearing different styles. As the most visible people in our society, celebrities are seen everywhere and their fashion is commented on in magazines and TV shows. What celebrities choose to wear can become not only fashion but also news. There has been a lot of fuss over the outfits that high-profile celebs wear during award ceremonies; for example, J. Lo is especially known for making headlines. If you are into a particular celebrity, you may show this by dressing like him or her. For example, many hip-hop and rap artists have influenced the fashion trends of the 2000s by bringing back tracksuits, throwback sports jerseys, and velour outfits. In fact, in 2001, people spent over $2 billion on hip-hop fashion. Britney Spears has a sense of style that is copied by young girls everywhere who are known as "little Britneys."

Lately, celebrities have been telling us what is in fashion by creating their own clothing lines. Jennifer Lopez, P. Diddy, the Olsen twins, and Russell and Kymora Simmons (founders of Phat Farm and Baby Phat) are some of the celebrities who have their own brands of clothing. So, now you can not only dress like your favorite celebrity, but you can actually buy clothes with his or her name on them.

THE THINGS YOU DO TO YOUR BODY

Tattoos—Your Body as a Canvas

Tattoos have a rich history, having been around for thousands of years. In the last fifteen years or so, however, they have been pretty popular and have made their way into the mainstream. Models and actors show off their tattoos nowadays.

The first people to wear tattoos were located in Polynesia and in Egypt; archeologists and historians believe that tattoos have been around since 4,000 B.C.[2]

43

What is different about tattoos today is their purpose. Long ago, tattoos had two primary purposes—to provide magical protection against sickness or misfortune, or to show that you were part of a group. Throughout history, tattoos served to identify the wearer's rank, status, or membership in a group—it was common to mark slaves with tattoos to show ownership in some countries, while in others only the elite were allowed to adorn themselves with body art. Often, the same tattoo was put on several different people as a way to show that they all belonged together somehow.

Today, tattoos are still used to denote group membership, but more often people choose to have tattoos instead of having tattoos put on them against their will. When people all have the same tattoo design, they can quickly and visibly declare membership to a particular group and can advertise this allegiance with their bodies in a permanent manner. Certain branches of the military, biker clubs, gangs, and even groups of friends might all get the same tattoo to show that they will always be together.

RECENT RESEARCH[3]

Of those people with tattoos, 34 percent say their tattoo makes them feel sexier and 29 percent say it makes them feel more rebellious.

However, 36 percent of people without tattoos say that they make a person *less* sexy and 31 percent say a tattoo makes some look less intelligent. And over half (57 percent) see people with tattoos as more rebellious.

Different people, different perceptions!

But sometimes tattoos have the opposite purpose. Tattoos are often used to express *individuality* as well as group membership. A person might get a tattoo with a particular, unique design to advertise a piece of himself or herself. A tattoo can represent a hobby (like skiing or music), someone you care about (your mother, or a religious figure), or something special about you (your astrological sign, or the flag of the country you were born in). Or it can remind you of a particular time in your life that was especially memorable. In these examples, tattoos are about personal expression.

However, in a sense, getting a tattoo in the first place can still reflect a sort of group membership. That is because some people get tattoos simply because they want to feel as though they fit in with a certain type of crowd; they want to be cool or make a statement. They get a tattoo because tattoos are trendy, or because they see their favorite celebrity or idol has one and they want to be like those people who are up to date on the latest looks. Or someone might get a tattoo simply as a way of rebelling against authority—either parents or other adults. (If you got told that you weren't allowed to get one, you might feel that getting one anyway would demonstrate that no one can control you or your body.) These reasons for getting a tattoo should make you think twice about getting a permanent piece of art on your body. Fashions and trends change all the time. How are you going to feel about having something on your body that will not go away, especially if it is no longer "in"?

Also, consider the different opinions people have about tattoos. Some people find them attractive, interesting, or cool. Others find them the exact opposite—ugly, silly, and pointless.

Problem is, you never know what type of person—pro- or anti-tattoo—you are going to be dealing with in different situations, such as a job interview, a date, or meeting a new group of friends. It is important to consider this before you decide to get a tattoo, because it may help you decide what design to get and where to put it, or whether you should get one in the first place. It is also important to consider whether tattoos are allowed in places where you spend a lot of time. Although tattoos are more socially acceptable now, there are places where they may not be permitted. Certain schools, places of employment, and clubs may not allow visible tattoos. When basketball player LeBron James was still in high school, he had to put bandages on his tattoos so no one could see them during games.

The most important thing to think about when you get a tattoo is the fact that it is permanent. If you are thinking about getting one, you have to remember that the tattoo you get today will stay on your body for the rest of your life. When your favorite band breaks

HEALTH WATCH

There are some health risks associated with getting a tattoo. Though it is normal for a new tattoo to bleed a little bit for up to twenty-four hours after you get it, and possibly ooze clear, yellow, or blood-tinged fluid for several days, bigger health problems can happen from getting a tattoo, such as:

- Infection.
- Skin reactions or raised scar tissue (keloid).
- Allergic reactions to the dye, which can cause hives, swelling, or difficulty breathing.
- A life-threatening medical condition such as tetanus, hepatitis, or HIV.

up, you'll still have the tattoo; when you've broken up with your "true love forever," you'll still have the tattoo. So, the decision to get one should not be taken lightly. Although there are techniques for removing tattoos, having one removed is much more expensive than having one put on. Laser removal can range from several hundred dollars to thousands of dollars, depending on the size, color, type, and location of the tattoo and the number of visits required. Plus, removal procedures are far from perfect; you can tell when someone has had a tattoo removed because it leaves sort of a smudge and discoloration on your body. Another consideration is that medical insurance generally doesn't pay for it, since it is considered a cosmetic, not medical, procedure and thus not necessary.

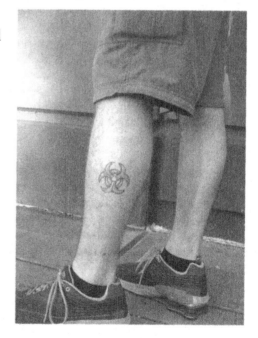

Finally, you need to think about how old you are before going out and getting a tattoo. First of all, in most states it is illegal to get one if you are under 18; in Oklahoma and South Carolina it is illegal to get a tattoo no matter how old you are![5] But equally important is the fact that most bodies are still growing during the teenage years. That means that the tattoo you get at age 16 or 17 may not be in the same place on your body when you are 25 or 26, and most likely will not be in the same place when you are 40, never mind 70. Think of all the sagging, growing, and stretching that your body will be doing as you grow and grow older. Then, think of where the design will be after a decade or so. You may want to reconsider your tattoo (or at least its location) after thinking about this.

PIERCING HEALTH

Another important thing to think about before getting a piercing is how well you will be able to care for it. Approximate healing times for different piercings:

Belly button	6–9 months
Ear lobe	6–8 weeks
Ear cartilage	6–9 months
Eyebrow	3–6 months
Nipple	3–9 months
Nostril	3–6 months
Tongue	2–3 months

There are many things that can affect the time it takes for a piercing to heal. Infections are common if you don't take good care of yourself. Other things such as stress, diet, physical and personal health, clothing, and of course how well you care for it will also determine how long it takes to heal and if there are complications or not. Don't forget to *clean* your piercing as it heals, and *leave it alone* when not cleaning it.

Piercings

Like tattoos, many different body piercings have a rich history. The first nose piercings were recorded over 4,000 years ago in the Middle East.[6] They then became popular in Africa as nomads wandered across the world. However, it wasn't until the late 1960s that nose piercings became popular in America, where they first appeared among the hippies who traveled to India. Piercing later became part of the Punk scene of the late 1970s, as a symbol of rebellion against conservative values (even safety pins were used instead of traditional jewelry).

Tongue piercing was practiced as a part of a ritual by the ancient Aztecs and Mayans of Central America. The tongue was pierced to draw blood to offer the gods. Even ear piercing (the oldest documented at 5,000 years ago) was first used for magical purposes.[7] However, belly-button piercing seems to be a modern invention and has never been recorded in ancient cultures; the first ones were seen in the 1980s or so.

Today, piercings are pretty common among young people. Although the most common place to be pierced is still the ear, one poll showed that 20 percent of teens who have at least one piercing have another body part pierced as well (such as nose, belly button, or eyebrow). When asked who helped them decide to get a piercing, about half of teens said no one influenced them, while about one out of four said that their friends influenced them. Only 4 percent said that their parents had any influence.[8]

Although piercings are less permanent than tattoos, you should still think carefully before getting one. Piercings can close up if you take out the jewelry, making them reversible in a sense, but they do not always heal completely and may leave a scar that never fades. As with tattoos, it is important to think about what part of the body you want pierced. Belly buttons are less likely to be seen by more conservative people like parents and bosses, who may not think too highly of them. A nose or eyebrow piercing, on the other hand, is pretty hard to hide. The good thing about a piercing, however, is that you can take the jewelry out (once the hole has healed properly), so you do not always have to draw attention to it if you are in a situation where having a bright object on your face may not be appropriate. That way, you do not have to let everyone know about it. Still, when a person looks closely at you, you can still see the hole.

Although you may not care what "other people" (read: adults) think about you right now, you may care—or have to care—in the future. So think about their possible reactions carefully before getting anything done—especially if you want to get a very visible (or controversial) body part pierced.

Branding

Another way that people change their body is by branding them, even though this procedure is currently illegal in the

United States. Historically, branding has been around since the 1800s. Back then it was a form of torture or used to mark criminals according to crimes they committed. Slaves were sometimes branded to show ownership. Today, some African American fraternities use branding as part of their initiation ceremony (athletes Emmitt Smith, Michael Jordan, and Shaquille O'Neal all have the brands of their fraternities). Even though branding is not required to become a part of a fraternity, some members choose to brand themselves as a way to show their permanent loyalty to the group. Those who support fraternity branding say it proves commitment—by undergoing a painful experience that marks their skin forever, people with a brand show what they are willing to do for their fraternity. Others simply think that it is too extreme and unsafe.

Plastic Surgery

There are some teens—though not very many—who think about getting plastic surgery as a way to improve their looks or make themselves feel more confident. It is pretty clear that plastic surgery is very common among models and actors. Boob jobs, nose jobs, tummy tucks, liposuction—who is getting what done to themselves makes entertainment headlines on a regular basis. Also, makeover reality shows have moved into using plastic surgery rather than clothes, haircuts, and makeup to help someone change his or her appearance.

Still, plastic surgery among teens is pretty rare. Only 4 percent of all the cosmetic surgeries performed in the United States were done on people younger than 18. Still, that small number represents an increasing trend; more teens are getting "unnecessary" plastic surgery than ever before.[9] Although no one is sure why this is the case, several reasons have been noted. For one thing, more plastic surgeons are available today than there were ten years ago. Also, plastic surgery has become a more public and visible solution to our unhappiness with our appearance (thank the celebrities and advertisers for that), and more and more Americans have been searching for a quick fix to their problems. But, unless you have unlimited income and a really good reason to want plastic surgery, chances are you are not going to get it. Still, there are some cases where you may decide it is the best thing for you to do. There are three main reasons why someone might get plastic surgery:

1. **For reconstructive reasons: This is when a person has a defect on their face or body either because they are born with it, or because they were in a horrible accident or suffered a traumatic injury and need to have something repaired.**

2. **For health reasons: Some people need to change their body in order to live a healthier life. For example, someone might need a nose job in order to be able to breathe more easily, liposuction to be able to get around better, or a breast reduction to help ease back pain.**

3. **For cosmetic reasons: This is when a person simply wants to change how they look because they are not happy with their appearance.**

If you are thinking of getting plastic surgery, think about which of these three reasons explains why you want to change part of your body *forever*. (You can't get the old *you* back, you know.) Some teens do indeed get plastic surgery for very good reasons. Someone who was caught in a horrible fire can have his burns fixed so that the scarring is not so bad and the wounds can heal better. Someone who is born with a cleft lip can have it repaired so that dental problems are prevented later on.

However, if you want to get plastic surgery simply for cosmetic reasons, there are many things to think about before going under the knife (they don't call it *surgery* for nothing!):

1. *Why do you want to change yourself enough to risk having a medical procedure?* **Many teens feel insecure about their bodies, and almost everyone (teens and adults) wish that they could change a thing or two about their looks. What makes your situation so different that surgery will solve the problem? Once you fix one body part, you might simply become unhappy with a different body part. It's a vicious cycle.**

2. *Are you still growing?* **If you haven't finished growing yet, it is not a good idea to get plastic surgery. The part of your body**

that may seem too big or too small now may grow right into proportion when you are done developing.

3. *Are you willing to deal with the consequences that come with your after-surgery body?* If you get liposuction, for example, you also need to change your eating and exercise habits. Otherwise, your body is eventually going to look like it did before your surgery. If you get your stomach stapled, your eating habits will have to change drastically; a person with a stapled stomach can only eat one cup of food at a time!

4. *Do you really believe that getting plastic surgery will make you feel better about yourself?* Sometimes you might feel down, lonely, or as though no one will ever think you are attractive. These feelings about yourself might make you think that changing a part of your body—your nose, your chin, your chest—will turn you into a different person. It won't. You will be the exact same person with a slightly different nose, chin, or chest after the surgery is done.

The most common cosmetic surgery procedures performed on people younger than 18:

- Rhinoplasty (nose job).
- Breast reduction (in both males and females).
- Chin augmentation.
- Lipoplasty (liposuction).[10]

If you think you might want to get plastic surgery, you will have to talk to many different people—your parents, so that they can give permission (if you are under 18, that is); a pediatrician or other doctor, so that he or she can figure out how much more growing you have to do; and the plastic surgeon, so that he or she can learn about what you want to have done, why you want to get it done, and whether he or she is willing to do it after hearing your story. A responsible plastic surgeon will meet with you at least two times before agreeing to any procedure and may even turn you away if he or she feels that your expectations for what the surgery will do for you are not realistic (for example, most plastic surgeons automatically turn away teen girls looking for breast augmentation). This is because chances are plastic surgery will not change your life.

It does not come with a guarantee that it will make you more popular, like yourself better, or improve your chances of getting a date with your sexy classmate. All plastic surgery can do is take one part of your body and make it look a little bit different, and as a result make you thousands of dollars poorer (it ain't cheap, you know). So think about it—is this the option you want for yourself, or is there another way you can help yourself feel better about the way you look?

HOW YOU TREAT YOUR BODY

Eating Habits

We all need to eat. It is one of the few basic needs that humans have. Yet there are many different eating styles and habits that make the act of

> On a typical day, 39 percent of teens eat fast food.[11]

eating a unique part of a person's life. It may not seem obvious, but the way you eat and what you eat are a part of who you are. Are you the sort of person who eats on the run? Do you prefer to sit down and have a meal with your family? Do you hold certain beliefs that restrict what you eat and when? The things you eat and the way you eat can say a lot about who you are and the sort of life you lead.

HELPFUL HINTS

People who eat "on the go" sometimes have a hard time making healthy food choices and develop poor eating habits. Fast-food restaurants and convenience stores are full of foods that are high in calories and low in nutritional value. In order to eat better without spending a lot of time, it sometimes helps to pack healthy snacks in advance so they are ready whenever you find a spare moment to replenish your energy. Carrots and fruit are easy to eat on the go, as are energy bars.

Your lifestyle might influence your eating habits. If you have a hectic life with lots of hobbies, friends, and commitments, sometimes eating feels more like a hassle than a need. You might find yourself eating alone, feeling rushed as you wolf down your lunch, and basically seeing eating as another thing to accomplish on your very long to-do list. For you, eating may not be all that much fun or even interesting.

There are also people who make eating a social time with their friends. They meet at a particular place every day at school, or they set a weekly time for a lunch date in order to catch up with each other. Some sports teams have breakfasts together on the morning of an important game in order to get the team together for fun before the competition begins. Eating with friends can be a way to have fun and build strong relationships.

Then there are families that place a lot of importance on eating together, if not once a day, at least once a week. The family meal is not there just so you can get your daily supply of vitamins and energy, but it becomes a time that you can talk, share, and just be with each other. Sometimes family meals emphasize your culture and traditions based on the food that is served. Your father may take time to cook up a dish that reflects your heritage. Your grandmother may grab an old family recipe for extra special occasions, like a birthday or for the celebration of a good report card. Or, for some families, Thanksgiving Day is just not the same without Uncle Antwon's famous dressing. You may even get into the spirit of family meals by trying a new recipe or thinking of topics to discuss at the dinner table, such as something you saw on the news, the last movie you saw, or what you would like to do over the weekend. For people who often eat with their families, food can be associated with social events, comfort, and good times. In fact, without mealtimes, it might become hard to connect with one another and keep up to date on family happenings.

Your religious or cultural beliefs may also affect your eating habits. For example, some Jewish people follow fairly restrictive and complex rules about food. They do this to obey the divine law contained in the Torah. Food that is okay to eat is called *kosher*, a Hebrew word that means "fit or proper" according to the dietary laws. Food is determined to be kosher if it conforms to the rules provided by the Torah. For example, the Torah states that kosher mammals are those that chew cud and have cloven or split hooves (so cows are kosher, pigs are not). Kosher fish must have both fins and scales. Fish and meat may not be eaten together at the same meal. In addition to what foods Jewish people may eat, kosher laws dictate how some foods are prepared. For example, these laws require that everything that comes in contact with milk products needs to be kept apart from things that are used for cooking or eating meat.

There are some Islamic laws, or *halal*, that concern food. The Koran, or the holy book of the Muslim religion, forbids certain foods and regulates eating patterns during certain holiday periods. For example, pork and birds of prey are forbidden foods. There are holidays designated as "feast" days, and holidays (most famously, the month of Ramadan) during which Muslims must fast, abstaining from all food and drink from dawn until sunset.

Among Asian religions, Hindus believe that the cow is sacred and are therefore never allowed to eat beef. They believe that milk, yogurt, and clarified butter are innately pure. Jainism, which is a branch of Hinduism, states that its followers must be *vegans*, which means they cannot eat any animal-related food (see the section on Vegetarianism following). They may even avoid root vegetables (vegetables grown underground), because insects clinging to the root may be hurt or killed during the harvest.

Christian faiths also have food restrictions. According to Roman Catholicism, Catholics should avoid eating meat on Fridays during Lent (that's why many restaurants serve clam chowder as their soup of the day on Fridays), and they should abstain from food and beverages one hour before taking communion. Mormons generally avoid alcohol and caffeinated beverages.[12]

Vegetarianism

Many people choose to adopt a vegetarian lifestyle. This means that they choose to not eat meat. There are many reasons people become vegetarians:

- To avoid cruelty to animals and harm to the environment.
- For health and diet reasons.
- For religious reasons.
- For financial reasons (vegetables and grains cost a lot less than most meats).
- To be different.
- To fit in with their friends.

Lots of people have more than one reason for not eating meat. Before becoming a vegetarian, it is important to think about your reasons for choosing this restricted diet. These reasons may influence not only your decisions about what you eat, but also what you might buy or believe in.

Flexitarian: **A person who chooses to eat vegetarian for health reasons but eats meat every now and then.**

There are different kinds of vegetarian diets. Some people, although not strict vegetarians, will eat fish but will not eat any other kinds of meat. Strict vegetarians will not eat meat or fish. Ovolacto vegetarians will eat dairy products and eggs, because no animals are actually killed when making these foods. Finally, vegans believe that they should not eat any animal products at all: meat, fish, eggs, or dairy products—anything that comes from an animal. True vegans will also avoid any processed foods that use animal fats, so they must carefully read the ingredients of all foods before having any of them. For example, many packaged cookies and snack cakes are made with animal fat, and many fast-food restaurants cook their French fries in animal fat. None of these foods would fit into a strict vegan diet.

If you are thinking of becoming a vegetarian or vegan for political reasons, it might be important to you to think about

REMEMBER

Not everyone chooses to become a vegetarian. Just because you don't eat meat does not mean that everyone else will agree with your decision. Don't force your beliefs on anyone, but talk to your friends and family to help them understand why you eat the way you do. They may not agree with you, and you might not agree with them, but at least you can learn to respect each others' choices.

how animals are used in other products that you may own. For example, some vegetarians do not wear leather shoes or jackets because it too comes from animals that are killed. Wool clothing might be okay for a vegetarian, but not some vegans, since the lamb or sheep was not killed for its coat, but strict vegans rule out wool. Also, some makeup and beauty products such as shampoo, lotion, and toothpaste are tested on animals before they are given to humans to make sure they are safe. If you are against animal testing for beauty products, read the labels of these things before you buy them. There are many brands that say something like "no animals were used to test these products" or "cruelty-free," meaning that using these products would be consistent with your beliefs about how humans should or should not use animals for their own benefit.

If you are thinking of becoming a vegetarian for health reasons, remember that not all meats are bad for you, and not all breads and vegetables are good for you. There are many meats that are low in fat and calories, while still rich in vitamins. There are also many breads and even some fruits and vegetables that are very high in calories—especially if they are prepared with a lot of sugar or butter.

No matter what your reasons are for becoming a vegetarian, it is important to make sure that you are getting enough iron, calcium, protein, vitamins D and B12, and zinc in your diet if you are not eating meat. Talk to your doctor about making sure you are getting all the nutrition you need as your body continues to grow.

Steroids and Supplements—
Body Image Issues Aren't Just for Girls Anymore

Although body image issues are usually associated with being female, males can also be insecure about their physical appearance. Many images in the media— perfectly toned men advertising the latest exercise equipment, hulking forms ready for battle in video games, and bigger, faster, stronger professional athletes—can make a guy feel like his body shape simply isn't good enough because he doesn't resemble those images. And this insecurity shows. One study found that men overestimated the body size that women think is most attractive. Whereas guys thought women wanted someone who was cut like the Incredible Hulk, in reality women said they preferred someone with at least thirty pounds less muscle.[14] But there is also competition among guys—who is the strongest, who can flex the best bicep—these situations can also cause a guy to try to bulk up in hopes of winning the admiration and approval of his peers.

Almost half of men are dissatisfied with their muscle tone. More than a third want bigger pecs.[13]

Going to the gym and exercising can be good ways to become stronger or more muscular—as long as you don't overdo it. The body needs time to heal between workouts in order to get the most benefit from the exercise, and lifting too much weight or lifting too often can lead to muscle damage. Yet even going to the gym regularly won't make you look like the latest superhero. In fact, today's G.I. Joe action figures have a body shape that would be almost impossible to attain just by working out (for example, G.I. Joe's biceps are as big as his waist in some dolls; his chest is bigger than those of most football players!). It would take a more dangerous strategy—steroid use—to even come close to that sort of look.

Unfortunately, it is becoming more popular for guys to turn to steroids or dietary supplements designed to enhance the body to help them feel better about their bodies or more competitive as an athlete. While it is true that taking steroids may make you stronger and leaner and give you more stamina, those appealing characteristics come with a cost. Steroids can cause shrunken testicles, impotence, difficulty or pain while urinating, the development of breasts (in guys, that is), baldness, and infertility. They can also stunt your growth. So, the question becomes, do steroids really make you more manly?

RECENT RESEARCH
More than half a million high school students currently use steroids.[15]

Those people who are aware of the dangers of steroids sometimes turn to other supplements that claim to be safer. While it is true that vitamins and minerals can help a body grow, many of the fancier supplements have not been proven to actually do anything. In addition, some are known to be dangerous for your health. Possibly the best-known supplement is creatine, which advertisers claim is the "legal and safe steroid." Many professional athletes such as baseball great Mark McGwire openly admit to having used creatine, seeing it as very different from taking steroids. However, there are side effects associated with this supplement. Taking more than five grams per day leads to kidney and liver problems. Some athletes stopped taking it because it can cause severe diarrhea and other digestive problems. So, even if it is legal, creatine can still be hazardous to your health. Getting a bigger body doesn't seem to be worth the risk.

Other guys use weight-loss supplements in order to help them in their athletics or simply to make them look better. Wrestlers, for example, sometimes use them in order to qualify for a particular weight class if they are a few pounds too heavy. Gymnasts and rowers will sometimes do the same thing. The problem is these weight-loss drugs can also be dangerous. Although the Food and Drug Administration has issued a consumer alert about the dietary supplement ephedra, it was

IN THE NEWS: STEROIDS IN PROFESSIONAL SPORTS

Steroid use by professional athletes was enough of an issue for President George W. Bush to mention it in his State of the Union Address on January 20, 2004. The president said:

Athletics play such an important role in our society, but, unfortunately, some in professional sports are not setting much of an example. The use of performance-enhancing drugs like steroids in baseball, football, and other sports is dangerous, and it sends the wrong message—that there are shortcuts to accomplishment, and that performance is more important than character.

Less than a month later, Greg Anderson, the personal trainer for baseball great Barry Bonds, was charged with drug and steroid conspiracy. Newspapers all across the country cried out that America's pastimes were full of corruption and deceit. Famous sportscasters, including Dan Patrick on ESPN, talked constantly about what would happen if we found out that some of our sports heroes used steroids and therefore basically cheated when they set new records. In January 2005, Major League Baseball unveiled a new, tougher policy on steroids that included stiffer penalties and heavier fines for players caught for using performance-enhancing drugs. The U. S. Congress set up a committee to investigate steroid use in baseball. Sportscasters and fans across the country speculate about the validity of records that have been broken by possible steroid users.
The issue continues . . .

very popular among athletes because of claims that it helped with weight loss and enhanced performance. However, the dangerous side effects of ephedra include high blood pressure and other stresses on the circulatory system (heart). Baltimore Orioles pitcher Steve Belcher's death at 23 was attributed to ephedra, which helped put major restrictions on the substance.

Body Image

Your body plays a major role in how other people see you. After all, your body is a significant part of yourself, along with your mind. Not only do other people form opinions about who you are by what your body looks like, but you do too. How you feel about your body has a lot to do with how you feel about yourself. Your feelings and thoughts about your body are known as your *body image*.

Body image: How you feel about how you look.

Unfortunately, our society creates very high and restrictive expectations about what bodies should look like in order to be considered attractive. Although bodies come in many shapes and sizes, very few body types are considered "acceptable" in the media. In order to conform to the ideal, girls need to be very thin, have big breasts, and be quite tall. Boys need to be muscular and tall and have a full head of hair. It's no wonder that most people end up feeling concerned about how they look.

But body image isn't only about how big or small you are. Usually, when we think about our body image, we mostly think about how we feel about our weight, chest, hips, stomach, legs, and butt (boys and girls tend to put different levels of emphasis on these body parts). However, there are other parts of us that can carry a lot of our image and/or identity. Hair, eyes, skin tone, noses, even our arms, can be very important to us. Different people see different parts of their body as important depending on what else in their life they believe is worth emphasizing. Family resemblance, athleticism, ethnicity, sexuality, your unique personality—if any of these things are important to you, you may find that different parts of your body are more important than others. For example, people who take pride in their Chinese heritage may love their eyes, with their particular color and shape; meanwhile, someone who prides herself on her rebellious nature may adore her blue hair, and a tennis player may find his arms his best feature to emphasize.

Why is it that people with curly hair seem to prefer straight hair, and people with straight hair wish theirs was curly?

It would be ideal if everyone was happy with his or her entire body, but we are realistic and know that this is rarely the case. (If you are one of those people who truly love yourself just the way you are, congratulations!) We hope at least that you will see that everyone, you included, has some great features worth emphasizing. Of course, there are parts of us that aren't our favorites. Instead of hating those parts, or wishing you could change them, work on accepting them. See your body as a complete package. Don't worry about each feature separately; instead, see yourself as a whole person whose various parts fit together just right to create your look. There is no point in obsessing over a particular aspect of yourself that you don't like. No one's body is perfect. And just think—that very feature that you don't like may be someone else's favorite part about you.

HOW YOU LOOK INFLUENCES HOW YOU ARE TREATED

Margie is a 19-year-old college student with a job as a manager at a copy shop. Although she is very bright and professional, she is also "energetic and outgoing." These characteristics, along with her appearance, make her seem younger than she is, which sometimes makes it hard for her to do her job.

Q: How would you describe yourself?
Margie: I am very driven. I would also say that I look very young for my age and I also have blonde hair.

Q: What is the most important thing people should know about you?
Margie: The most important thing people should know is that even though physically I may look immature, I am more intelligent than my years would indicate. I am also more mature than many people assume I am.

Q: How do you think others see you?
Margie: People see me as a young girl. Even though I am a supervisor at work, when someone (usually a male) comes into the shop, they don't approach me first. People have even said to me that they do "not need to be told what to do by some girl." I believe that I am not taken as seriously as someone with brown hair.

YOUR BODY'S INFLUENCE ON YOU

Obesity

People often make a lot of assumptions about someone based simply on their body size. Today, American society has a negative image of overweight people. Larger people are often assumed to be lazy, slow, stupid, ugly, and have no willpower or motivation. On the other hand, thanks in part to the media and fashion industries, being thin is often associated with being happy, confident, loved, and ambitious. Of course, these generalizations are not necessarily true. There are larger people who achieve great happiness and have wonderful, successful careers. For example, Oprah Winfrey is a successful talk-show host and businessperson, no matter what her size! And there are thin people who are very unhappy, are not in a relationship, or do not do so well in school. I'm sure you know some.

But the stereotypes sometimes become self-fulfilling prophecies. For example, research shows that overweight people tend to do less well in school—but not because they are not as smart as thin people. Instead, their school performance suffers because of how they are treated by classmates and teachers. Thinner people sometimes treat heavier people poorly for two reasons:

1. They believe that how much a person weighs is completely under personal control. Therefore, they think a person can become thinner if he or she just tries hard enough. Their logic continues that if a person is overweight, that just means that the person is too lazy or doesn't care enough to do anything about it. Since heavier people don't care about themselves, why should others care about them?

2. Since people who are heavy face a lot of prejudice, thinner people may make fun of overweight people because they are afraid that somehow they will be associated with being fat if they associate with someone who is not thin.

Neither of these reasons stands up to common sense. First of all, there are many people who try to lose weight without

Ronald McDonald is the second most popular fictional character among children today (Santa Claus is #1).[16]

success. Scientists have discovered that a person's size is due in part to genetic makeup. This means that a person's biology helps determine body size and shape (but it is not the only cause). Some people's bodies have a natural "set point" of a higher weight than others, meaning that their bodies naturally tend toward a certain weight that is heavier. Other things also affect a person's weight, such as depression, cultural influences, and the fact that fast food is cheaper and more accessible than lower-calorie options (think about how hard it is to find nutritious food at or near school). Then there is the fact that almost all diets—95 percent—fail. That means that 95 percent of people who lose weight on a diet gain it all back eventually.[17] So many people are trying to lose weight, but are not having much success.

And another thing, pounds are not contagious. A person does not gain weight by standing or sitting next to someone who weighs more than they do. But some people act as though it is possible to become overweight just by associating with heavier people. Even online medical information sees the need to assure its readers that "obesity is not contagious."[18]

The bottom line is no matter why people are teased about their weight—whether they are "good" reasons or not—the fact is that teasing hurts. And people who are teased about their weight often end up feeling guilty, lonely, embarrassed, and even full of self-hatred. Body image and weight issues face extra complications when a person becomes depressed because of the teasing and then eats to make him- or herself feel better, which only makes the weight problem worse. It's a vicious cycle.

If you are a thin person, there is no reason to tease a person who is heavy. People don't need to be reminded that they are overweight—they know they are already. Overweight people are rarely happy about their body size and shape and usually know that they are putting themselves at risk for various health conditions because of their size. Pay attention to the attitudes and opinions you have about people who are overweight. Think twice before you trust those thoughts—just because someone is heavy doesn't mean they aren't fun to be with.

While it is important to try to lose weight for health reasons, believing that you will become a happier, more successful, and more popular person simply by losing weight is a dangerous mindset. Thinness is not the ticket to a better life, though there are health benefits to being of average weight. There is the sad reality that some people

---

THE HEALTH RISKS OF OBESITY

People who are overweight have a greater chance of developing:

- High blood pressure
- High cholesterol
- Type 2 diabetes
- Heart disease
- Stroke
- Breathing problems
- Cancer
- Depression

In fact, obesity is the second leading cause of preventable death in the United States.[19] And experts believe that it will be the main cause of preventable death within a few years, passing smoking sooner than you think.

HISTORICAL PERSPECTIVES ON BODY SIZE

Large people have been perceived differently throughout different cultures and historical times. When food and other resources are scarce, being heavy carries a positive image, because larger people are thought to be able to afford the food and other luxuries that others cannot. Simply put, being big means you have wealth and a comfortable lifestyle when those around you don't have their basic needs met. You can see this in the paintings and sculptures of certain time periods, for example. The Rubens ideal woman is very fleshy and curvy and would probably be seen as fat by today's standards. Back then, it was ideal beauty. However, when there are plenty of resources to go around, as there are today (for the most part), being larger is associated with laziness and poor willpower.

might treat you better simply because you are less heavy, but life is not that simple. If you feel that you need to lose weight for health reasons, that's great. But if you think that losing weight will change you into a completely different person, be careful of setting your expectations too high. Work with a doctor, counselor, or even friends to remind yourself that you have a lot more to offer the world than just a shapely body. And even if you are a few pounds less, you will still be the same person with the same interests, goals, and passions that you have now.

The Other Side of the Story

Although it is usually heavier people who are teased, sometimes a person is teased because he or she is skinny. Guys may get teased for being "weaklings" while girls may be called "anorexic" (see below—this is nothing to laugh about). Again, being teased about one's body is difficult to deal with. You may not be able to help how your body is shaped, although often there are things you can do to make sure you are healthy. Talk to your doctor if you are concerned that you do not weigh enough.

And, if you find yourself making fun of people because of their smaller body size, ask yourself why you do it. What is it about a thin person that you believe deserves ridicule? Are you seeing that person as someone who is weaker than you are? More successful at conforming to the ideal body image created by the media? Whatever your reasons, chances are that when you are making fun of someone, you are revealing an insecurity you have within yourself. By exploring your own attitudes about your body and what people are "supposed" to look like, you may no longer feel the need to tease people who look different than you.

Eating Disorders

While it is important to care about your appearance and weight, sometimes this concern can go too far. When this happens, it is possible to develop unhealthy eating patterns that can result in an eating disorder. Although most of the time (about 90 percent) girls are the ones who are diagnosed with eating disorders, boys can get them too. There are basically three different types of eating disorders:

1. **Anorexia Nervosa: a condition in which a person has an intense fear of becoming fat and therefore either refuses to eat or severely restricts food intake.**

2. **Bulimia Nervosa: a condition in which a person has a sometimes secretive cycle of binge eating and purging (or other compensation for caloric intake, like exercise or laxatives) in order to control his or her weight.**

3. **Binge Eating Disorder: a condition in which a person will occasionally binge, eating beyond the point of being comfortably full. Unlike Bulimia Nervosa, however, the teen will not purge afterwards.**

What Causes Eating Disorders?

Even though eating disorders are often about food and weight, what causes an eating disorder is usually more complicated than just having poor body image. Many people do not like their bodies, yet thankfully most of then do not develop eating disorders. So what are the things that separate those people who develop eating disorders from those who do not suffer from these illnesses?

THINK ABOUT IT
How much happier are you really going to be if you lose ten pounds? How much is your life going to change if you develop bigger biceps?

One thing that contributes toward eating disorders is something called *body image disturbance*. This is when a person misjudges how large or small they really are. When people with body image disturbance think about what they look like, or even when they look in the mirror, they perceive themselves to be a different shape than they are in reality.

Many of us might look in the mirror and not be completely happy with what we see. That is because no body is perfect, and we all have flaws. However, most of us end up shrugging our shoulders and telling ourselves that we are good enough. Sure, there are parts of us that could be better, but as a whole, we tell ourselves that we look pretty darn good.

But not everyone is able to look in the mirror and accept what they see. A girl with body image disturbance may think she looks fat when she is really just skin and bones. A boy with body image disturbance may see himself as a weakling when really he is a slender guy with a highly toned body. When people think that poorly of their bodies, they start thinking negatively about themselves. This self-concept—which is based on inaccurate visions of body size and shape—might cause some people to develop an eating disorder in hopes of changing their body into something more "acceptable." Problem is, since people with body image disturbance do not see themselves accurately, they are never satisfied with the results.

People with eating disorders will sometimes use food and their ability to control how much of it they digest in order to put some control and structure into a life in which they feel out of control. Oftentimes, people with an eating disorder feel unloved, depressed, or overwhelmed. Excessive dieting, bingeing, and purging become ways to cope with the bad feelings they have about themselves. However, sometimes these coping strategies take over; the teen loses control over her sense of what is healthy and unhealthy, and places herself in great danger both physically and emotionally.

The prevalence of bulimia increased dramatically in girls living in Fiji after American television programming was introduced to the country.[20] Think our culture plays a role in whether people like their bodies or not?

Many people believe that America is to blame for eating disorders. American society places great pressures on people to be thin and attractive. Many products are available for sale that promise that by using them you will be happier, more beautiful, and a better person. When we sit down and think about this, we know that nothing could be further from the truth. A miracle diet will not win you friends; a special cream will not make you more popular. Yet advertisers design their commercials to make you feel bad about yourself so that you end up buying their product in hopes that it will make you feel better. It won't, of course. In fact, the opposite could happen. You may end up buying something, hoping it will make you feel better or look better, but it doesn't live up to its promises, which makes you feel worse, which might make you tempted to buy something else in hopes that the new product will change the way you feel and how you look. But of course it doesn't and the cycle continues. Unless you put a stop to it. Don't fall for advertisements that promise you popularity or a significant other if you buy their product. Remember that people can be

WHAT TO DO IF SOMEONE YOU KNOW MIGHT HAVE AN EATING DISORDER

- *Express your care and concern.* If the person feels that you are attacking him or her, he or she will not want to listen. Let your friend know that you are only talking because you are worried and care.

- *Collect evidence of your concern.* Note times when your friend does any of the following: purges, skips meals, overeats, overexercises, abuses laxatives or diet supplements. Also note your friend's moods and level of stress and irritability.

- *Ask if the person wants to get help.* You might say something like, "I am concerned about your health. I am not sure if you have an eating disorder or another concern, but a professional might be able to tell. Would you consider getting help?" Offer to help make the call or go with your friend.

- *Know where to get help.* An online source is www.somethingfishy.org, which has a great list of resources—both local and national.

- *Do not feel rejected if the person does not want help.* Denial is very common among people who have trouble. Seek help or advice from a professional or adult if you want to, for your own well-being.

- *Tell the person you will always be there for him or her.* It may take time, but eventually your friend may come to you when he or she is ready for help. Or your friend may just be happy knowing you are a true friend.

beautiful and not look like the models in the magazines. Does a guy really have to have a six-pack in order to look cute? Does a girl really need to show some cleavage in order to win someone's heart? No! An attractive person is someone who cares about what he or she looks like on the outside and has a great personality inside. No commercial is going to admit that—otherwise, a lot of companies might go out of business.

The bottom line is that having an eating disorder is not about dieting or simply needing to lose a little bit of weight. When someone has an eating disorder, it consumes his or her life. It's about believing that one's weight and appearance are the keys to happiness and satisfaction with life. It's about feeling in control. One of the biggest myths a person with an eating disorder believes is that "Life will be better and I will be happy when I lose the weight." However, the reality is that people do not necessarily feel better when they lose weight. The only way a person with an eating disorder can feel better is by getting help and being treated for the illness.

Physical Disabilities

Teenagers with physical disabilities face extra challenges when it comes to forming their image and their identity. First, it might be hard to get people to see beyond your crutches, wheelchair, braces—whatever—and have them see the person behind the limitation. What are the things you can do that will help people see the whole you? Second, spending your life with a serious or chronic health condition can be a stressful and often painful experience. What can you do to help yourself live life to the fullest?

Unfortunately, teens with disabilities can both stand out yet be ignored in a group of people. Their physical disabilities or the equipment they use to get around may make their presence pretty obvious. But often, people ignore those with a disability out of fear, misunderstanding, or awkwardness. People may worry about saying the wrong thing or being unable to deal straightforwardly with them—sometimes people are very shy and awkward around situations they do not understand, and simply avoid them in order to avoid embarrassment. Since many people are not familiar with physical disabilities, they may steer clear of people who have them in order to avoid the unknown.

Even if people with disabilities are noticed, sometimes they may feel that their disability is ignored—which can be like pretending not to notice the elephant in the middle of the room. Hopefully there is a balance between assuming that someone is defined by a disability and treating the person as if he or she isn't disabled at all. If you think about it, either way could be kind of offensive. It would be difficult to have other people assume there is nothing else important about you but having a disability, but having people pretend something isn't true about you might communicate that having that characteristic is wrong, shameful, or weird.

REMEMBER
You can't ignore your disability, but you can't let it dominate you either.

If you have a physical disability, it is important to consider how it fits into your sense of self. Although your disability most likely plays a part in who you are and what you like to do, it is by no means the only thing. When you describe yourself, is the first thing that you mention your disability, or is it your love of video games, your friendships, or the fact that you are an excellent trumpet player? Chances are, you are

CHECK IT OUT!

Encourage Online: www.encourageonline.org
A place for teens with chronic illness and their family and friends to talk and connect.

Adolescent Employment Readiness Center: www.dcchildrens.com/about/abt2c1_mn.asp
A national program that helps teens with disabilities and chronic illnesses obtain useful job skills.

a very well-rounded person just like most people—in other words, you are not just your disability. Do you show all these sides of yourself to others?

Even though you are a complex person, it is wise to figure out how your disability does influence your life. What sort of control do you have over different parts of your life? Are you able to drive? Dress yourself? Live on your own when you get older? These are things that many teens take for granted but that you need to take seriously. Even though there might be things that you will never be able to do independently, there will always be things that you can do on your own (no one can ever take away your thoughts or your creativity, for example).

Instead of torturing yourself over what is not fair, and what could be, learning to accept your limitations can actually

be empowering. There is no sense in wasting time over things that you cannot change, no matter how frustrating they may be. Instead, see yourself realistically—make a list of all that you can do, and note your challenges as well. Then look at your challenges and assess which ones you may be able to conquer with hard work and which ones will always be difficult for you. By focusing on what you can and hope to do, you can help the true you emerge—a person who happens to have a disability, not a person who is a disability. Other people will see that and react to you as a person—not a person who needs extra attention or help.

While you are thinking about your abilities and limitations, it's also a good idea to be aware of your feelings about your disability. Different people have different attitudes about their physical limitations. Some people accept them, while others deny them. A disability can make a person feel resentful, bitter, guilty, helpless, lonely, embarrassed, or shy. But it can also make a person feel lucky, thankful, or appreciative of the little things that many others take for granted. A disability can sometimes even lead you to develop greater skills in other areas. Some blind people have amazing abilities to hear and distinguish sounds—an ability they might not have developed without the inability to see. People confined to wheelchairs may develop incredible arm strength.

Some people embrace their disability and see it as an opportunity to express their uniqueness and ability to connect with others. They speak at different places to inform people about their particular condition, or they start support groups or websites to connect people like them to each other. Your attitude toward yourself shapes the image you present to the world. If you are angry or miserable because your body doesn't work the way it is "supposed to," people may be able to sense that and stay away from you. They aren't staying away because you are different—they keep their distance because you give off an image of being unapproachable and not very fun. Nice, happy people are more likely to make and keep friends, no matter who they are or what they look like.

TAKING ADVANTAGE OF A SUPPOSED DISADVANTAGE

Some people who live with a disability choose to dedicate their lives to helping people understand their condition and how people like them manage everyday activities. For example, in 1995 Heather Whitestone-McCallum, who is deaf, was crowned Miss America. In fact, when host Regis Philbin announced she was the winner, Whitestone-McCallum couldn't hear and the runner-up had to nudge her to let her know that she had won. Since then, Whitestone-McCallum has dedicated her life to visiting kids who are deaf and telling them that their disability should not limit their goals and dreams.

Living with a Chronic Illness

Cancer, diabetes, asthma, depression, lupus, cystic fibrosis—many illnesses can affect a person for the rest of his or her life. How each person chooses to cope and adapt to his or her health condition will help determine not only quality of life but also the length of that life. Although a chronic illness may not be as obvious to others as having a physical disability, being in relatively poor health can alter the way others see you and how you see yourself.

Learning how to cope with a chronic illness can be challenging. Although different health conditions have their own sets of challenges, living with any chronic illness requires you to accept your health condition, learn how to care for yourself, and adjust your lifestyle so that you can live the best, healthiest life possible. The more you take an active role in

STAGES OF COPING

Although everyone needs to cope with the life they have, it is often more difficult for someone with a disability or chronic illness to adjust. Here are the three stages of the coping process for people with poor health:

1. The first stage is highly emotional. A person who has just been diagnosed, or whose life is changing in other ways (by moving to a new school, wanting to start a new hobby, or trying to make new friends, for example), will feel a lot of things. Anger, confusion, worry, sadness, frustration, disappointment—or any combination of these feelings—are all common reactions to one's health, body, family, or the world in general when you think about how your body is not as healthy as a young person's body "should be." All feelings are normal, and it's important to acknowledge them.
2. The second stage of the coping process is learning. The more you know about and understand your health condition, the stronger you feel and the better able you are to take care of yourself. As the saying goes, "Knowledge is power."
3. Finally, a person has learned to cope with an illness or disability when he or she is able to incorporate the condition into regular life, and start living again. In this third stage, your life does not always focus on your health (although sometimes it has to), and you are able to become a well-rounded person, taking things as they come.

your health, the better you will feel about yourself both physically and emotionally. Managing your health, asking questions about your condition, and understanding your body will all give you a sense of power and security, which will build up your confidence in your ability to live a great life.

Still, all the hassles of having a chronic illness might cause you to go through a time of denial or anger about your condition. These feelings might tempt you to not take your medications or follow a particular diet. Although you should acknowledge your feelings about your health, it is also important to keep taking care of yourself during these times. Continuing to manage your health will help you not only keep control over the illness, but also show a level of responsibility and independence that you are capable of having. You will also be able to prove to yourself that you are able to be strong during rough times.

Sometimes people, despite their best intentions, slip up and do not follow their treatment plan for a while. Nobody's perfect. But the sooner you get back on track with managing your health, the better you will feel both physically and emotionally.

However, no matter how well you take care of yourself, how others perceive you and your health can still affect you. Sometimes, your appearance changes because of your illness or the medication you take. For example, going through chemotherapy will most likely cause you to lose your hair. Although wigs and hats can cover up your head, people may still stare and make you feel embarrassed or awkward. Other medications can make you shake or twitch, which can also make you—and others around you—feel weird. When your illness draws unwanted attention to you, it can make it more difficult to be your whole self—the person you are outside of your illness.

When this happens, try to accept other people's fears about your health. Maybe they feel sad or afraid for you. It is not easy to see a young person be sick. In our society, young people are perceived to be strong, healthy, and able to conquer the world. Seeing a teen in a fragile and vulnerable state can be very threatening to a person. Although on some level you are the one who probably needs the support, maybe you can offer some support to those who feel awkward around you. Tell them that your appearance may look strange to them, but that to you, these changes in your looks represent getting better. Because that is what these medical treatments are doing—sending you on the road to recovery. Hearing that side of the story makes everyone feel stronger and hopeful, which is important to feel as you continue to manage your health.

Your illness also might make it hard for you to become more independent from your family as you get older. You may have health needs that require you to get some help. Or your parents might have been so involved with your health care since you were little, that they may find it difficult to let go of their role as primary caregiver and let you take care of yourself. Although it is great to have support from family (and friends), make sure you try to take care of yourself as much as possible. This will help with your confidence and make you a stronger person.

YOUR TURN

Here are some questions for you to think about:

1. **How do you describe your fashion style?**

2. **What do you want your clothes to say about you?**

3. **What other styles do you see in your school? What stereotypes do others attach to them?**

4. **How do you feel about being required to wear uniforms?**

5. **Do you have any tattoos or piercings? What do they say about you?**

6. **Have you considered getting a tattoo or piercing? Why or why not?**

7. **If you could change one thing about your body, what would it be? What is your favorite part of your body?**

8. **Do you think minors should be allowed to have cosmetic surgery?**

9. Describe your body. What do you look like? What are your most important physical characteristics?

10. What attitudes do you have toward food?

11. How do you take care of your body?

12. How does your physical condition affect what you can and cannot do?

13. How do the media affect how you feel about your body?

NOTES

1. Harris Interactive, *Trends & Tudes Newsletter* 2, no. 2 (2003).

2. "Skin Stories: The Art and Culture of Polynesian Tattoo," PBS (2003), accessed March 12, 2004, at www.pbs.org/skinstories/history.

3. Harris Interactive, "A Third of Americans with Tattoos Say They Make Them Feel More Sexy," news release, October 8, 2003, PRNewswire.

4. TalkSurgery.com, "Tattoo Trauma: Now That You Have Got It, How to Get Rid of It?" accessed March 14, 2004, at www.talksurgery.com/consumer/new/new00000084_1.html.

5. Channel Oklahoma, "Tattooing Illegal in Oklahoma . . . Except," accessed March 14, 2004, at www.channeloklahoma.com/news/2167172/detail.html; "State's Tattoo Proponents Eager for Legal 'Ink,'" *Greenville News*, http://greenvilleonline.com/news/2004/03/14/2004031427040.htm.

6. C. Morrison, "Body Piercing History" (1998), accessed March 14, 2004, at www.painfulpleasures.com/piercing_history_htm.

7. Morrison, "Body Piercing History."

8. Teengrowth.com survey results, accessed March 2, 2004, at www.teengrowth.com.

9. C. Kuzma, "Unnatural Beauty," Teenwire, accessed March 2, 2004, at www.teenwire.com/infocus/2003/if_20030711p240_surgery.asp.

10. Kuzma, "Unnatural Beauty."

11. S. A. Bowman et al., "Effects of Fast-food Consumption on Energy Intake and Diet Quality among Children in a National Household Survey," *Pediatrics* 11 (2004): 112–117.

12. P. G. Kittler, K. P. Sucher, and Four Winds Food Specialists, "Religious Food Practices," accessed February 14, 2004, at http://asiarecipe.com/religion.html.

13. H. G. Pope, K. A. Phillips, and R. Oliverdia, *The Adonis Complex: The Secret Crisis of Male Body Obsession* (New York: Free Press, 2003).

14. Pope et al., *The Adonis Complex.*

15. P. Zickler, "NIDA Initiative Targets Increasing Teen Use of Anabolic Steroids," *NIDA Notes* 15, no. 3 (2000).

16. E. Schlosser, *Fast Food Nation: The Dark Side of the All-American Meal* (New York: Perennial Press, 2002).

17. National Eating Disorders Association, "Listen to Your Body" (2002), accessed May 15, 2004, at www.nationaleatingdisorders .org/p.asp?WebPage_ID=286&Profile_ID=54933.

18. WebMD, "Obesity: Topic Overview" (2003), accessed May 24, 2004, at http://my.webmd.com/hw/weight_control/hw252867.asp.

19. American Obesity Association, "Obesity Research," accessed May 24, 2004, at www.obesity.org/subs/fastfacts/Obesity_Research .shtml.

20. A. Becker, R. Burwell, S. Gilman, D. Herzog, and P. Hamburg, "Eating Behaviours and Attitudes Following Prolonged Exposure to Television among Ethnic Fijian Adolescent Girls," *British Journal of Psychiatry* 180 (2002): 509–518.

Who You Hang Out With

3

Who you choose to spend your time with says a lot about who you are. That's because humans are social creatures. We like to belong to groups of people who share common interests and passions. We like to spend time with those who make us feel liked, loved, and special. It feels good to hang out with people who think we're neat. Who you choose to be with and the kinds of people you like also say something about you to others. Your choices can say that you feel you are like certain people, or they can imply that you find certain activities fun, or that they are at least okay with you. The people you hang out with are a public representation of parts of yourself. Finally, the people you hang out with can also influence you and your decisions; we can learn a lot from the people we spend time with.

For all these reasons, it's important to "be yourself" when you hang out with people you want to like you. If you put on an act and behave in the way you think they want you to, what happens when you show a side that is more genuine? What happens if you make friends while you are pretending to be something or someone you aren't? You will never know if they like you for you or if they like the act that you put on. If you present yourself to others the way you feel naturally, you never have to worry about what others will think about you if they only knew the truth.

Besides, it takes too much energy to be someone you are not—you always have to think about what you should be saying and how to say it. You always have to think much too hard about what to be like, the same way an actor needs to "stay in character" when working on a play or movie. Being yourself is a lot easier in the long run than putting on a show for everyone else.

This chapter talks about the different relationships we have with friends and acquaintances and how those relationships influence the sort of person we are. It also looks at how other people may perceive us based on whom we associate with.

GROUPS

It's great to hang out in a group. By spending time in a group instead of with only one or two others, or with no one at all, you get a chance to learn how to interact with a variety of people, meet new friends, experience how others deal with certain problems or social situations, and see that there are others out there who have interests similar to yours. One of the most important things you can do in your teen years is find a group of people to spend time with that you like. It's a part of growing up.

However, who you spend your time with can have a lot of impact on your image. Other people make lots of assumptions about who you are by the people you hang with. "Birds of a feather flock together" is an old saying that means those who spend time together have a lot in common. For example, if you hang out with members of the drama club, people are going to think you like acting or at least attending plays. If you chill with people who smoke, people might assume that you smoke too (whether there is actually a cigarette between your fingers or not). While it may be true that you and your friends have similar interests, it does not mean that you are exactly the same as people you are seen with. Still, you should at least be aware of the way others think when you associate with particular crowds and individuals.

So, who are the people you hang out with? What are their reputations? How might these reputations influence how others perceive you? What consequences or benefits are there to being associated with your group of friends?

LABELS

Many groups of teens have labels, and these terms carry a lot of meaning. Think about the labels you have heard in your life. Some of the more popular ones are burn-out, freak, goody-goody, gamer, goth, hippie, jock, loner, loser, nerd, player, raver, skank, skater, and stoner. As you read each of these words, a picture of a person probably pops into your head. You know what that person looks like, what they wear, what they are interested in, what sort of music they are into, and maybe even how well they do in school or how well they get along with their parents. That's a lot of meaning to get out of a single word! Thing is, all people who get the same label are assumed to be alike. Deep down, you probably know that people are more than the group they are in, or whom they hang out with, but you can't help the associations you have learned to have about various labels.

THINK ABOUT IT
Think about a time when you decided not to approach someone just because he or she was in a different group than you are.

It's hard to shake the label once we hear it used on someone. It's easy to look at a person, form an impression, or see which group he or she hangs with, and feel that we already know quite a bit about who that person is. From that, we

81

sometimes decide whether or not we want to get to know that person better or even want to be associated with him or her in the first place. For example, a goth may decide not to say hi to that cute guy in the hallway simply because he is a jock, even though she really appreciates his sense of humor in class. And a geek might feel that she has no time for a drama queen even though she was impressed with her performance in the school play.

The problem is, making assumptions about people solely based on their group is stereotyping. We usually associate the word *stereotype* with race, ethnicity, gender, and even sexual orientation. But to believe that you know things about someone simply by observing whom they hang out with or what they look like is also stereotyping. And this sort of thinking can be oppressive, limiting, and lead to false assumptions about other people.

It might be hard for you to see beyond someone's label or reputation, and it might be even harder to shake a label once it is used on you. Just as you stereotype people based on what they look like and whom they hang out with, others look at you and your crowd and make similar assumptions. Taking an honest look at yourself from the perspective of those who simply see you from the outside can help you understand why people treat you the way they do. Understanding these reasons does not make it okay for people to judge you based on your peers, but it can help you decide whether you want to change the first impression you make on people (if you feel you can) or see why people seem to treat you a certain way before they even get to know you.

For example, you might hang out with people who wear only black and listen to depressing music. As a result, others may think you are not all that fun to be with. Is that the impression you want others to have of you? What if you are interested in meeting new friends, or what if you are tired of looking on the downside of things all the time? You might want to put on a brightly colored shirt, or smile as you walk down the hallway. Sure, you are taking a risk by changing your normal ways of doing things, and you are also separating

FEELING TRAPPED BY YOUR LABEL?

Tired of being known by who you hang out with and not who you are? Here are some things to do to shake things up:

1. *Say hello to someone new every day.* Smile at someone you want to get to know. Or say hi to someone who doesn't seem to know too many people. Even if you don't make any friends this way, you will feel better about yourself.
2. *Try talking to someone outside your circle.* Don't think about social status or who is supposed to be cool, friendly, whatever. Just talk to someone you have never talked to before.
3. *Expand your social circle.* If it's too hard to meet new people in your school, try meeting people in your community through volunteer work, or at your church, synagogue, or mosque.
4. *Join a new club.* Do something you have always wanted to try, or are at least interested in. Meet people who like the same stuff you do.
5. *Do things that contradict your label.* Wear different clothing, listen to different music, take a different class. Do something that shows you are more than the label people have given you.
6. *Focus on being yourself and ignore people who stand in your way.* Do what you want to do—whatever feels right. By being yourself, you will at least grow out of your label in your own mind; others will figure it out soon enough.

yourself from your usual crowd. But that doesn't mean that you don't like your old friends anymore—it just means that you are willing to try something different and show others a side of you that they are not used to seeing.

We all know that people are more than labels. Just because you belong to one group and another person belongs to a different group does not mean the two of you have nothing in common. In fact, you may be more alike than different. Or just because you belong to a certain crowd does not mean you do all the things that the group tends to do. An individual is much more complex than a group label. It's up to you to not only make sure people understand that about you, but to also make sure that you do not make generalizations about other people based on whom they associate with.

CLIQUES

Cliques aren't the same thing as a group of people. Cliques usually form in junior high or middle school, but they sometimes still play a pretty big role in high school. The term *clique*, unlike *group*, carries negative associations. That's because cliques are *exclusive* groups of people. Of course there are groups of people who hang out together and are not judgmental or exclusive. Those groups are not cliques, because they are open to new people and new ideas. A clique, on the other hand, is a group of people who:

1. **Leave other people out on purpose.**
2. **Act as though members are better than other people.**
3. **Are often mean to those who are not in the clique.**

Why do people in cliques tend to treat others so poorly? A couple of reasons come to mind. For one, the exclusiveness of a clique helps those in the group feel better about themselves because, by not letting certain people into the group, the group puts on a strong, powerful image. This image makes those in the group feel better about themselves because they were chosen to be a part of it. The group gives them a sense of belongingness—and let's face it, it feels good to belong.

CONSIDER THIS
People who are part of the popular crowd are not always happy and secure. They may be afraid that they will slip up and lose their acceptance. Or they may not feel as though they deserve to have such cool people be their friends.

The obvious downside, of course, is that those people not invited to be a part of a clique, or are made fun of by a clique can end up feeling lonely, insecure, unhappy, and not liked. If a group of people teases you, it can obviously affect your self-esteem and confidence. Although it is much easier said than done, try very hard not to take criticism from a clique too seriously. Instead of focusing on what other people say about you, spend time focusing on your own life and accomplishments. Don't worry as much about what other people think about you—even the supposed "popular crowd"—or how you compare to others. Constantly comparing yourself to others only leads to trouble because no matter how great you are (and we are all pretty great in our own ways), there is always someone out there who is better than you are in a particular talent or skill (unless, of course, you hold a world record in something, but even those are often broken). Knowing and liking yourself—both your strengths and the things that could use a little improvement—gives you a sense of pride and confidence that you can accept yourself the way you are and work to change the negative parts on your own time.

This brings up another reason people in cliques are often not nice to other people: they do it to hide their own fears and insecurities. Some people believe it is very important to be a part of a particular group because it increases their self-esteem. They feel the need to "be popular" not because they actually like the popular crowd, but because they want to feel liked by people who seem to matter. What does it actually mean when someone says "I want to be popular"? Does it mean he or she wants to feel important? Be well liked? Feel good about who they are? People who make a big deal out of being popular often have little sense of self-worth on their own and thus need to be part of a group in order to feel good about themselves. They figure that if the popular crowd accepts them, then they must be okay, even though deep down inside they are not so sure. The security of clique membership can provide them with protection from their own self-doubt.

Because these people need group membership in order to feel okay about themselves, they feel a need to separate themselves from those not chosen to be a part of it. By seeing nonmembers as not as good as they are, they justify their group membership and their coolness that results from it. They tease and put down others (or simply ignore them) to make themselves feel as if they are better

REMEMBER
Bad-mouthing people gets old quickly and doesn't earn you any respect from your peers.

85

than those who do not fit in. This helps them hide their own insecurities about who they are and who likes them. Sometimes people in cliques tease others because they are afraid that if they don't target someone else, they will become the target.

Of course, basing your self-esteem on whether you are part of a certain clique or not is a dangerous mindset. Because, sometimes, a clique can boot a member out pretty quickly and for no apparent reason. Maybe someone didn't date the right person or didn't go to the party on Saturday or stuck up for the "wrong person" in an argument. Any of these things can anger the group and—in order to preserve its exclusiveness—a clique will remove anyone who does not follow their code. So, if a person finds self-worth based on a particular group membership and then ends up being dismissed from the clique, this might cause him or her to end up feeling no good. As you can see, basing your self-worth on whether or not a certain group accepts you is a losing proposition.

GANGS—THE ULTIMATE CLIQUE

Sometimes people hang out in a particular group and refer to themselves as a crew, posse, or a particular name ("The Street Survivors," for example, or "The 41 Club"). Then there are groups of people who hang out together and are sometimes

WARNING SIGNS THAT THE PEOPLE YOU HANG WITH MIGHT NOT BE REAL FRIENDS

- There are rules about what you can do and what you can wear.
- You feel pressured to uphold an image that you don't feel is real.
- You don't feel so happy when you are with your supposed "best friends" and would rather spend time with someone else.
- You feel pressured to conform to ideas and opinions that you don't agree with.
- Your friends exclude other people—even those you think are fun and interesting.
- You feel fake.

involved in violent, illegal, or criminal activity. These groups are gangs. Gangs usually associate themselves with a common name, symbol, and color; they might wear a certain type of clothing or identify themselves in another way. Gangs have a very distinct image. One of violence, drugs, and fear.

This image of gangs isn't far from their reality. A gang is a very risky group of people to get involved with. Gang members are much more likely than others to commit serious and violent crimes. Violent conflict between gangs is common, and gang members are about sixty times more likely to be killed than everyone else. People involved with gangs are also three times as likely to be habitual drug users.[1]

Why would someone want to join a gang? Despite the fact that gang membership can be very dangerous, people do have understandable reasons for joining them—some reasons are related to the need to fit in and belong, while others are related to gaining a certain image. Some people join gangs for the following reasons:

- *To find a family who cares.* People who don't feel close to their families sometimes see a gang as a substitute family that can help them feel less lonely and unwanted. They see the gang members as people who will accept them and stick by them, no matter what; the gang provides them with the love and sense of belonging that they don't get at home.

◎ *To escape a bad family situation.* Sometimes a person is abused by his or her family. In order to feel safe, and to get away from a bad home life, a person may join a gang. Even if the gang is not all that safe, at least it might be safer than home—or at least the violence may be more predictable.

◎ *Peer pressure.* If everyone else a person knows is in the gang, it only makes sense to join too. Sometimes, gang members are particularly popular, and that makes it appealing to join.

◎ *Safety.* When a person lives in a very unsafe neighborhood, joining a gang can seem like a form of protection against a violent community. In a gang, you have people who are "watching your back" no matter what. However, this protection is not as real as one might think. Being a member of a gang often means that a person is more likely to be involved in violence—becoming a more likely target for rival gang members and others than before.

◎ *The thrill.* Some people are attracted to gang life because it seems thrilling, and even glamorous. "Gangsta rap"—the songs of Snoop Dogg, Dr. Dre, Tupac, and others—often glorifies the violence associated with gang life. They see the illegal activities and violence of gang life as exciting and wild instead of dangerous and life-ruining. Or a person can see being a gang member as the ultimate rebellion.

◎ *Respect and power.* Some young people join gangs in order to gain respect and power in their neighborhood. The problem is: whose respect are they getting? And under what circumstances? Sure, they may earn the respect of fellow gang members, younger kids, and some peers. But they certainly are not respected by adults, or peers who choose not to be involved in gangs. Within the neighborhood, gang members are often feared, and this gives them a sense of power. Though this power may be real in some respects, it is also limited. This power is not bigger than the law; it is not enough to leave a person feeling safe or untouchable.

◎ *Money.* Gangs make money through illegal activities such as robbery, theft, and selling drugs and weapons. For people who do not believe they will be able to get a more traditional (and

**legal) job because of their schooling or learning difficulties,
or because they don't know anyone with a successful career,
they may see gang work as the only way to earn a living.
Or they may be tempted by what looks like "easy money"
in large quantities and the immediate results of their labor.**

Despite the appeal of being a member of a gang, the bottom line is that the risks of gang membership outweigh the benefits. Also, the solutions that gangs seem to offer are not very secure. The feeling of safety is limited because the violence of gang activity leads to more violence; the power one gets is limited to a small area and a select group of people. Most people realize the fleeting nature of gang benefits. For example, gang membership has decreased over the past ten years or so. And for those who still end up joining a gang, their membership usually doesn't last long. One-half to two-thirds of gang members leave the gang by the end of their first year, growing tired of the scene or realizing that gang membership causes more trouble than it is worth.[2] So, with time, gang membership is losing its appeal and prestige among youth. The benefits simply do not outweigh the dangers.

You can save your image and sense of self by taking the first step and avoiding joining a gang in the first place—you will be far ahead of those friends who join for a little while and then (hopefully) drop out before more serious consequences result.

GROUP, GANG—WHAT'S THE DIFFERENCE?

When is a group just a group or crew, and when is it actually considered a gang? Here are four differences:

- *Gangs tend to be exclusive.* Members don't spend much time, if any, with nonmembers. People in gangs might cut themselves off from friends and family not involved in the gang.
- *Gangs are involved in crime.* Gangs tend to do things that are criminal, or at least anti-social. Gangs are involved in illegal activities for several reasons: interacting with rival gang members, in order to build a reputation in the neighborhood, and as part of the initiation process (being "jumped in").
- *Gangs have rivalries with other gangs.* Rivalries among different gangs are traditional and are rarely questioned or evaluated. These rivalries can be dangerous, even for those not directly involved in a particular situation. This is because anyone associated with a gang may be in danger from either known or unknown rivals.
- *Gang loyalty is very extreme.* Members are expected to stay with the gang once they have been "jumped in." They are also expected to do whatever activities the gang as a whole thinks are okay, regardless of personal feelings about such activities. So, even if you are not interested in doing drugs or carrying a weapon, you may "have" to do these things in order to be part of the gang.

In other words, gangs are exclusive, are violent, and have distinct enemies. Groups of people who happen to hang out together will welcome new friends, are rarely violent, and do not seek revenge or hate a particular group just because other members do.

FRIENDS—THROUGH THICK AND THIN

Even though we spend a lot of time hanging out in a group, often there are a few people that we feel especially close to and think of as our closest or even best friends. Our friends are often one of the most important parts of our lives, and we often feel that being a good friend is one of the most important parts of ourselves. So what makes someone important enough to be considered a real friend and not just a pal, buddy, or acquaintance? Real friends are people who don't mind if you do something different from them, say something stupid, or make a mistake (as long as you apologize later). They accept you for who you are. That doesn't mean that they like everything about you, but they understand that you come as a whole package and don't try to change one part of you so that you fit in better. Real friends know the truth about you, and you can trust them with your biggest secrets and fears. They are people with whom you probably have things in common, like activities and experiences. They're probably fun to be with, and they make you feel good about yourself.

Having good friends is important because they accept you in ways that adults may not understand or see things about you that most others overlook. They understand what you are going through, either because they identify with your situation or because they are going through the same things themselves.

But even if you and your friends have similar problems, good friends see things not only from their own point of view, but from your point of view as well. And sometimes a friend can see your problems from a more objective point of view than you can. Because a friend might see things differently than you do, he or she may say things that you might not want to hear. But a friend's opinions about and insight into a particular situation may make sense because he or she is able to see things and observe parts of the problem that you are not able to. Because a friend cares about the problem (because they care about you), but is not directly involved in the situation, he or she can step outside the issue and take a look at it from all perspectives. Your friend may point out that you are being mean to someone and hurting the person's feelings, or that your parents might actually have a point when they are concerned about your grades. By listening to your friend's opinions about a particular situation or issue, you can learn these new perspectives and really understand how other people might feel

THINK ABOUT IT
How did you and your best friend meet? Did you like each other right away? It can be fun to take a trip down memory lane and think about how you and your friends first met.

or think. Or you may be able to solve a problem you are having in a way that you could not have thought of yourself. Keeping an open mind about what your friends tell you can help you see things in a new light and either challenge or help reinforce your own beliefs.

How good a friend you are says a lot about what kind of person you are. Most close friendships evolve naturally over a period of time. Seeing someone a lot, going to the same activities, or having a lot of the same classes allows you to get to know someone and see him or her in different settings. After a while, certain people become interesting, fun, and personable to you. Those people eventually become your friends.

However, it takes time and effort to both make friends and maintain a friendship. If you neglect a friend, or assume that a friend will be there for you even if you are never there for him or her, you are in danger of losing that friendship. You need to have one-on-one time with someone in order for the friendship to truly survive. Friendship requires give-and-take and sacrifice; sometimes you need to put your problems and needs aside in order to give full attention to someone else. Friendship also requires flexibility; friendships should be flexible enough to survive certain types of change, like when a friend starts dating someone or moves to a new school but still lives nearby. Or maybe you need to be a little flexible about when the two of you get to hang out. Sometimes you may need to be understanding when your friend has a last-minute change in plans. However, if a friend flakes on you too much, that may be a signal that your friend is taking you for granted and is not willing to put in the effort and dedication it takes to keep your relationship going.

In yearbooks, it's common to sign "BFF"—"Best friends forever." But not all friendships last. It's sad to think about, but just like romantic relationships, sometimes friends break up or stop hanging out with each other as much as they used to. Over

time, you may not feel as close to someone who was very important to you in the past. You may find that your interests or priorities have changed, which can mean you have less in common with a friend than you did before. Ending the friendship may be the best thing for you, since you are no longer relating to that person like you used to. Friendships can also just end on their own. This might happen because two people don't spend enough time together, or they just don't talk anymore.

> **REMEMBER**
> Sometimes it's better not to have a close friend than it is to stay friends with someone who causes you pain.

Some "friendships" can even be damaging; friends can be abusive, needy, or encourage you to engage in risky behaviors. If a friend causes you nothing but sadness, trouble, and stress, then you might want to question why that person is your friend. Remember: if someone fills your life with more hurt and trouble than happiness and support, that person isn't really a friend.

When a friendship ends, it may involve not just the two friends but several people who are part of the same group. It may be difficult for you to stay part of a group once you end a particular friendship. This may be a lonely experience, as you may find it hard to turn to someone after leaving a core group of people. It can also cause you to question your decision to end the friendship and make it hard to move on. Talking to someone you trust, like another friend outside the group, a family member, or even a counselor may be helpful. They can help you see that losing a friend, even by your own decision, can be painful; however, sometimes it is an important part of your growing process and becomes necessary in order for you to feel comfortable being who you are.

Overall, friendships should make your life more fun and enjoyable. People seek the company of others because it makes things more interesting, more meaningful, or easier to deal with. Of course there are times when bad things happen to you or your friend, and it is important for friends to stick together through those rough spots. But overall, having a best friend is one of the most important experiences a person can ever have.

GOOD FRIENDS ARE PEOPLE WHO:

Show respect.
Are kind.
Want to be with you.
Are supportive.
Stick up for their friends when they need it.
See things from another's perspective.
Understand and appreciate different points of view—even if
    they don't agree with them.
Are honest about their thoughts and feelings.
Are not afraid to be different.
Say they are sorry—and accept apologies.
Keep secrets and promises.
Accept people for who they are and don't try to change them.

KATHLEEN ON BEING A FRIEND

Kathleen describes herself as "15 going on 35." She lives with her step-mom and her step-mom's lesbian partner, though technically her father has custody (she doesn't get along with his girlfriend, though, and likes her step-mom's partner a lot more). Because Kathleen "is always putting others first, before me," she believes that being a good friend is a very important part of who she is.

Q: What is the most important thing people should know about you? Why is this most important to you?

Kathleen: They should know that no matter what, I will stand by my friends' side and always be there for them, no matter if it's advice they need or someone to stand behind them when no one else will.

Q: How does being a good friend affect who you are?

Kathleen: It makes me strong and willing. Also, I have many friends who come to me in the time of need for help. It also boosts up my self-esteem and shows me that my life so far hasn't been a complete waste of time. But sometimes when I don't put myself first, it makes my life worse. And I go back a space instead of forward one. I have had a lot of things happen in my life, and no matter what it was/is, I will get through it. I will stand by people when no one else does because I know what it's like to be standing by yourself. Also, because of what I've been through, I have a lot of advice to share. I think my hard life and hard times was all worth it because of all the people I get to help in return.

Q: How do you think being a good friend influences how other people see you?

Kathleen: People trust me because they know I am not B.S.'ing them. They know I am strong, hard working, and always will speak my mind. That's why they see me as they do. A great friend to have around.

RELATIONSHIPS AND DATING

Relationships are a very important part of human life. Healthy relationships help babies grow faster and stronger, help people have better self-esteem, and make communities safer places to live. One example that illustrates how people need human contact is an experiment that was conducted in the 1950s.[3] Babies in an orphanage were raised in two different ways. The first group of babies was fed and bathed and clothed but otherwise were kept away from people in order to prevent them from catching any diseases. These babies experienced almost no talk, play, or contact with anyone. The second group of babies was raised in a group setting where there was a lot more social stimulation (some would even say chaos). They were held when fed, soothed when they cried, and interacted with both other babies and adults. After three or four months in these two different environments, the babies in these two groups began to differ from one another. The babies in the first group became withdrawn and expressionless. They rocked themselves, and hugged themselves, curling up in a ball. Some babies even got sick and died, even though doctors could find nothing wrong with them. The babies in the second group were happier and healthier. From this study, among others, researchers have concluded that people need human contact simply in order to survive.

Social contact is an important part of our lives, and for the most part, we get it from all sorts of places. On a typical day, we talk to many different people who have various relationships with us. We talk to bosses, friends, family members, professionals, store clerks, neighbors, teachers—the list goes on. And the types of relationships we have with these people also vary. We have casual, professional, loving, respectful, and even adverse relationships. The type of relationship you have with someone often determines how you interact with that person. For example, how you interact with your doctor is probably not the way you interact with your best friend—people have different ways of interacting in different relationships, and this is perfectly normal. Your ability to adjust to a particular situation and relationship helps you with the social contact you need to thrive.

However, even though social contact is beneficial, many people have taken the need for relationships to the extreme. They believe that they absolutely need to be in a romantic relationship in order to be somebody, feel loved, or simply fit in with the rest of the world. Our society supports this belief by placing a great deal of importance on whether someone is in a relationship or not. Questionnaires often ask people whether they are married or single. We hear things like "I was not whole until I met you," or "This person is my better half." Then there's the infamous line from the movie *Jerry Maguire*: "You complete me!" The message is that somehow a person is not whole without a special someone. Movies and television shows also make it seem as though being in a relationship is more normal than being single. Think about it: When was the last time a movie ended with someone walking off into the sunset alone? Or the final scene didn't feature a kiss between the leading actor and actress? Most television characters have a significant other, too, and if they don't, a lot of the plot of the show focuses on the character's dating life. Your peers may also pressure you into believing that you should be in a relationship. You might feel that you need to be in a relationship in order to fit in or feel popular.

Out of all the different reasons a person would want to go out with another, there are two basic types of reasons. The first type of reason is a personal reason. Personal reasons are reasons that concern you and your partner only. There is no consideration of anyone else in your decision to date each other. If you like each other for who you are, get along well together, are attracted to each other, and like and respect each other, then you are dating for personal reasons.

The second type of reason to go out with someone is a social reason. Social reasons are reasons that consider other people and how they think about you or the person you are with. For example, sometimes people want to be in a relationship simply in order to be accepted by a certain group. Or they want to go out with a particular person not because they actually like that person, but because that person is popular or somehow seen as quite a catch. How they feel about the person they are dating isn't even the main reason for going out! So, if you are dating someone just because that person is popular, so that you will be invited to the right parties, or simply because you think only lame people do not date, then you are dating for social reasons.

People who get involved in relationships in order to improve their social standing may expect too much from the relationship. They might believe that simply being in a relationship will make them more popular, feel better about themselves, and make them more mature. They may hope that by dating someone who is liked by other people, more people will like them too. All too often, these expectations are not met

97

by the relationship. This puts a lot of pressure on the couple and makes it hard for the relationship to last. Relationships are more successful if they happen for reasons that are personal to the people involved and are not determined by social pressures.

In fact, before entering a relationship, it is a good idea to ask yourself "What is it that I want to get out of this relationship?" or "Why do I want to spend so much of my time with this one person?" Don't go out with just anyone for the sake of being with someone—anyone—even though it might be tempting. Sometimes people get into a mindset where they believe they are nothing without a boyfriend or girlfriend. They feel unwanted or unloved and believe that they are not important if they are not someone's significant other. They believe that being in a bad or unenjoyable relationship is better than being alone. If you start to feel that way, you need to tell yourself that you are an important person with or without a significant other. The best thing you can do for yourself is to make sure that the person you *choose* to be with is a good person for you.

So, how do you go about figuring out what sort of person is right for you? Make a list of qualities that you believe are

ARRANGED MARRIAGES

An arranged marriage is when family members, usually the parents, choose a spouse for their child. (This is in contrast to a "love marriage," where spouses choose one another.) Since most parents want what is best for their children, their choice is thought of as likely to be the most appropriate for kids. They select spouses for their children based on class, shared family values, status, and perceived compatibility. Sometimes this happens when the child is still very young, as young as two or three; other times it happens when they are much older. In India, approximately 95 percent of marriages are arranged; worldwide, about 60 percent of marriages are arranged.[4] At present, no one is sure how many arranged marriages there are in the United States. However, arranged marriage is still a custom for many immigrants to the United States from countries such as Cambodia, India, Pakistan, China, and Japan.

essential for a good relationship partner, such as the person is kind, supports you, and makes you feel good about yourself. Make another list of qualities that are absolute deal breakers, such as the person smokes, mistreats a pet, has dropped out of school, doesn't believe in the same causes that you do. After you get a good sense of your relationship essentials, you can continue to make a list of qualities that would be nice to see in a person, or ones that you would prefer not to see in a person, but that are optional rather than essential. Remember—there is no perfect person out there for you. No matter how serious the relationship is, or how much you may love a person, there will always be things about that person that you do not like. That is okay. The trick is to look for someone who is the right kind of imperfect for you. And that sort of looking takes a lot of time, so don't worry about figuring it out right away. If you look for perfection, you are setting your expectations too high. And that means you will never be happy sharing a part of your life with another person.

Being in a close relationship with someone—or even just going out on a date or spending time together—gives you a chance to see how you interact one-on-one with people who have different personalities and to see if these different personalities click with you or not. Being in a longer-term relationship also lets you see how the combination of your personality and your partner's personality works in various situations. For example, how well do the two of you get along in a group? How well do the two of you study together? Try something new together? Talk about serious things? What happens when the two of you disagree on something? Spend time apart? It is important to experience your relationship under different circumstances so that you not only learn about what characteristics you like in a partner, but you also see how you react in different situations when you are with someone you care about.

Relationships let you discover what you are like when you get close to another person. You learn how you show affection, how you care for another person, how being cared about makes you feel. But in order to really learn and grow in a relationship, you need to be yourself. Too often, especially early on in a relationship, people are tempted to act in a way that they think the other person finds attractive. They may try not to mention things that bother them, or they may do things that they don't find fun, or they may lie about their own background or experiences just to impress the person they are with. That sort of fake behavior never works out in the long run. It's hard to keep up the act. And if you do manage to have someone fall for your fake self, what's in it for you? You won't know if that person will like the real you—the one that is most important. Although it isn't always easy, the best strategy is to be yourself from the start. That way, you have an honest sense of whether you are being liked for who you really are.

If you find someone you really like and they like you— congratulations! At first, you might feel all-consumed by this new relationship and want to spend all your time with this new special person in your life. However, don't let that "honeymoon period" last too long. Your friends, hobbies, and schoolwork need attention too. So does your family. Abandoning the rest of the things in your life that make you "you" will make you a one-dimensional, boring person. Everyone knows some inseparable couple who are "glued at the hip" or so constantly all over each other that it's annoying. Once your relationship becomes more secure and the two of you are more comfortable with your situation and each other, it can be very healthy for the relationship for the two of you to spend some time apart. And we mean time during the day, sure, but even perhaps over several days. That way, you will have things to talk about when you see each other again. You will also continue to grow as a person as you continue to do the things that you love to do. Remember, the person who fell for you liked the person you were before the two of you got together. Keep those pre-relationship activities and people in your life so that you can keep on being that exciting, well-rounded person.

Your Dream Comes True[5]

How can you tell if you are interested in being in a relationship for personal as opposed to social reasons? Do the following exercise and see!

Okay, now I want you to imagine you can go out with *anyone* you want for a day. Someone in your school, your neighborhood, an athlete, a movie star, an author, I mean *anyone*. Imagine you are with that person, and it's the most perfect day ever. You two have the best time possible. Get a good picture of that person and your day together. Imagine what you would do together (don't get too excited now . . .). You will always remember that day together as the most perfect day with this completely gorgeous, wonderful person. Picture the person that will be with on your perfect date.

Now there is a catch to this perfect date. (Of course! There is *always* a catch!) You *can't tell anyone about it*. And if you *do* try to tell someone—*anyone*—about it, *no one would believe you*. In fact, if you tried to tell anyone about it, you would be the laughingstock of your friends. How does the catch to the story make you feel? Does it change the person you want to be with? Why or why not?

Going through this imaginary exercise might help you figure out if you are more interested in dating a particular someone for personal or social reasons. If you were annoyed when you heard the catch to the story, or said to yourself "Then what is the point of being with that person?," chances are you

ASK YOURSELF
Do I really want to be with this person, or am I just feeling lonely?

want to be with that person for *social* reasons. If you still choose the same person, despite the catch to this game, because you knew it would still be the perfect day, congratulations! You are probably choosing that person for *personal* reasons.

Being in a relationship with someone should make you happy. However, over the course of your life, you are going to have good relationships, but there is also a good chance that you are going to have some not so good ones. The key is to know when to leave if a relationship is not going well. Only you know your own limits as to how much you are willing to work on a relationship. You may be someone who looks for a low-maintenance arrangement (a relationship that

One in four teens admits they have cheated on a partner.[6]

doesn't need a lot of work or effort, one that doesn't take up a lot of your time), or you may be more willing to deal with both the highs and lows of a relationship because you know that it takes time to make a true connection with someone. But even if it is hard to break up with someone, it is important to get out of a relationship if you are being mistreated or taken for granted. Ultimately, you learn something about yourself and other people from all of your relationships, not only while you are in them but as you reflect back on them once they are over.

WHEN TO END IT

You are more valuable than a relationship, and you deserve the very best. Not sure if you should bail out of the relationship you are in? If you see yourself in any of the following items, it is time to walk away.

- The relationship has more bad moments than good moments.
- You're being abused in any way—mentally, physically, or emotionally.
- Your partner lies or cheats on you.
- Your partner treats you poorly in front of other people, blaming or criticizing you when you don't deserve it.
- The two of you have different levels of commitment in mind (you are serious but he or she is not, or vice versa).
- You feel pressured into having sex or doing something else you do not want to do.
- Your friends warn you that the relationship doesn't seem healthy and you are way too quick to defend it.
- You've stopped hanging out with all of the friends you had before the relationship.
- Your partner's life is dangerous, involving guns, drugs, or other illegal things.

YOUR TURN

Here are some questions for you to think about:

1. Who are your closest friends? What makes each of them a good friend?

2. How do you spend time with your friends?

3. What are some of the social groups in your school or community? Where do you think you fit in?

4. Do you know people in other groups besides your own? How do you relate to them?

5. What are some of the negative effects you see of tight-knit groups or cliques? Positive effects?

6. Have you ever felt excluded from a group? How did you react?

7. How important is being in a relationship to you?

8. What kind of importance does your social group place on being in a relationship?

9. Describe your ideal date.

10. What is the dating scene like in your school or community? How do you feel about it?

11. What does it mean to be "in a relationship"? How do you know if you're going out or not?

12. What do you look for in a romantic partner? Are there any qualities that you see as "deal breakers"?

NOTES

1. J. C. Howell, *Youth Gangs: An Overview* (Washington, D.C.: U.S. Department of Justice, Office of Justice Programs, Office of Juvenile Justice and Delinquency Prevention, 1998).

2. National Youth Violence Prevention, "Facts for Teens: Youth Gangs," accessed June 12, 2004, at www.safeyouth.org.

3. Excerpted from L. K. Gowen, *Making Sexual Decisions: The Ultimate Teen Guide* (Lanham, Md.: Scarecrow Press, 2003).

4. J. Mackay, "Global Sex: Sexuality and Sexual Practices around the World," presented at the Congress of the European Federation of Sexology, Berlin, June 29–July 2, 2000.

5. Gowen, *Making Sexual Decisions*.

6. S. S. Feldman and E. Cauffman, "Sexual Betrayal among Late Adolescents: Perspectives of the Perpetrator and the Aggrieved," *Journal of Youth & Adolescence* 28 (1999): 235–258.

The Things You Do

While the things you *are*, or the categories you fall into, and the people you associate with are big parts of your identity, so is the way you spend your time. To a certain extent, you have even more choice here than in other areas. You get to pick what you want to do, within reason. So what you spend your time and energy on is a really public way of expressing who you are on the inside and what is important to you. Think about how the things you do both express who you are and become a part of your image of yourself.

SCHOLASTIC ACHIEVEMENT

You gotta go to school—at least for a while. Most states require that children attend school through age 16, but everybody feels a little bit different about it. School is an opportunity to learn information and skills that will hopefully be useful to you throughout your life. For some people, the education aspect of school alone makes it worthwhile. Curiosity is a strong motivating factor for some of us (the nerdy authors of this book included)—we just want to know things and enjoy learning. And even though school is something that is "good for you," we like it anyway. You might even enjoy learning outside the classroom, on your own time. For some people, being

The authors of this book have accumulated forty-five years of formal schooling between them!

intellectual, learning new things, or adding new skills is a huge part of who they are. They are always looking to pick up knowledge or see how things work. And for some people, school is pretty easy; they do well in most of their subjects. Being intellectual or intelligent has some obvious advantages, among them getting good grades, getting approval from parents and teachers, being qualified for a good college, and being considered for advancement in a job. People who are really into school and work hard at it can become very successful. You can earn the support and admiration of adults and peers by investing a lot of energy in school.

> In 1930, about half of people between the ages of 14 and 17 were enrolled in school.[1]

Unfortunately, we have a lot of derogatory terms for people who really like learning or who are particularly good at it. Nerd. Geek. Dweeb. Brain. And these names carry with them the connotation of social rejection. Those are powerful stereotypes, and they assume that kids who like to learn are unable to fit in or be liked by other kids. Or perhaps that they don't like the same things that "normal" kids do. We don't really have the same kinds of nasty names for people who don't care much about school—sure, you can call someone stupid or moron, but that doesn't seem as mean or socially rejecting. Somehow the world has decided that it is uncool to be smart or to like trying to be smart. So if you enjoy school or like to learn, you might find yourself facing people who want to make fun of you because of it. Molly still remembers being called a brain in second grade and being mocked when she didn't get something right.

Kids who are gifted, or who have particularly impressive talents or intelligence, face some unique problems as teenagers. Gifted kids sometimes get bored, frustrated, or ignored, in addition to feeling scrutinized or under pressure for being smart. It can be frustrating to feel that others look at you and your interests and make fun of them. Even though it seems like a contradiction, sometimes gifted teens fail in school for these sorts of reasons. This occasionally even leads them to drop out on their own, deciding that even though they could do

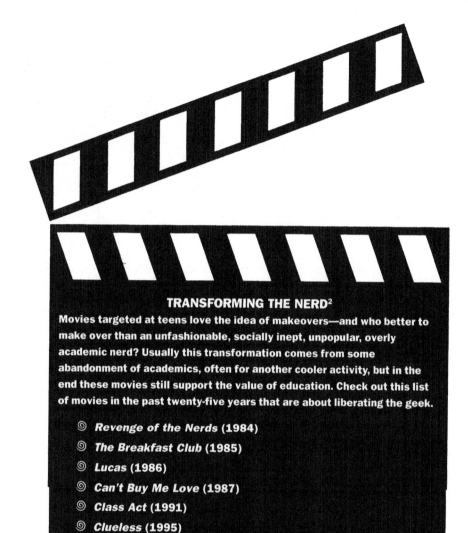

TRANSFORMING THE NERD[2]

Movies targeted at teens love the idea of makeovers—and who better to make over than an unfashionable, socially inept, unpopular, overly academic nerd? Usually this transformation comes from some abandonment of academics, often for another cooler activity, but in the end these movies still support the value of education. Check out this list of movies in the past twenty-five years that are about liberating the geek.

- *Revenge of the Nerds* (1984)
- *The Breakfast Club* (1985)
- *Lucas* (1986)
- *Can't Buy Me Love* (1987)
- *Class Act* (1991)
- *Clueless* (1995)
- *Can't Hardly Wait* (1998)
- *She's All That* (1999)

everything they are asked to do, it's just not worth their time because they don't get challenged enough.

Additionally, while devoting yourself to school can certainly get you important accomplishments and recognition, there is such a thing as overkill. Getting into a good college is important if you want that, sure, but there is so much more to being a teenager than school. And there is much more to life after adolescence than where you go to college. There are lots of kids who spend all their time doing homework, playing sports,

participating in activities, and volunteering their time—all to get into the best college they can—who never really have time to enjoy themselves. They might not get to just hang out with other teens or have strong friendships or get to do something just because it's fun. As we said in the introduction to this book, thinking of yourself as only one thing or choosing only one part of yourself to devote time to can be harmful. You can miss out on a lot if you pick only one thing when there are so many options available to you. School is a difficult thing to manage in your life, because there is a lot of pressure from teachers and parents to work hard at it—and we think you should—but even teens need to have balance. Good grades alone won't make you happy.

Although being a brainy teenager can be tough, the good news is that being smart seems to be more acceptable as you get older. As you age, the advantages of trying to be academically successful become more obvious. The environment you are in makes a big difference as to whether being smart can be compatible with being cool. There are high schools where students compete to get the best grades, and there are also schools where smart teens try to hide their academic success. As you advance in education, you may find more people like you who want to do well academically and will support and challenge you along the way. As time passes, being smart becomes a little bit cooler and worth trying for.

What if you're not a genius? The vast majority of us aren't. You can still like school, even if you aren't a straight-A student.

Most people aren't good at everything; instead, they have a few areas that they really like and are talented at. You might be a whiz with Spanish or make amazing pottery or be able to argue anything, but still get average grades in English or science. There are many different kinds of intelligence and many different ways to think about being smart or talented. The most obvious is academic intelligence—people who can remember lots of information or analyze things thoroughly. There are people who can solve math problems quickly or who understand every poem. But you can also have strong abilities in things like physical tasks, building or construction, music, communication or persuasion, art, design, foreign languages, and more things than we can think of here. And these are all things that can be not only rewarding to spend your time and energy on, but also fun. We can think of school as about reading, writing, and arithmetic, but it can definitely be more than that. You may find that there are things other than traditional academic subjects that you love and are talented at.

It is also worth mentioning that just as everyone has different areas of talent, everyone may have different styles of learning. For example, Molly loves to read things—seeing them down on paper helps her remember them. But her sister seems to remember everything she hears, so she would rather go to a lecture and hear someone talk about a topic. Some people like to learn by doing—Kris would rather take on a task or problem and solve it herself, or work with her hands to understand how something works or is put together. In the same way, some people need rules or activities to be organized and given to them, while others would rather be flexible and do things on their own schedule. School can be biased toward the reading and hearing styles of learning, as well as the organized assignment method. If those ways of learning don't work for you, think about what helps you remember things or know them well. You might be able to find a way of learning things that can get you more excited about school or help you perform to your highest ability.

While we've spent a lot of time talking about the education part of school, there are reasons to enjoy school other than academics. There are lots of extracurricular activities that go along with high school: sports, arts, music, literary publications, academic clubs (debate, foreign languages, etc.), and community service. School and its activities can be great socially—after all, it is one of the few chances in your life that you will have to spend most of your time with people your own age. You get to see lots of different people, have different interactions with them both in and out of class, and learn about yourself as a social person through activities and events, like drama productions, sports teams, and even school dances. Imagine you didn't go to school every day; how many fewer people would you talk to on a daily basis? School might be important to you for those reasons.

So there are several reasons that you might be invested in the time you spend in school: education or knowledge for its own sake, the social contact it gives you, activities you can't get outside of a school organization—heck, even getting away from your family for a while every day. However, while there are many reasons we think school could (and probably should) be an important part of who you are and what you do, some teens find themselves questioning the purpose or relevance of high school and formal education. If this is you, you might simply suffer through high school and decide not to pursue any further education. Or you might decide that finishing school is not for you. Teens give many reasons for choosing not to attend school. You might think you're not learning as much as you would like, or you may find it hard to keep up with the demands of school. You may think your time would be better spent on other activities (e.g., sports, music) or feel like you don't belong. You may find yourself in a situation where you have to spend a lot of time doing other things, such as working to support your family or taking care of a child, making school seem like less of a priority. Whatever the reason might be, you do have options other than attending school.

Some kids get their education at home, through homeschooling or distance learning, rather than going out of their house to school every day. In 1999 it was estimated that around 850,000 children were being homeschooled, including

INTERNET HIGH SCHOOL

There are several institutions that offer online learning leading to a high school diploma. Enrolled students take courses such as English, history, math, and science via online classrooms. Students can participate from any geographic location, and all interaction with instructors takes place online. Richard Milburn High School (www.rmhs.org), an alternative school with several campuses that has expanded to offer high school classes online, offers a lot of freedom in instruction, with most classes conducted via asynchronous communication, or a series of e-mails or posted messages. Choice 2000 (www.choice2000.org), a charter school in California that operates entirely online, requires that students "attend" class at set times and log in every day. Students must participate in physical education and submit a P.E. log documenting their activity, signed by their parents. They must also visit the campus office three times a year. Students enrolled in Choice 2000 include kids with serious medical disorders, highly gifted students, and inattentive students who struggle in regular classrooms. Internet schooling is not for everybody, to be sure, and schools such as these ask a lot of questions to determine if it's the right placement—you need to be a pretty self-motivated and technologically aware student to do well in online high school.

approximately 235,000 children in grades 9 through 12.[3] This adds up to about 2 percent of teens who are still "in school." Parents say that they choose to homeschool their children for a number of reasons, such as moral or religious reasons, dissatisfaction with public schools, or concern about school issues like drugs and peer pressure. They choose to take their children out of the public education system and provide academic instruction privately. Sometimes teens live too far away from a regular high school to attend on a daily basis. If you lived in a remote area, it might take you several hours to get to school. In this situation, some kids stay with families closer to the school or in a dorm during the week and go home on weekends. Sometimes, however, they can get much of their instruction and do lots of their homework over the Internet, attending school only when necessary (to take formal exams, for example).

FAMOUS DROPOUTS

Albert Einstein—high school dropout who studied on his own to get into college.

Abraham Lincoln—dropped out after only one year of formal schooling, obtained a law degree by self-study.

Thomas Edison—had no formal education, was entirely homeschooled.

Homeschooling definitely has its advantages. When you get more personal attention from a parent or whoever instructs you outside of school, you may be able to learn at your own pace, moving quickly through things that come easily. You may get to focus on areas that are more naturally interesting to you, or get extra help when topics are hard. Some teenagers feel that they can learn better when they are away from the distraction of classroom dynamics and peer relationships. For kids who struggle socially and are generally uncomfortable in a traditional classroom, more individual learning can free them from worrying about what other people think and help them succeed.

UNSCHOOLING

There is a movement known as "unschooling" or "natural learning."[4] Kids who elect this decide to educate themselves at home, engaging in "experience-based learning," in contrast to formal curriculum education. The idea is that learning happens wherever you find it, not just in the classroom, and teens learn better when they go out and get the knowledge that they need. There is even a book of advice about this called *The Teenage Liberation Handbook: How to Quit School and Get a Real Life and Education* by Grace Llewellyn. The book suggests that teens who are seriously motivated and want to educate themselves outside the school system might actually learn better when allowed to learn what they find interesting rather than what is programmed by the traditional academic system.

Learning at home has its costs as well. Given that there is much more to high school than just the academics, teens attending school at home might not have the same opportunities for extracurricular activities that those in a traditional high school have. Teens being educated at home don't always miss out on the traditions or events conducted at formal high schools, though. Some homeschooled teens attend a school part time, for example. Some states even put together a "homeschool prom" for teens who are being educated at home, so that they can have a formal dance experience without the formal high school.

Some kids just drop out of school and decide not to pursue further education. In 2001, about 11 percent of kids age 16 to 24 had left school without a high school diploma or General Educational Development (GED) certification. Boys are more likely to drop out of school than girls, and Hispanic teens have the highest dropout rate, with almost a third of Hispanic teens no longer enrolled in high school.[5] Teens who drop out give a variety of reasons for their choice: they didn't like school; they were failing or couldn't keep up with the work; they didn't get along with their teachers; they felt like they didn't belong with other students; and they had to deal with substance abuse, pregnancy, or criminal involvement.

What happens to kids who drop out? Some go to work full- or part-time. Some eventually get a GED instead of a traditional diploma. Some stay home to take care of family members or their own kids. We'd love to tell you that everyone can be happy in school, but some teens just decide that isn't the case. However, you should know that high school dropouts are 72 percent more likely to be unemployed, and they earn 27 percent less than high school grads.[6] And while you can get a GED, which may open some doors for you, it is not the same as a high school diploma. While high school can be a challenge, both academically and socially, there is no avoiding the fact that graduating will give you benefits that you can't get if you drop out. But if you do choose to leave high school, you do have other choices. Only you get to decide what you want and how you think you should get it. Keep in mind that in most states,

In 2001, 62 percent of students who had graduated from high school or completed a GED by June were enrolled in college in October.[7]

you have to be above a certain age before you can drop out of school without a parent's permission.

There is life and more learning after high school, as well. Lots of teens choose to go on to further education rather than entering the workforce right away. What kind of choices do you have? Think about these options:

- *Technical/career college*: These programs last anywhere from three months to two years. You receive a certificate or diploma after training for a specific career, such as truck driver, cosmetologist, medical assistant, chef, and so on.

- *Community college*: This usually takes two or more years. You can get an associate's degree or transfer to a four-year college after two years. Most community college students train for careers such as sales, nursing, legal assistant, accounting, and the like.

- *Four-year college/university*: These schools typically take four or more years, leading to a bachelor's degree. You may study areas like English, education, engineering, social science, and biology.

- *Graduate school*: These programs take anywhere from one to five or more years. You can receive a master's degree, a PhD, MD, JD, or MBA in areas like law, history, medicine, or education.

Choosing one of these educational options can help you get more specific training for the kind of work you might be interested in, or a degree that might be flexible for you in later career choices. You have many options in terms of how you take on higher education. There are definitely the traditional four-year colleges, where you live on or off campus and are a full-time student, focusing your attention on your education. Or you could attend school part-time while you work. You can take classes through online universities as well, which can even free you up to work full-time and still make progress on getting a degree. If more learning or training is something that is important to you, you can probably find a way to do it. And it's important to remember that you can always go back to school—you are never too old. You may decide right now that you don't want to be in school any longer, but you can change your mind and get more education later. Like most things that you choose to have as part of your identity, you can also choose to change the importance of school and education as you get older.

> **In 1999, 39 percent of all students enrolled in two- and four-year colleges were age 25 or older.[8]**

WORK—BRINGING HOME THE BACON

Even though teens have a lot going on with all the activities we've talked about—family, school, hobbies, friends—the majority of kids between the ages of 16 and 19 have jobs at some time during the year. When school is in session, about 38 percent of high school students have jobs; during the summer, that rises to about 62 percent.[9]

> **DID YOU KNOW?**
> **Shawn Fanning started the music download site Napster when he was only 19 years old. Brad Ogden started a webpage design company, Virtual Web Pages, when he was 13. Elise Macmillan, age 14, owns and runs www.chocolatefarm.com.**

What kinds of jobs do teens have? Teens regularly hold jobs like babysitting, paper routes, yard work, grocery store work, retail sales, fast-food/restaurant work, summer camp counselor, office work, and park and recreation work (e.g., lifeguarding). Some teens even own their own businesses—landscaping and yard work, for example, or computer consultation. The Internet has allowed many kids to make money in ways that didn't exist before.

The primary reason to work is pretty obvious: when you work, you make money. Having your own money to spend can make life easier, whether you choose to spend it on clothes, CDs, games, or your family, or whether you save it for college or a car. Some teens feel that they have to work in order to contribute to their family. The extra income that another worker brings into a family can make a big difference. But lots of teens choose to work for other reasons. Working can make you feel more independent. Sure, earning and spending your own money can free you up from asking your parents for money, which might give you more freedom to decide what you spend your money on. But having a place to go on a regular schedule and managing the responsibilities that go along with being an employee can feel more like grownup activities than some other things you do. You might feel really good about yourself and what you have to offer the world if your contributions at work are noticed and valued.

Learning to handle multiple responsibilities can be a valuable skill that may even help you academically. Some teens feel that working teaches them to manage their time and tasks better, and they do better in school because of it. Work can be a social experience, as well; you can meet people through work whom you might not otherwise come into contact with. Employment could also teach you something about what you might want to do for a career; knowing that you love or hate certain types of work can help you make decisions about what to do for a living. You might also gain knowledge about the world of work that can prepare you to enter the workforce after school more easily than those who don't work.

Another reason to work might be because it's fun, believe it or not. Some of the jobs that teens have may actually be more

HOW DO YOU GET A JOB?

Start by going to the places you might like to work—local stores, the mall, tourist attractions, parks and recreation departments, restaurants, small businesses, golf and tennis clubs, hotels and resorts—and ask if they are hiring and if they would consider hiring someone your age. You can look on the Web, too: www.snagajob.com has listings for students and teens; www.quintcareers.com/teen_jobs.html offers a bunch of resources for teen job seekers.

fun than the kinds of jobs you will have during the rest of your life. Babysitting, for example, can be a great job—you get to hang out with and play with kids and get paid for it. If you work in a retail store in a mall, you might get to have more social contact with all kinds of people than you will in future jobs. Of course, some summer jobs let you be outdoors doing fun things the whole time—for example, lifeguard, camp counselor, tennis instructor. The jobs you hold as an adult may not be as relaxed or as much fun as these positions can be.

However, while working has some strong benefits, for a teen it also has its drawbacks. Work is one more responsibility in addition to many other things that are expected of you. If you are spending a lot of time at work, that reduces the number of hours available to you for fun things and homework. Research shows that teens who work more than twenty hours per week are at greater risk for failure at school and psychological distress. The stress of going to work can really add up. Because of these demands, you might find it hard to eat well or eat regularly, or you might be unable to keep up with your sleep, so you might often find yourself being tired and run down.

Some parents and experts feel that teens' earning and spending money can be a problem as well, as teens learn lessons about money and economics that affect them throughout their lives. Generally, teens spend a lot more money than they save, and this habit can be difficult to shake later on, when you may need to save for something. If you are making money that you are allowed to spend however you want, without needing to cover expenses like rent or groceries, you may develop a skewed sense of how essential fun things (like CDs or stylish clothes) are to your lifestyle. Additionally, teens usually don't need to adhere to a budget or do much research on what to buy, and again, these financial habits can become a problem later in life.

Teens are often subject to regulations that other workers are not, however. Federal child labor laws prohibit 14- and 15-year-olds from working more than eighteen hours a week. The consensus from research on teen employment is that kids do pretty well up to about twenty hours per week, but above that amount, the negative impact of work on teens' other

117

responsibilities is simply too great to ignore. Also, there are jobs that are off-limits to you because they are considered hazardous. For example, in some states, only teens who are 16 and older can actually cook or prepare food, so you'll see the 14- and 15-year-olds selling burgers at the counter while the older teens are behind the grill. These regulations are often for good reason, as the workplace can be a dangerous place. Lots of teens (about 100,000 per year) suffer injuries while at work.[10] This is something to take into account as you think about where you might want to work.

If you do work, how much you work and how seriously you take your job will inevitably be parts of your identity. You might find something that you love to do for a living early on and be able to devote yourself to getting really good at it. But it's important to watch that work doesn't take over your life too early, blocking out other aspects of your life that might become really important parts of who you are. While it can be exciting to work and earn money, work is just like any other part of your identity—you are much more than this one thing. Learning this as a teenager can help you lead a more balanced life as an adult.

HOBBIES—WHAT DO YOU THINK IS FUN?

Think back to the online profile example we talked about in the introduction to this book. Imagine that you are about to register at a particular website, maybe to chat. You'd probably include somewhere in there a list of things you like to do, right? The things that we *choose* to do for fun are one of the ways that we express who we are on the inside. Hobbies are usually all about us and what we like or enjoy. You might work at something you don't enjoy because it pays well. Or you might not like school, but you go because of what you'll get from graduating. But the things you pick to do for fun? In a way, that's more purely a demonstration of what you are about. In addition, your hobbies, or the things that you like to spend time on (other than work or school, mostly), impact what your schedule is like, how you spend your money, and who you run into and hang out with.

Almost any activity you can think of is someone's hobby. Even things that you might think of as boring may be fun for someone else. There are physical hobbies—sports, martial arts, outdoor activities. There are creative hobbies—writing, painting, knitting. There are learning hobbies—reading, being a fan of movies or music, collecting things, traveling, playing trivia games. There are spiritual hobbies—church groups, religious study. In the same way, there are solitary hobbies and group hobbies, indoor hobbies and outdoor hobbies, difficult hobbies and easy hobbies, skilled hobbies and novice hobbies. The lists can go on and on and on, but we know you get the idea. As we consider the things that you do for fun, we want to introduce you to some unusual ways you could spend your time, but mostly encourage you to think about how your choices express what you think is important and what those choices show to the world at large. (Note: we will talk specifically about sports in its own section later.)

We choose hobbies for a whole variety of reasons. Sometimes it's just that doing a particular activity is really darn fun or makes you feel good—it's simply enjoyable. You just like the way it feels to be doing something. We also pick hobbies because they can be an opportunity to spend time with people who are like us. For many people, hobbies are a social thing. Take collecting baseball

TEEN HOBBIES

Here is a list of hobbies teens participate in, as taken from various message boards on the Web: acting, beading and jewelry, cartooning, collecting things (baseball cards, coins, stuffed animals, etc.), computers, cooking, dancing, fashion design, filmmaking, graffiti, knitting and sewing, drama, painting, drawing, digital art, photography, sculpture, Web design, travel, role-playing games, movies, aquariums, basket weaving, skateboarding, gardening, hiking, volunteering, 4-H, Boy Scouts, Girl Scouts, ham radio, dinosaurs, raising animals (chinchillas, iguanas, etc.), reading, writing poetry, scrapbooking, radio-controlled vehicles, beauty pageants.

cards or being a *Star Trek* fan, for example. Every year, there are several conventions for both of these hobbies that offer an opportunity to get together with other people who are as enthusiastic about the hobby as you are. You can even go to conventions on things such as scrapbooking, beauty pageants, cooking, raising pets, and video games. For other people, however, hobbies can be a way to escape their regular lives. You might want a chance to get away from others. People can do things like bird watching, hiking, or reading—all of which can be great solitary activities. It's worth mentioning that some hobbies are more involved or expensive than others. Anyone can write, for example, with little expense or training other than pen, paper, and inspiration. But making pottery involves material, tools, storage space, appliances like a kiln, and sometimes instruction. And cost does influence what people choose as hobbies.

One of the other ways that hobbies differ is in their scale, or the intensity with which you pursue them. If reading is one of your hobbies, it might be something that you do occasionally but generally don't spend a ton of money or energy doing. It's pretty easy to have that as a limited hobby. But if you are into something like acting or singing, you might find yourself devoting lots of time and energy. With lessons, rehearsals, and practice, performing arts hobbies can be pretty intensive endeavors. Even though it is hard to keep some hobbies limited (for example, if you want to fly planes, at least for a while you have to spend a significant amount of time flying to get certified), you can take almost anything as far as you want and spend a lot of time doing hobbies. You can have a large number of hobbies that you do and enjoy, or you can be more exclusive. Some people play around with a variety of things, and others find one thing that really excites them and devote themselves to it.

This brings up another cool thing about hobbies: for many people, doing an activity that they really love as a hobby can actually lead to a career. What could be better than getting to do something for a living that you would do for fun anyway? Say you like collecting stuffed animals. You could just do it in your spare time, occasionally giving it your attention. Or you could peruse catalogs and online listings, learn about the history of different manufacturers of types of stuffed animals, and even become a buyer and seller of stuffed animals through something like eBay. A surprising number of people have turned their passion for specific things into their life work.

Of course, you can go the other way as well. Many people enjoy their hobbies for the simple reason that they are *not* what they do for a living. If you work all day with people, you may need a hobby that allows you to spend time alone or interacting less with others. If your job involves being very organized and deliberate, you may want to spend your free time doing something more creative, unpredictable, and messy. That's the great thing about hobbies—they allow you to balance your life

NATHAN LOVES MOVIES

Nathan is a 16-year-old guy who lives in the Pacific Northwest. He attends public school and is very interested in expressive arts like film, music, and writing. His father was a serious record collector, and his brother used to pay him to read books—both of which influenced his strong interests. He volunteers at a funky revival movie theater one evening a week and would love to be a movie director.

Q: How would you describe yourself?
Nathan: I fluctuate a lot; I'm very inconsistent. When I'm around people, it's showtime—I'm different all the time. I think I'm made up of the people I respect and the stuff I like, like movies. I want to make movies and write prose. I have a real need for communicating something—I don't always know what I say, but I know how I'll say it.

Q: How do you think others see you?
Nathan: People talk about how "cultured" I am because I know a little bit about everything. They think I'm a novelty because I'm all over the place, and I hate that.

Q: How do you think your hobbies influence how others see you?
Nathan: I think that many other people don't have a major drive for life or a passion about something. Because I've been really into several things, like movies and writing, I think that alienated people. In middle school, being cool is not associated with being passionate about anything. I just thought that lots of other things were pointless and boring.

and get what you need by allowing you to do what you truly love. But it's also why, when you think about what your hobbies say about you, you need to remember that no one is defined by a single thing that they are or do.

A really big hobby for most teens is listening to music. People can get really into music. There are tons of fan clubs, fan sites, and get-togethers for people who really like and admire particular musical artists. Other ways people express their musical interests involve reading about groups and artists that they like, going to concerts, watching videos, and talking about them with other fans. Your taste in music is assumed to communicate lots of things about you. Many of the labels that we apply to people are linked to particular kinds of music—hip-hop, hippies, goth; in fact, it's one of the top five ways that people label others.[11]

The problem is that sometimes other people assume that if you like a particular kind of music, you are automatically like the people who make that music or the music itself. For example, if you listen to heavy metal or industrial music, others may think that you are really angry or violent or hate the world. But you might not be like that at all. There are many reasons to like different kinds of music other than because the artists are like you—sometimes certain music just makes you

feel good. But the music industry is a lot about image, and that trickles down to the people who buy music and determine what is considered popular or profitable. It's important to be aware of what your musical choices might say to others, but keep in mind that you get to fight those assumptions too. Listen to what you like, but be prepared to argue against the assumptions others might make about you because of your particular tastes.

SPORTS

There's a dream shared by many. It's the dream of becoming a sports hero. Becoming a professional athlete can bring fame, fortune, and a chance to play a sport for a living. It sounds like the ultimate fantasy life.

Our society talks up the lives of professional athletes who started out with nothing—no money, a broken home—yet their love of the game vaults them into fame. The stories of Allen Iverson and Alex

Over half of all teens played on at least one sports team in 2003.[12]

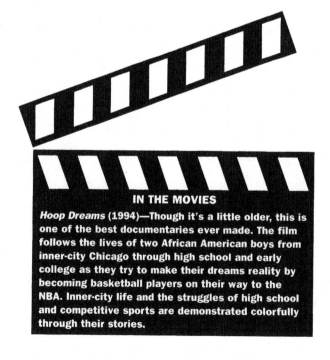

IN THE MOVIES

Hoop Dreams (1994)—Though it's a little older, this is one of the best documentaries ever made. The film follows the lives of two African American boys from inner-city Chicago through high school and early college as they try to make their dreams reality by becoming basketball players on their way to the NBA. Inner-city life and the struggles of high school and competitive sports are demonstrated colorfully through their stories.

Rodriguez, who grew up in poor communities without their fathers, make for great news. Their current paychecks and lifestyle can lead many others to think that they can make it into that world if only they try hard enough. This dream brings lots of people to play organized sports.

However, reality plays a huge role when it comes to aspirations of making it in professional sports. First, the chance of going pro is a numbers game, and the odds are not in anyone's favor. For guys, only about 5 percent of high school athletes make it to college-level sports, and only 3 percent of college athletes make it to the pros.[13] That means that your odds of making it are less than two in a thousand. And those aren't the odds of making it BIG—they're just the odds of making it at *all*. For the hundreds of people who spend a little time in the pros (and that includes the minor leagues, because you are paid there, giving it professional status), there are only a handful who become household names and the owners of fancy cars, shoe contracts, and recording deals. The odds of a female making it into pro sports are even worse, because there are fewer ways women can earn money as a professional athlete than there are for men.

So if sports aren't going to be a career for most people, what is it about sports that has so many people participating in them? Being involved in a sport means being involved in an activity that brings people together. Practicing and playing competitively can teach you skills and values (such as working as a team, responsibility, dedication, and sportsmanship) that you can use in whatever career you choose. And these lessons

"There are over 360,000 NCAA athletes, and most of them will be going pro in something other than sports."

—NCAA commercial slogan

can be learned whether you are the star of the squad or even if you "ride pine" (sit on the bench and rarely play) the whole time you are on the team. Studies also show that being involved in sports can increase your confidence and self-esteem.

Choosing a Sport

Although sports have many things in common, such as the need to practice, the chance to be on a team, and a way to get exercise, sports also have many differences among them. How did you decide what sport was for you? If you are thinking of trying out for a team, which team are you considering? Here are some ways that sports can be a part of someone's image or identity.

Different sports have different images associated with them. There are many things that influence our impressions of athletes, such as how the sport is played and how the media portrays the sport. For example, many people see football and hockey players as tough and strong, because of all the hitting that goes on in those sports. However, if you ever watched a gymnastics tournament, you can see how strong those athletes need to be in order to complete their routines. Yet rarely do we think about gymnasts as the strongest people around; we think of them as being delicate and graceful instead.

The superstars affiliated with sports on television also influence image. A professional athlete's character—how they talk to the media, what they wear, whether or not they are in trouble with the law—all shape how the sport they represent is portrayed. Some people think that professional athletes influence how younger people see and play the sport and therefore should be better role models for society. For example, some people blame the level of violence and taunting that goes on in high school sporting events on the fact that there is a lot of that going on at the professional level. These people go on to say that there is no room in professional sports for people who play dirty and get in trouble with the law, and that those athletes who do not obey the laws of their sport and the laws of society should not be able to play.

125

Not only do professional athletes have a particular image, but the sports themselves have images as well. For example, some sports such as tennis, golf, and croquet have more of a "rich" image while other sports are seen as more "street"— basketball, soccer, and even baseball to some extent. The reputation of a sport varies in different schools and communities. In different areas of the country, different sports are seen as cool, whereas others are ignored or seen as somehow "lesser" activities. For example, in Indiana, basketball rules, whereas in Minnesota, the high school hockey tournament gets tons of press. These reputations might be based on the success history of the sport in that particular place,

JONATHAN CHOOSES HOCKEY

Jonathan is 16 and describes himself as "fun and outgoing." He has been playing hockey for eight years; he started playing with his dad when he was young, and the two of them still play together on recreational teams. Jonathan also plays in a youth league, competing in regional tournaments several times a year.

Q: How does hockey help shape you into the person you are?
Jonathan: I like the roughness and the brutality of it. But at the same time, it's all about finesse. Because it is both rough and smooth, it fits all sides of my personality. It makes me a happy person and keeps me from being too lazy.

Q: How does your dedication to hockey influence how others see you?
Jonathan: People think I am crazy to spend so much time playing hockey. It's not a big sport out here in California like it is in other places. People wonder why I bother with it because I am not going to go pro or make any money or anything. They think I am weird to spend so much time doing something just to do it. I play in tournaments sometimes, and sometimes the team does pretty well. But that is as big as I am ever going to make it.

or how cool a particular sport is in the media or in a particular area, but otherwise are not really based in reality. Still, local support for a popular sport can make it more appealing to join.

As you can see (and probably already knew), different sports have different images. And that image may influence your decision whether or not to participate in it. You may see one sport as matching your image (or the image you want to portray) better than another. Although it is important to be involved in a sport that you are proud of, be careful of being on a team just to look good. Choosing a sport that matches your personality and your true self is a better way to go.

So, how do different sports suit different personalities? First, there are team sports and individual sports. Some people prefer to play on a team—they practice together, play together, and their ability to work with others influences how well they do. Winning and losing depends on a group effort, not on the play of a single person. Hockey, basketball, football, volleyball, softball, baseball, and soccer are examples of popular team sports. People who play on team sports may like the interaction, the close relationships that are formed on a team, and the experience of working with others to make something happen.

Then there are other people who prefer participating in individual sports, such as tennis, track, swimming, gymnastics, and golf. Although in competitions sometimes a team score is created by adding the scores of all the different members, in these sports one person is usually in competition against other individuals, with everyone not only trying to beat the others, but also trying to beat his or her personal-best scores or records. People who participate in individual sports might like to be around others but prefer the feelings that come with competing one on one. They may also like the way they are working mostly by themselves during practice; for some, the work becomes a sort of meditation.

However, being involved in a sport takes not only time and dedication, but sometimes it also takes money. This might be a deciding factor as to whether your dreams of participating in a particular sport are realistic. Some sports, such as basketball and soccer, can be played almost anywhere and you don't need a lot of equipment (shoes and a ball, basically)—therefore, they are pretty accessible to everyone. On the other hand, there are some pretty expensive sports out there. Sports like tennis, snowboarding, and golf often require memberships at clubs or equipment fees that can cost hundreds or thousands of dollars a year. (In some places, though, there are courts and courses available to the public for free or a reduced fee.) In order to excel at a sport such as gymnastics or ice skating, it could cost from $30,000 to $70,000 to hire a personal coach as well as rent the practice facility. Even a sport camp can cost $200 for a week. You can see how money might limit your options.

When Is a Sport Not a Sport?

Sometimes, however, being involved in a sport can lose its benefits. This happens if it becomes too stressful or you depend

More than one in four boys (27 percent) and one in five girls (20 percent) worry about doing well in sports.[14]

ARE PROFESSIONAL ATHLETES ROLE MODELS?

When someone gets as much media attention as professional athletes do, should they have to serve as role models for today's youth? Over ten years ago, former NBA star Charles Barkley created quite a controversy when he told the media, "I am not a role model. I am a professional basketball player. I am paid to wreak havoc on the basketball court. Parents should be role models!"[15] Many people disagreed with his point of view—including retired superstar basketball player David Robinson, and many other Americans who believe that because kids look up to professional athletes, they have an obligation to live a decent, respectable life that can serve as an example for the millions who admire them.

But the image of many of today's athletes is anything but wholesome. Think about the murder and manslaughter charges against football players O.J. Simpson, Ray Lewis, and Ray Carruth. Or Mike Tyson, the infamous boxer, constantly getting in trouble with the law over his violent behavior. In the National Hockey League, there have been more suspensions for more severe incidents on the ice than ever before. Even the "bad boy" image of tattoos and talking trash seems more common in sports than the "All-American" squeaky-clean style of the past. Sure, there are still many people in sports with good character—but they usually don't get their name in the news, and they don't always get the sponsorships. True, an athlete's actions can become too extreme and as a result contracts are lost; basketball player Kobe Bryant lost his relationship with fast-food restaurant chain McDonald's when he was accused of rape. But other basketball stars like Kevin Garnett are rarely seen in the media, yet he is one of the best in the game today. Many say this is because his image is too clean and therefore not as interesting.

The bottom line is that many adults are concerned about the image of today's athletes and how that affects youth behavior. They worry that violence both on and off the field influences how youth play the game themselves and also what they see as acceptable behavior—and possibly what they think they can get away with because of being an athlete.

What do you think?

too much on your success in a sport for your sense of who you are. There is a famous quote by former football coach Vince Lombardi: "Winning isn't everything, it's the only thing." If you believe that, being an athlete is no longer about fun and learning about yourself and others. It's about pressure, stress, and an intensity that may get in the way of you enjoying yourself—or playing well. If you are no longer having fun, there is something the matter. If you believe it is okay to "win at any cost" and become tempted to cheat, injure an opponent, or use steroids to enhance your performance (as mentioned earlier in the "Your Body" section), there is something the matter—and other people are less likely to enjoy playing with you and having you as a teammate.

Chances are very likely that you are not always going to win. And you are also going to make mistakes. You may think these events are damaging your image, but all they do is show that you are human. So instead of being angry or embarrassed by a loss or error, learn from your mistakes. That will make you not only a better athlete, but also a better person. Even baseball pitchers Roger Clemens and Pedro Martinez get shelled once in a while. And guess what? They show up for their next start, ready to succeed.

EXERCISE

Although not everyone wants to join a sports team or club, that should not prevent anyone from exercising. Even outside of being a member of a sports team, exercising can be a part of and influence one's image and identity—and usually for the better.

The most obvious way that exercise can improve your image is by improving your physical fitness. People who are physically fit look healthier and have well-defined body shapes that can make them look more attractive to others and themselves. This may increase their popularity or the attention that they get from others. Therefore, exercising regularly can help you improve your appearance and self-image, which may boost your self-esteem and self-confidence, which will improve your appearance and self-image, and the cycle continues.

Exercising can help you sleep better.

Exercise clearly has physical benefits, such as helping a person maintain a healthy weight and blood pressure, and improving one's bone and muscle strength. There also can be meditative benefits from exercise. Some people get into a "zone" when they exercise, which allows them to clear their head or empty their minds of things that are bothering them. When they are done exercising, the problems they had earlier don't seem as pressing. And then there are people who simply find exercising fun.

However, many of the benefits of exercise are more subtle. Exercising greatly enhances your self-esteem—in other words, exercising makes you feel better about yourself. One of the theories as to why this happens is that endorphins (chemicals that the pituitary gland in the brain produces during vigorous exercise) biologically improve your mood. It's endorphins that give you a sort of rush after you exercise hard. Another theory as to why exercise improves your mood is because it gives you a feeling of accomplishment. By pushing your body physically hard, you feel good about what you have done and gain a sense of pride in yourself. Working out can teach you more about what you are capable of doing and encourage you to challenge yourself to reach higher goals.

Exercise can also help your public image and self-image by reducing stress. First, exercising actually helps balance the stress hormones in the brain, so you are better able to relax. This is because regular exercise helps flush out the byproducts of the body's stress response—hundreds of chemicals released in

WHO EXERCISES, ANYWAY?

In today's society, there seem to be fewer and fewer American teens exercising than before. In 2001, one-third of teens reported that they did not participate in any vigorous or even moderate physical activity on a regular basis. Only half of all teens have physical education class. On average, boys are more likely than girls to report exercising, and younger teens are more likely than older teens to report exercising, although these differences are not very big.[16]

response to a stressful situation. This body cleansing helps you return to a normal, more balanced emotional state quicker. Also, studies have shown that by making the body stronger and healthier, exercise improves your ability to respond to stressful situations. And less stress also means less anxiety and depression, so overall, exercise makes you a more balanced, pleasant person to be around.

GO ONLINE

The Internet provides many people with a great opportunity to express their opinions or simply let people from all over the world get to know them. First off, instant messaging (IM) and chat rooms allow people to "talk" to others on the computer instead of talking on the phone or sending e-mail. Although chat rooms are a place where people can talk about a particular topic, meet new people, or just vent about the bad day they had with whoever is signed on at the time, more and more teens are using IM to communicate instead of going to chat rooms. IM is a way to hang out and chat with friends in the virtual world— in fact, IM allows you to talk to more than one friend about different things at the same time. One study showed that out of sixty teenagers, only one said that he never had multiple IM conversations.

Three-fourths of teens who are online use instant messaging (IM). About 70 percent use it several times a week.[17]

But IM has other advantages. It can help maintain relationships with friends or relatives who live far away; it's usually cheaper to IM someone than it is to talk to him or her on the phone. Also, IM can strengthen the friendships you have with people you see every day. In fact, most of the time, people IM friends that they know in real life and see quite often. They simply log on and chat with friends when they can't hang out in person.

IM can also help people with certain communication problems. It can make it easier for you to overcome shyness;

some people say that they find it easier to approach someone they like over IM and talk with him or her first online instead of going up and saying hi in person. So it's possible that relationships can start online even though two people already know one another in real life. IM also can be used for emotional support and getting advice because it might be easier to talk about a sensitive issue online than to talk about it in person or even over the phone. Sometimes it's easier to write out how you feel than it is to talk about it.

Overall, different people have different communication styles. For those who are shy or find it easier to write out their feelings than talk about them, IM may be one of the best ways to get to know someone better or talk about a difficult problem. For those who are more outgoing and social, IM is great for talking to several people at once. No matter how you use it, IM can help maintain friendships and develop new ones.

Of course, there are disadvantages to communicating online. For example, some people rely on the Internet too much for meeting people or talking to friends about difficult topics. Although the Internet can be a helpful communication tool, depending on it as your main source of communication can make your relationships less personal. Make sure you say really important things to people face to face, or at least in the most intimate manner possible (the telephone is second best).

> **REMEMBER**
> **Do not use your real full name (first and last) as a user name. It makes it easier for strangers and stalkers to find you!**

Some people also "say" things online that they would never say in person and that can come back to haunt them. Remember—never write anything in an IM or e-mail that you would not say in person. Electronic messages can easily be saved and printed by the person you send them to, so be very thoughtful about what feelings you put in writing.

Another way the Internet provides you with a way to express yourself is through message boards (some of the biggest ones are www.alloy.com and www.bolt.com). On boards, teens get a chance to voice their opinions about everything from music to politics to fashion. Usually there are different message boards for different topics (though not everyone stays on topic!). And not only do message boards allow you to type about what you think or how you feel, but they also allow you to express yourself through your user name and icon. For example, your user name can let people know about your appearance (crazyredhead), your favorite band (iluvblink182), or a hobby you love (hockeyrulz). Your icon can do the same; at bolt.com, we saw icons of devils, lips, a dollar bill, and American Idol stars, just to name a few. For the more artistically inclined, you can even design your own icon to represent yourself. So before anyone even reads a message from you, they can already begin to get a sense of who you are by the name and picture you use to represent yourself.

An even more personal and detailed way to talk about yourself on the Internet is through an online diary—a Web log, or blog. A blog is basically a journal that is kept on the Web and updated by the author often—sometimes even several times a day. People can also choose whether to let people respond to their blog, making it a sort of interactive diary. Check out www.teenopendiary.com or www.blogger.com to read about the lives of thousands of people.

Finally, for the truly computer savvy, there is the option of creating your own webpage. In fact, it is estimated that there are about 2 million independent websites created by people age 6 to 17! Terra Lycos, a company that offers people tools to help build their own websites, estimates that about half of its 32 million members are teenagers (though not all of their members have actually built webpages).[18] Creating a homepage is almost like inviting anyone in the online world into your personal space. It can be a way to let your real life and online friends get to know you better. On a homepage, you can let people know about your likes and dislikes, your thoughts on certain topics and issues, and even keep a journal of your life (see the Blog section).

Even if your homepage does not directly talk about you, it does reveal your interests and your opinions about them—

otherwise, why would you make the page in the first place? Many teens have started online businesses, or created websites to support causes they are active in. Others have created online support sites for teens facing particular situations like a death in the family, a chronic illness, or an unexpected pregnancy.

GLBT TEENS ONLINE

Teens who do not identify as heterosexual often face discrimination, a lack of support, and loneliness in their real-life communities. Thanks to the Internet, however, gay, lesbian, bisexual, and transgender (GLBT) teens have an entire virtual community to reach out to and find connection. (See the section on sexual orientation in chapter 1 for websites to check out.) On the Internet, there is a chance to meet others from all around the world and share common thoughts, feelings, and troubles. Because it offers a relatively cheap and easy way to communicate with others, the Web has been a great way for GLBT teens to cope with their everyday lives, where they may feel different and alone. School may be hard, and their social life may be full of lies, but on the Internet they can express themselves honestly and know that they will find support and validation from people who feel the same way they do.

However, most homepages focus on the interests of the creator. A homepage gives people the opportunity to show a side of themselves that they would not want to show in public. You may have a certain image or label in school but a different one online. However, you should remember that even though a homepage may feel very private, the Internet is a very public space. Search engines and links can easily lead strangers and people you know to your website, whether you want them to see it or not. It's tricky, because a homepage can seem like the most personal, intimate expression of who you are, yet it is out there in the virtual world for anyone to see.

Although the online world is a great place to express yourself and learn about other people, use of the Internet can be taken to the extreme. If you're spending a lot of time online and it's really interfering with your life, you may actually be addicted to the Internet. Anytime an activity causes you to let go of important tasks and responsibilities, or interferes with work, home, or relationships, then your involvement in that activity may be a problem. If you think you may be addicted to the Internet, ask yourself questions such as: Are you spending more time online than doing anything else? Do you think about the Internet when you are not online? Are you keeping it a secret from people? Do other people think you might have a problem? Answering yes to any of these questions may mean you are addicted. If you are at all concerned about your Internet use, talk to a counselor or adult you trust. They can help you find other ways to express yourself that do not involve a computer.

ALCOHOL, SMOKING, AND DRUGS

There are three different areas that we'll talk about in this section: cigarette smoking or tobacco, drinking alcohol, and using other drugs. While they're all versions of the same thing—using a foreign substance for some physical or emotional effect—they are still pretty different. You can get cigarettes at a much younger age than you can legally buy alcohol. There is no legal age at which to obtain other drugs, usually. And they have very different effects—no one has ever been stopped for driving while smoking cigarettes, for instance. Additionally, tobacco, alcohol, and other drugs each have their own kind of reputation—and your decision to use different ones can impact your image and your ideas about yourself. Making the choice to use or not use these substances can be seriously related to your sense of personal identity. We want to talk about the specific issues around your decisions for each of these activities, but also more generally about the philosophical assumptions that might motivate you to make those decisions. Your outlook about why or why not to use substances is a deeply personal part of your identity.

Tobacco

Cigarettes are kind of like the Average Joe of substances. You must be 18 years old to purchase cigarettes in the United States, but a lot of teens have no trouble getting their hands on them before they reach that age. As of 2002, about 28 percent of kids in high school reported that they used tobacco during the previous thirty days—so about one in four high school students has used tobacco in the last month. Rates of teen tobacco use have declined in the past several years. However, while the number of kids who regularly use tobacco has declined, lots of teens still try cigarettes (about 64 percent in high school say they have tried tobacco).[19] While cigarettes are the most obvious example of tobacco use, there are also cigars, smokeless tobacco (chew, snuff), pipe tobacco, clove cigarettes, and bidis (flavored cigarettes). Since the most prevalent way to use tobacco is cigarettes, we're choosing to focus on smoking in this section.

Health advocates have taken on smoking pretty intensely, and as a result, antismoking information and advertisements are everywhere.

Vietnam has banned smoking scenes from all Vietnamese movies.[20]

Most teens are pretty aware of why smoking is bad for you and why not to start smoking. Among them, of course, are that smoking causes cancer, increases health risks for other illnesses, is extremely difficult to give up, affects even nonsmokers, can make you short of breath even if you're mostly healthy, causes significant public health expense, can lead to sexual dysfunction, and other not-so-fun things. In addition, there are places that smokers can't go—in California, for example, bars and restaurants have banned smoking indoors entirely, meaning that smokers have to leave and go outside to have a cigarette. Smoking causes bad breath and can leave a very distinct and strong smell in your clothes and hair. And, don't forget, cigarettes are awfully expensive. If you add up how much money a pack-a-day habit costs you per year, you are spending $1,000 or more per year on cigarettes alone.

GREAT RESOURCE
Check out www.thetruth.com—this website provides some straight talk about cigarettes and their impact.

So, if smoking is bad for you, and most people agree on this, why do teens even start?

1. Smoking is supposed to make you feel good—taking in nicotine, which is a stimulant, can make you feel alert, energetic, or relaxed.

2. Nicotine is also terribly addictive, so once you start putting it into your body, your body continues to want more. So to a certain extent, people who've started smoking feel that they have to continue in order to not go through withdrawal from nicotine.

3. With recent changes in rules about where you can smoke, smoking regularly generally means having to take a break from what you're doing and go outside or someplace you're allowed to smoke. Some people really like that they have these regular breaks during their day—they find the ritual of smoking comforting and feel that it relieves stress for them.

4. Smokers may also feel a bond with other smokers. You might see groups of people outside office buildings or restaurants sharing cigarettes now and again.

5. Cigarette smoking is everywhere—if you just look around, you see characters smoking on TV and in the movies; there are ads in magazines promoting different kinds of cigarettes. With all those images around us, it's not that surprising that people might consider trying tobacco. After all, if it's everywhere, it must be worth it or okay, right?

6. In addition, these ads tend to portray smoking as an "adult" activity. You're not supposed to get your hands on the things until you're 18, so if you want to be seen as older and more independent, why not do something that only older people can do? A lot of teens who smoke say they like how it makes them feel older.

7. Some girls who smoke say they do it because they think it will help them with their weight, keep them thin. Whether or not this is true, it still motivates some people to try cigarettes.

So how do you decide about smoking? We certainly understand the allure of trying things just once—figuring out what all the fuss is about can be really hard to resist. However,

with smoking, it's often not just trying it once. It should be pointed out that because smoking is so addictive, deciding whether to smoke or not may actually be deciding to be a smoker or a nonsmoker. While it would be great if you could just decide at each moment whether you wanted to have a cigarette or not and feel free to change your mind whenever you

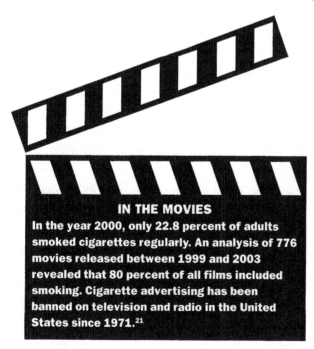

IN THE MOVIES
In the year 2000, only 22.8 percent of adults smoked cigarettes regularly. An analysis of 776 movies released between 1999 and 2003 revealed that 80 percent of all films included smoking. Cigarette advertising has been banned on television and radio in the United States since 1971.[21]

wanted, it never seems to work that way. A tiny group of people can do this, sure, because for some reason they are able to avoid the addiction of nicotine. But because nicotine is so powerfully addictive, the decision to smoke tends to have a longer-term impact than just what you are doing for the next five minutes. This is definitely worth thinking about. We talk some more about making decisions about using substances in general at the end of this chapter.

Alcohol

In all U.S. states, you must be 21 years old before you can legally purchase and drink alcohol. Despite this, it can still be incredibly easy to get your hands on booze—through your parents, relatives, or older friends—even well before you turn 21. So even though most people reading this book aren't legally supposed to consume alcohol, you will probably be asked to make some decision about drinking before that, if you haven't already. Alcohol is the most commonly used substance by teens. In 2002, 34 percent of twelfth-grade boys and 29 percent of twelfth-grade girls reported having five or more drinks in a row in the preceding two weeks.[22] And the National Center on Addiction and Substance Abuse reports that 78 percent of high school students have tried alcohol, with 14 the average age for trying one's first drink.[23]

Why shouldn't teens like you drink? After all, there are beer ads on racecars, businesses built around drinking (bars, pool halls, dance clubs, etc.), and sometimes it can seem like everyone does it. Well, there are many reasons to consider:

1. **It's illegal. If you are under the age of 21, you can be arrested, fined, or even jailed if you are caught purchasing or possessing alcohol. Pretty obvious.**

2. **Alcohol affects your brain—it can cause slowed reflexes, impaired coordination, distorted vision, and altered perception. It also lowers your inhibitions and affects your judgment, and can even lead to blackouts, where you don't remember what happened. Because of this, people who drink sometimes do silly or stupid things. When teens are under the influence of alcohol,**

they might do things that they wouldn't do if they were sober. Risky behavior, like unprotected sex, is more likely when people are intoxicated.

3. Teens tend not to drink in moderation; they binge drink. Binge drinking is defined as five or more drinks in one sitting for boys, and four or more for girls. Alcohol in small amounts can be handled by your system, but in large quantities it can have really negative effects (like hangovers or something more life threatening). In addition, teens' bodies aren't really ready to handle alcohol metabolically—your body doesn't process the substance as readily as adult bodies do. Because of this, the effects of alcohol can be more intense for teens. Alcohol use can hurt your liver and your stomach, among other organs.

4. People who drink don't just do stupid things, sometimes they do dangerous things. Alcohol use is linked to car accidents, injuries, and deaths. As you have probably noticed, drinking and driving injures and kills surprisingly large numbers of people every year. Drinking is also related to fighting, crime, and other serious consequences.

5. The younger you are when you start drinking, the higher your risk for problems with alcohol like alcoholism. Also, it's important to remember that research suggests that the tendency for alcoholism is inherited, so if your parents had a hard time with addiction to alcohol, you are at risk for the same problems.

We can't go into every reason in favor of abstaining from alcohol here, but we hope this gives you a good idea of the arguments against teens drinking.

Despite the fact that most teens are aware of these reasons not to drink, you probably see many people like you who choose to use alcohol. So, if all these things are true, why do teens choose to drink, then?

1. First of all, alcohol is supposed to make you feel good. It's a relaxant of sorts and can lessen anxiety and act as a disinhibitor. Many people feel that alcohol helps them to relax, let down their hair, and feel more at ease. They believe that it is fun.

2. Alcohol is often a very social thing to do. Lots of activities get arranged around drinking, such as parties. So if you're going to be social with other people, in some cases you'll probably be with people who are going to drink. It might become sort of expected that when you are hanging out socially, you're drinking. (See our Partying section for more on this.)

3. Alcohol is sometimes linked to cultural traditions. Wine is part of the communion ceremony and is served at a Passover seder. In certain countries, France, for example, wine is an important part of the dining experience—and few dinners are served without wine to accompany them.

4. Some teenagers are introduced to alcohol in their families. Their parents might let them try a little wine with dinner or have an occasional beer at home. They are given permission by their families and so decide that they want to drink because it is an allowed activity.

5. For adults, drinking alcohol is a socially accepted activity. It's not only not unusual, it can seem kind of expected that people drink. We hear about the husband who comes home from work and has a martini, or people who drink champagne at weddings. Many teens probably feel that it's going to be okay for them to drink eventually, so why not start now?

So how do you personally make a decision about whether or not to drink alcohol? Sometimes this decision is made for you—you live in a dry county, for example, where obtaining alcohol is inconvenient even for nonminors. But since we know that teens can often get alcohol despite being underage, you will probably find yourself making a decision about it. We hope that you will think about your reasons for drinking and consider whether doing so will actually meet your expectations. You should also weigh the risks—you might want to evaluate what the penalties would be for you, both from the actual drinking itself (e.g., hangovers, disinhibited behavior) and getting caught (e.g., punishment from parents, school or legal consequences).

Drugs

Drugs are common and can have a large presence in teen life, whether you choose to use them personally or not.

Statistics show that in 2002, 21 percent of tenth graders and 25 percent of twelfth graders reported using an illicit drug within the preceding thirty days.[24] Commonly used drugs (other than tobacco and alcohol) include marijuana, inhalants (huffing, nitrous oxide), cocaine, crack, methamphetamines, LSD, PCP, heroin, Ecstasy (MDMA), and prescription medications (Vicodin, Oxycontin). Something important to think about when considering taking drugs is not just whether you do it, but if you choose to do it, *why* or *how* you use them.

Again, even though we are probably telling you things that you have already heard a million times, it is worth thinking about the reasons you have to choose not to use drugs.

1. **Drugs are illegal. Marijuana, heroin, methamphetamines, X or ecstasy—they are all illegal. Possessing, selling, or using these substances can result in being arrested or charged with a crime. And drug offenses often carry severe punishments that can affect you for a long time.**

2. **Overdose or incorrect use of some drugs can result in serious injury or death. The effect of using can be permanent.**

3. **Drugs can have some serious side effects while you are on them. While they vary, they can affect your judgment, perception, reality testing, memory, and moods. Because of this, you might behave differently when under the influence— taking more risks, for example.**

4. **Even though drugs do have a powerful effect on you, generally this effect is temporary. While you might forget about stress or being depressed while high, when the drug wears off, usually you're still under stress or you still feel depressed.**

5. **Drug addiction is a risk with many substances. If you start using some drugs, you may feel compelled to continue using. Addiction leads many people to do destructive things, make poor decisions, and lose a lot of opportunities and assets.**

With all these reasons to avoid using drugs, why do teens sometimes choose to use them anyway? People have a whole variety of reasons for using drugs, despite some of the reasons not to that we have listed above.

1. The most basic reason is because most drugs make people feel good. Marijuana relaxes some people; cocaine is a stimulant that makes people feel they have more energy; hallucinogens can make the world seem distorted or different. People use drugs to get these effects, or to feel differently than they believe they can naturally feel.

2. Some people use drugs because they want to change the situation. Taking drugs may change how they feel, which will make a particular situation feel different. If they are stressed out and want to relax, taking something might make the stress disappear for a while. If they are bummed out and want to feel happier, they might think that using a drug will make them happy. Or if they're bored, they might hope that drugs will make the world more interesting.

3. Some teens hang out with older friends, perhaps those who can smoke or drink legally, and using drugs makes them feel older.

4. In some cases, drugs are cheap—even cheaper than alcohol. And they are sometimes easier to get.

5. Some teens differentiate between drugs, like "soft" drugs and "hard" drugs—saying that marijuana is less of a big deal than heroin, for example. They believe that it's not a big deal to use certain drugs and will not have significant consequences. They think that substance use is harmless.

Making Decisions about Smoking, Drugs, and Alcohol

We've tried to help you understand the reasons that might underlie a decision to use or abstain from tobacco, drugs, and alcohol specifically. But thinking about what role substances will have in your identity is a big issue, with some big questions behind it.

First, teenagers have a tendency to feel that they are invincible or invulnerable. Because you are young—your body works, your mind works, you feel like you have all the time in the world to do things—it is easy to fall into the trap of thinking that certain things aren't dangerous. When you feel this way, it is tempting to try things that other people consider risky—after all, if you can't be hurt by it, why not check it out? Unfortunately, this sense is an illusion; teens are damaged by things like tobacco, drugs, and alcohol more often than you might think. Just because you're young, you are not immune to danger.

Another reason that tempts many teens into trying and using alcohol and drugs is the fact that they are forbidden. Somehow the things that we aren't allowed to do can seem more appealing to us—it must be really good if they try to keep it away from us. Or, you might feel that since you get so many messages that smoking, drugs, and alcohol are bad, deciding to go against that and trying them anyway is an act of rebellion. It can seem like you're saying that you don't care that it's bad for you; you are going to do it anyway—sort of a "screw the system" attitude. Keep in mind that when you let this reason motivate you to do something, the people who are denying you things are still affecting your decision, whether you like it or not. If you are doing something just to defy your parents, society, whatever, then you are not just making up your mind on your own. Drugs and alcohol are off-limits to teens for some very good reasons, and you should think about those before reaching your decision.

Some people think that using drugs and alcohol is a personal decision and that every individual should have the freedom to

choose based on personal reasons. Then again, some people feel that drug and alcohol use is completely wrong. Statistics show that anything from secondhand cigarette smoke to injected heroin can cause negative effects, including death. And some people feel that this cost is too high—whether or not you want to, you shouldn't be allowed to, because you aren't the only one who pays. The consequences can affect more than just yourself. Think about this—whom else will your choice affect?

You will probably also consider how choosing to smoke or use alcohol and drugs affects your image, or what other people think of you. It's important to remember that every choice you make can be seen as positive or negative, depending on who is evaluating you. Some people think that smoking cigarettes makes them seem older or look cool. But other people might not see it that way—they might see you as someone who smells like smoke and always has to hang out outside. In some groups, your choice to drink might make you feel just like everyone else—and to others that might make you look like one of the gang, but it might also make you seem like you'll just do anything your friends do. Your parents will almost certainly see your choice to drink, smoke, or use drugs as a negative thing, not something that makes you cool or more grown-up. So while your decision to use substances might seem like it is about creating a certain image, in truth, your image can be both enhanced and degraded by this choice—it all depends on who you ask.

The decisions you will have to make about tobacco, drugs, and alcohol aren't just *whether* to try them, but if you choose to do so, *what kind* of user you will be. There are several kinds of drug/alcohol users and many different patterns of drug use. There are social drinkers, who only drink when they are out in social situations or hanging out with friends. Casual drug users may be more opportunistic, choosing to use when drugs are available but not really seeking them out on their own. There always seems to be someone who claims that they only smoke cigarettes when they are drinking. Addicts generally have a need to continue using regardless of the consequences, so they tend to take drugs or drink as often as possible and to the point of excess. All of these choices have an impact on your identity—they determine how much time you spend under the influence, how much energy and money you might expend to get your fix, what kinds of people you find yourself around, and even how you behave, both while under the influence and while straight or sober.

SIGNS OF ADDICTION

If you are worried that you or someone you love is addicted to drugs or alcohol, consider the answers to the questions below:

1. Do you have withdrawal symptoms if you try to stop using drugs or alcohol?
2. Do you see drugs/alcohol as the solution to problems?
3. Do you spend a lot of time figuring out how you can get drugs/alcohol?
4. Have you been withdrawing from your relationships with friends or family?
5. Have you lost interest in school, sports, or hobbies that used to be important to you? Have your grades slipped?
6. Are you experiencing anxiety or depression?
7. Are you keeping secrets from your friends or family?
8. Do you only hang out with friends who drink or use drugs?
9. Have you tried to quit but can't?

So, what happens when you can't live without a drug or booze? Teens can become addicted to drugs and alcohol just like adults. You could say that you are an addict when using drugs or alcohol becomes such a huge part of your identity that it takes over—you exist only to drink or use, and the idea of living without it is unfathomable. It can be hard to quit. The good news is that you don't have to try quitting on your own. Talk to a friend, teacher, or parent and let that person know that you need help—after all, they may have noticed anyway. There are drug and alcohol treatment programs that will give you the tools to figure out why you got so involved with substances and the skills to take on activities other than using.

Finally, you're probably asking, does deciding whether or not to use drugs or alcohol mean it's part of your identity? After all, if you drink water every day, that's not really a huge part of "who you are," right? Some smokers say that they keep smoking because "it's who I am," for example. They feel that being a smoker is closely tied up with their identity—and for good reason, since smoking takes a lot of time and investment, like many identity characteristics. Or people who hate being told what to do, for example, might choose to smoke because we are given such a strong negative message about nicotine. But as you are learning throughout this book, you can make choices about your identity. Just because you are or were something doesn't mean that you have to remain that for the rest of your life. You can take on the identity of a nonsmoker, too, or nondrinker—or just happen to be a nonsmoker or ex-smoker.

We also want to emphasize that you can change your mind. You can try smoking once, and never again. Or smoke for a while, and then stop. The same goes for drinking or taking drugs. Quitting smoking is hard, sure, but it can be done. And you may decide that once is enough or back off from drinking or using. That's okay too. We hope that as you think about the role that substances have in your life, you'll consider the costs and benefits, how a substance impacts the way you spend your time and money, and you can make a balanced decision that you are comfortable with.

Partying

To see or be seen—that is the question. To be or not to be part of the scene—that is another question. The party scene tends to be a place where larger groups of people get together and just . . . well, that's the point. What do people do at parties anyway?

For the most part, people at parties just hang out and chat, and do a lot of people watching. When you're at a party, you tend to hang out with the people you know and look around to see who else is there. It's almost as if the whole point of going to a party is to make sure people know you are there and to see who else is there too. Then, on Monday, you can talk about who was or was not at the party and feel included in those conversations. The point is going to a party makes you feel included.

There is another reason people like the idea of going to parties. Often they occur without the supervision of adults. Parents may go out of town, or the party may be in a location that has no monitors (like a rave held in a warehouse or other large space). This might make parties more appealing; they can feel risky, rebellious, and thrilling. And what goes on at parties that lack adult control may increase that feeling of the forbidden.

What's strange about the party scene at many schools and/or communities is the fact that you don't really have to be invited to a party in order to attend. Just hearing about a party pretty much gives you the okay to go. You don't even have to know the host or anyone who knows the host to end up at a party. So who ends up going to parties? People who have very little in common, who really are just looking for something to do or a place where they can be seen by others to make sure that others know they exist and are "important enough" to go to a party.

> **RECENT RESEARCH**
> Over half of eleventh graders (64 percent) said that a person becomes popular at school by "partying a lot."[25]

In other words, what a party sometimes ends up being is a group of people who don't really know each other very well, who are simply there to see and be seen. It's as if by going to a party, a person is validating his or her existence to peers, if not to him- or herself. And this sort of environment can make people feel pretty insecure. So what you have is a bunch of people standing around, trying to figure out how to act, what is cool, and what are the right things to say.

One way people deal with feelings of insecurity is by drinking or using drugs. Alcohol is pretty common at parties (some say that it simply isn't a real party without at least beer) and drugs might or might not be there. Alcohol is a drug that lowers people's inhibitions and loosens them up. It can bring people together and smooth out awkward meetings, help with shyness and embarrassment, and make people feel more comfortable. At least in theory, a few drinks helps replace the insecurity with a sense of belonging and commonality among partygoers. In this way, drinking becomes the thing to do at the party. Alcohol is the main event.

The problem is that alcohol can make you do pretty stupid things (it's also illegal to consume if you are under 21, but that is a whole different issue). It can make you act more violently, stupidly, or sloppily.

Alcohol can literally turn you into someone you are not. Think of the terms we sometimes use like the "happy drunk," the "sad drunk," or the "angry drunk." Does this mean that these people are not happy, sad, or angry at other times?

RECENT RESEARCH
Well over half (69 percent) of teens said that drinking or using drugs would influence what they might do sexually with someone.[26]

Alcohol can also alter your judgment and cause you to do things that you would not normally do when sober. It can make you wreck a person's home, have sex with someone you barely know, or get into a car you have no business driving. As discussed earlier, alcohol and other drugs can make it hard to think clearly and make it hard to set limits or honor the limits you set for yourself when sober, so you end up making bad decisions about your health and safety, all in the context of having fun at a party.

Given the risks of a typical party scene, what is a person to do? You can decide to go to a party and not drink or use drugs.

TIPS FOR PARTYING

- Go to the party with people you can rely on.
- Set up a system where you make sure you all check in with each other and make sure you are all safe.
- Decide what you are and are not willing to do before going to the party. Tell your friends your intentions and limits and have them help you stick to them.
- If you drink alcohol (and remember the legal age!), drink one glass of water after every alcoholic drink you have.
- Don't mix alcohol with other drugs—you don't know how they will react with each other.
- Arrange for a safe way to get home from the party. Have a backup plan.

This can be difficult to do because many people might be drinking and it can be hard to not follow the crowd. It can feel weird to be the "only sober person" in the whole place and you might feel left out. Other people at the party may look at you funny, and even accuse you of being "too good" for them or a member of the moral police. People who say these sorts of things do so because they may feel unsure about their own decision to use alcohol or drugs. To help with the awkwardness of feeling you are the only one abstaining, have a friend agree to not drink too. Together, the two of you can have fun watching people who are acting like idiots because they aren't in control of themselves. Be a hero and help a person who couldn't handle what they put into their bodies—give them a ride home, "baby-sit" them if they are feeling sick (but do *not* hesitate to call 911 if you find they are having trouble breathing or look extremely ill). Finally, think about how much better you will feel than most of the partygoers the next morning. It may make abstaining from alcohol and drugs at a party a whole lot easier.

You can also decide not to go to these parties. This is also hard to do, because you can feel as though you missed out on something big if you choose not to go. The stories at school told on Monday morning often make the party seem as though it was the best event ever held. But think about other parties you might have gone to. Are they really the most amazing times in a person's life? Sometimes they can seem like it, but often they are not. And there will most likely be a party next weekend (or even the next day). If you feel as though you are really missing out by not going, just tell yourself there is always next time. Then go and see if the next party is really as fun as everyone seems to believe the last one was.

Whether to be part of the party scene may depend on your personality. If you are the type of person who loves to go to big gatherings, then getting out and being part of the party scene might be the thing for you. If you are outgoing enough, you may not need alcohol to feel comfortable mingling in a crowd and meeting new people. But not everyone is like that. If you are not really someone who feels all that comfortable in the party environment, that is okay too. Instead, invite a smaller

151

group of people out to dinner, dessert, or some activity like bowling or paintball. In smaller groups, it can be a lot easier to really get to know someone and have others know you.

The point is, the party scene can seem like an important place to build up your image. But is it really a place for you to learn about yourself and others? It depends on who you are. Think about what you would go to a party for. To meet new people? To relax? To be seen? To not miss anything? To get drunk? Think about whether the type of event and actual party will help you achieve those goals and how important those goals are to you. And if you are not the type of person who enjoys going to a large party, there are other ways to make friends and have fun. The more comfortable you are in whatever setting, the easier it is for you to relax and be yourself.

SEX—DOES IT REALLY TURN YOU INTO SOMEONE DIFFERENT?

Everyone is sexual in one way or another. You don't have to be sexually experienced to be sexual because your sexuality is so much more than your actions. Your sexuality is about your senses, feelings, and attractions to other people. The better you feel about yourself and who you are, the sexier you become. The more alive, happy, and confident you are, the sexier you feel to yourself. Your sexuality can be a central part of yourself or something that is more on the sidelines. It all depends on how important you believe it is to your life.

But no matter how important your sexuality is to you, our society places a great deal of emphasis on both sex and sexuality. For example, people—especially teens—are given conflicting messages about *having* sex. On the one hand, they are told to "just say no" to sex until they are married or at least in a very serious relationship. On the other hand, they are bombarded with glorified images of sex and sexy people from the media. These images tell us that sex is a critical part of life and that everybody wants it. Sex sells everything from beer to cleaning products. Sex, in many ways, is portrayed as the ultimate experience a person can have and should want.

When you think about it, the idea that sex is used as a marketing tool is sort of creepy. It's strange how something so intimate, so personal, can be such a dominant theme in our culture. It's also strange to realize that whether or not you choose to have sex seems to become everybody's business. Your sex ed class tells you not to have sex. Your parents tell you not to have sex. The news has tons of stories warning about how today's teenagers are sexually active at early ages. Other television programs and the music you listen to seem to be insisting that you should be having sex. Your friends are dying to know every little detail about what you are doing sexually and with whom. The focus of both celebrity gossip and the rumors in the school hallways is often sex. What's the big deal about sex?

The bottom line is, the decision whether or not to have sex is a very personal decision. Sure, your parents, friends, favorite television show, or celebrity crush might influence your sexual choices, but none of these should have the final say in your decision. Only you can decide whether or not you want to have sex. And that personal decision isn't just for the first time you have sex, but every time you have sex. Just because you had sex once does not mean you want to have it again. Or just because you have had sex with a particular person, and want to have it again with that person, does not mean that you want to have it at a particular moment. Each time, you have to think about whether you want to have sex or not.

There are just as many reasons to not have sex as there are to have sex. For example, the number one reason teens who have not had sex yet give is that they are not ready or haven't met the right person. But there are other reasons: your religion may state that you should wait until marriage, you may be concerned about pregnancy or sexually transmitted diseases (STDs), or your parents or friends

> **REMEMBER**
> **Anyone who tries to force you to do something you do not want to do is not worth being with.**

may disapprove. The main reason teens give for having sex is that they are in love with their partner. But there are other reasons as well: curiosity, loneliness, pleasure, for fun.

153

In order to figure out how you feel about sex, and what your reasons are to have or not to have sex, you are going to have to think about it. Seriously. Pick a quiet time and really think about how you feel about sex. Think about the reasons you have certain attitudes and opinions about sex. Write them down. Then make a list of everyone and everything that has influenced your attitudes about sex. Doing this will help you understand what you believe about sex and how you arrived at those beliefs, and it may even help you see whether the beliefs you have about sex are really your own or if they are just messages you have heard. It will probably take more time than just this once to really understand how you feel about sex, and to figure out when and under what circumstances you would and would not want to have sex with someone. But even trying this thought exercise once will really help you understand how you feel about sex and why. And the more you think about it, the more you will know who you are and what your values are when it comes to sex. Researchers have found that 75 percent of teens think that choosing not to have sex can be a difficult decision.[27] But if you take the time to think about this important decision, you will be one of those in the minority who is more certain about what he or she wants to do.

One-third of teen girls worry about being forced to do something sexually.[28]

After you make up your mind about what feels comfortable to you, you need to discuss that decision with your partner. So, in a sense, the decision to have sex is a decision *two people* make *together*. But talking about sex and your feelings about sex is not easy. It can be embarrassing and it is also a very revealing experience, leaving you open for ridicule and pain. That is why talking about how you feel about sex is one of the most intimate things you can do with someone you care about. That is why the talk can also be a very rewarding experience. Once you are able to talk about one of the most personal topics to someone else, someone who really matters to you, you take a giant step toward learning about yourself, and you also let those who are important to you understand more about who you are and what is important to you.

So, while in the ideal world it would be great if the decision whether or not to have sex was a private one between two consenting individuals, that is not always the reality. In your social circles, whether or not you have had sex may be an important part of how your friends or peers think about you. Some people may pressure you to have sex by thinking of you as a "prude" or "tight," a "tease" or "mamma's boy." Others may look down on you for having sex by calling you a "slut" or "dawg" or simply someone to watch out for if you ask them out on a date. Your sexual reputation—whether it is true or not—can influence how others treat you. For whatever reason, your sexual decisions become everyone's business.

About one-third of teens said that what their friends are doing sexually influences what they might do sexually. Over half of the teens who said they have had sex (62 percent) admit that their friends' sexual experiences influenced their decision to have sex.[29]

Sometimes you don't get direct pressure from the people you hang out with, but all their talk about sex can make you feel as if you don't fit in. Maybe you end up in a conversation where everyone is saying that only "stupid people" have sex and that is why they decided to all sign a virginity pledge at their church. You stay quiet because you and your partner are having a very loving sexual relationship. Or you are in the locker room, overhearing "everyone else" brag about their sexual conquests at the party last weekend. You didn't "score," so you get changed as quickly as possible before anyone can ask you who you ended up with on Saturday. In these cases, the person not saying anything might feel abnormal, or as though he or she is doing something "wrong" because their experiences can't contribute to the conversations. While it's only natural to want to fit in, it's *more* important to make sure the decisions you make about sex are your own. So, keep listening to your friends to hear what they think are right and wrong things to do in a sexual situation. But when what you do does not match with what they are saying, try hard not to worry. Instead, feel confident, knowing that you are making your own decisions about a very important part of your life.

YOUR TURN

Here are some questions for you to think about:

1. How do you feel about school? What is the most important part of attending school for you?

2. What are your plans for the future?

3. What do you like to do in your spare time? What do you enjoy about these activities?

4. What do you do to stay physically active? What do you like about these activities?

5. What are some activities you've never tried but are interested in? What do you find intriguing about them?

6. Are you employed right now? How do you feel about your work situation?

7. What are the attitudes toward drugs and alcohol in your school and community? What are *your* attitudes toward drugs and alcohol?

8. What is the party scene like in your circle of friends? How do you fit into it?

9. Do you spend time online? What do you use time online for?

10. Have you ever met people online? How is it the same as or different from meeting people in person?

11. What are your attitudes and beliefs about sex? Where did these come from?

12. Do you think having sex makes someone a different person? Why or why not?

NOTES

1. U.S. Census Bureau, "Education Summary: Enrollment, 1900 to 2000, and Projections, 2001," No. HS-20, in *Statistical Abstract of the United States: 2003* (Washington, D.C.: U.S. Census Bureau, 2003).

2. T. Shary, *Generation Multiplex: The Image of Youth in Contemporary American Cinema* (Austin: University of Texas Press, 2002).

3. National Center for Education Statistics, *Parent Survey of the National Household Education Surveys Program, 1999* (Washington, D.C.: U.S. Government Printing Office, 1999).

4. A. Quart, *Branded: The Buying and Selling of Teenagers* (New York: Perseus, 2003).

5. National Center for Education Statistics, *The Condition of Education 2003*, NCES 2003-067 (Washington, D.C.: U.S. Government Printing Office, 2003).

6. U.S. Bureau of Labor Statistics, "So You're Thinking about Dropping Out?" accessed May 24, 2004, at www.dol.gov/asp/fibre/dropout.htm.

7. U.S. Census Bureau, "Enrollment and Employment Status of Recent High School Graduates 16 to 24 Years Old, by Type of School, Attainment Level for People Not Enrolled, Sex, Race, and Hispanic Origin: October 2001," in *Current Population Survey, 2001* (Washington, D.C.: U.S. Government Printing Office, 2001).

8. U.S. Department of Education, NCES, Digest of Education Statistics 2001, NCES 2002-130, accessed May 14, 2004, at http://nces.ed.gov/pubsearch/pubsinfo.asp?pubid=2002130.

9. U.S. Bureau of Labor Statistics, "Declining Teen Labor Force Participation," Summary 02-06, in *Issues in Labor Statistics* (Washington, D.C.: U.S. Department of Labor, 2002).

10. F. Blosser, "Most Teen Worker Injuries in Restaurants Occur in Fast Food, NIOSH Study Finds" (2002), accessed July 3, 2004, at www.cdc.gov/NIOSH/teenfast.html.

11. A. Muharrar, *More Than a Label: Why What You Wear or Who You're With Doesn't Define Who You Are* (Minneapolis: Free Spirit, 2002).

12. Customized analysis using the Youth Risk Behavior Surveillance System, 2003 data, accessed April 13, 2004, at www.cdc.gov/HealthyYouth/yrbs/index.htm.

13. W. M. Leonard, "The Odds of Transiting from One Level of Sports Participation to Another," *Sociology of Sport Journal* 13, no. 3 (1996): 292.

14. Harris Interactive, *Trends & Tudes Newsletter* 2, no.1 (2003).

15. G. Sailes, "Professional Athletes: Cultural Icons or Social Anomalies?" *USA Today Magazine*, September 2001.

16. Customized analysis using the Youth Risk Behavior Surveillance System, 2001 data, accessed April 13, 2004, at www.cdc.gov/HealthyYouth/yrbs/index.htm.

17. A. Lenhart, L. Rainie, and O. Lewis, "Teenage Life Online: The Rise of the Instant-Message Generation and the Internet's Impact

on Friendships and Family Relationships," Pew Internet and American Life Project, 2001, www.pewinternet.org.

18. E. Edwards, "Generation www: Kids Create Web Sites," *Washington Post*, March 24, 2004, C-1.

19. Centers for Disease Control, "Tobacco Use among Middle and High School Students—United States, 2002," accessed February 14, 2004, at www.cdc.gov/mmwr/preview/mmwrhtml/ss5004a1.htm.

20. "Vietnam Bans Smoking Scenes in Movies," Reuters Health Online, accessed January 9, 2004, at www.reutershealth.com.

21. J. R. Polansky and S. A. Glantz, "First-Run Smoking Presentations in U.S. Movies 1999–2003," University of California San Francisco Center for Tobacco Control Research and Education, 2004.

22. National Institute of Child Health and Human Development, *America's Children: Key Indicators of Well-Being 2003*, accessed July 23, 2004, at www.childstats.gov/americaschildren.

23. National Center on Addiction and Substance Abuse, "Teen Tipplers: America's Underage Drinking Epidemic," accessed July 23, 2004, at www.casacolumbia.org/pdshopprov/files/Teen_Tipplers_February_26_2003.pdf.

24. Customized analysis using the Youth Risk Behavior Surveillance System, 2002 data, accessed April 13, 2004, at www.cdc.gov/HealthyYouth/yrbs/index.htm.

25. Council of Ministers of Education, *Canadian Youth, Sexual Health and HIV/AIDS Study* (Ottawa, Ont.: Canadian Strategy on HIV/AIDS of Health Canada, 2003).

26. Kaiser Family Foundation, *Decision Making*, part of the Sex Smarts series co-sponsored by *Seventeen Magazine*, 2000, accessed August 27, 2004, at www.kff.org/entpartnerships/seventeen_surveys.cfm.

27. Kaiser Family Foundation, *Virginity and the First Time*, part of the Sex Smarts series co-sponsored by *Seventeen Magazine*, 2003, accessed August 27, 2004, at www.kff.org/mediapartnerships/seventeen-3366-100303.cfm.

28. Harris Interactive, *Trends & Tudes Newsletter* 3, no. 3 (2004).

29. Kaiser Family Foundation, *Decision Making*.

What You Believe

VALUES

Values is a kind of buzzword that means very different things to different people. You hear the word *values* all the time—the president wants to support family values, your parents want to make sure that you grow up having good values, the media think that teens have no values, and so on. So what are values? Values are things you believe, codes you live by. The dictionary says values are the beliefs of a person or social group in which the person has an emotional investment (either for or against something). But there are several different ways to consider values: you might talk about moral values, political beliefs or values, and personal values, for example. To an extent, your values are the foundation of your personal philosophy; they indicate what you think is right and wrong, important or inconsequential.

Your values are developed from a variety of sources. You learn them from your family, culture, peers, religious organizations, social pressures, and other sources. For example, in some Asian cultures, respect for one's elders is a strongly held value, which is demonstrated through multigenerational households and responsibility for caring for one's parents in their later years. In the United States, this value isn't nearly as important.

We are constantly taught to believe that certain behaviors and beliefs are okay and others are not. Some experts think that adolescence is a time period when teens distance themselves from the values instilled in them by their parents. The way your friends choose to look at the world or behave may seem more sensible to you than the way that your parents encourage you to act. Some of the task of adolescence is figuring out which of your values have come from which sources (friends, family, media, etc.) and which of those you agree with and want to keep. In any case, your values are deeply connected to your sense of identity. (Note: we talk about religion and religious values separately in the next section.)

Consider *moral values*—which could be thought of as very similar to the *family values* often discussed by politicians. Moral values are things like definitions of power and the legitimate or illegitimate use of power; definitions of crime and honor; good and evil. Our moral values are our beliefs about how people should act or what is good to accomplish. Think about how you feel about lying, for example. Do you think lying is always wrong? Why? Because dishonesty shows disrespect for other people? Or because it is fundamentally wrong to deceive people? Or do you think that there are situations in which lying is okay? Perhaps you think that lying can be justified when you are avoiding hurting another person or when there is no real impact from it. In either case, your belief about whether lying is always wrong or occasionally okay represents a moral value. Some other areas about which you probably have moral values are:

- ◎ *Good and evil:* Are there clear guidelines about what is good and what is evil that apply to all people at all times? Or does what is good and what is evil depend on the circumstances at the time? For example, are there situations in which killing another human is not evil, such as self-defense?

- ◎ *Humans and nature:* Should humans master and control nature for their own purposes? Or should humans co-exist with nature and not seek to alter or control it?

- ◎ *Altruism:* Is it more important to consider how your actions will affect other people, or is your priority to look after yourself first and foremost?

If you think about some of these questions, you'll see that values are important because they impact your behavior. When you are presented with a dilemma, your values are rules that help you decide what to do based on what you believe. Your values will sometimes conflict with each other or with the values of other people, and you will be forced to rank or prioritize them. Say you have a friend whose parents are getting divorced and he has been having trouble in school because of it. This friend tells you that he is in danger of failing English, so he stole a copy of the English final examination. He asks you to keep this a secret. However, the next day, someone else in your class is accused of stealing the exam and is going to be expelled for cheating. What would you do? How important is protecting your friend's secret? What is the value of seeing that innocent people aren't punished for crimes they didn't commit?

Some of the ways that values affect our behavior are through our political choices and our personal lives. Your political beliefs are often an outgrowth of your core values. If you think that human nature is fundamentally good and people look out for one another because it's the right thing to do, then you will support certain political ideas. On the other hand, if you think that people tend to be selfish and only look out for themselves and not others, then you will support different ones. These values will become more important and influential as you reach voting age. However, even though you may not be old enough to vote, you definitely get to have opinions and to be a political person or active citizen.

You may have noticed that people seem to be trying to get teens more involved in political activities. Organizations like MTV's Rock the Vote and Mobilize American Youth are an

MAKING THE WORLD A BETTER PLACE

Think one person can't make a difference? Think you are too young to influence others? Take a look at these examples:

Craig Kielburger founded Free the Children, an organization for
   children's rights, in response to reading an article about a
   boy in Pakistan who was murdered for protesting child
   labor. Craig was 12 years old when he began speaking out
   about children's rights.[1]
Seeds of Peace is an international organization that sponsors
   an International Camp every summer, where young people
   age 14 to 16 from many sides of the conflict in the Middle
   East get together to work for peace. They believe that "by
   teaching teenagers to develop trust and empathy for one
   another, Seeds of Peace is changing the landscape of
   conflict. It is enabling people blinded by hatred to see the
   human face of their enemies. It is equipping the next
   generation with the tools to end the violence and become
   the leaders of tomorrow."[2]

attempt to get young people interested in politics and active as
political participants. Teens everywhere express their political
values through activism and advocacy—in areas like
environmentalism, animal rights, public funding for education,
gay and lesbian rights, abortion issues, and more. If you can
think of an issue confronting society, there is a teen somewhere
who feels strongly enough about it to devote time and energy to
educating and influencing other people about it. It's up to you to
decide how big a part of your identity your political beliefs and
values are.

Although you express your values through your sense of
morality and your political beliefs, the way that values are most
obviously a part of who you are is through your personal
conduct. Your personal values guide your interactions with the
world and other people. What sorts of beliefs could be
considered personal values? Personal values have to do with the
importance of things like family, friends, leisure, politics, work,
religion, and service to others. Your values might have to do

WHERE DO I DEMONSTRATE MY VALUES?

Some examples of areas in which you may hold values about political or social issues are:

- What responsibility do citizens have to run their own communities? Should everyone be required to vote or participate in making decisions about how their neighborhoods, cities, and states are run? Or is it acceptable to choose not to be involved?

- How far does freedom of speech go? Do you support the free expression of all kinds of speech? Or are there things you shouldn't be able to say publicly? For what reasons? How about "hate speech" directed at particular groups?

- Should all people be entitled to the same things, or are unequal distributions of money, services, and access acceptable or helpful to society? Is it acceptable that some people have things like health insurance while others don't?

- Is education a right that you are entitled to or a privilege that you are lucky to take advantage of? How much responsibility do you think the government should take for the education of its citizens?

- Is it more important to ensure that life is easy or manageable for people right now, or should you consider how current policies affect future generations? If so, how much? Think about environmental policies—is it okay to make life easier for individuals and corporations now if it will have a negative effect on people in the future?

with important personal qualities, how one should act, or what one should accomplish: for example, being ambitious, logical, self-controlled, tolerant, well-paid, saving money. And personal values get expressed through your sense of ethics and things like: I won't cheat on a test; I will never lie to a friend; my family will always be the most important thing in my life; I think it's important to not have sex before marriage.

Think about two beliefs you could have about parents: (1) "Regardless of what the qualities and faults of one's parents are, one must always love and respect them." And (2) "One does not have the duty to respect and love parents who have

COMMON PERSONAL VALUES[3]

Accuracy, accountability, achievement, adventure, challenge, change, cleanliness, commitment, competence, competition, continuous improvement, creativity, decisiveness, discipline, equality, efficiency, fairness, family, friendship, fun, gratitude, hard work, honesty, justice, knowledge, leadership, love, meaning, money, peace, pleasure, power, practicality, privacy, punctuality, respect, safety, self-reliance, service to others, status, stability, strength, tolerance, tradition, trust, variety.

not earned it by their behavior and attitudes." Your relationship with your parents would be pretty different depending on which of those things you believe.

Some people are very principled—their beliefs are a powerful and obvious part of who they are. You probably know someone who holds a particular value as more important than anything else. Think about how highly you personally value "following the rules." There are still some people who get considered a "goody-goody" because of their adherence to a set of personal beliefs that others consider being good—not ever breaking the rules. But you might choose to follow the rules not because they're rules, but because you think they're a good way to live your life. You have decided that obeying customs or rules given by parents or schools is an important value to you, and that guides your behavior. On the other hand, you might decide that telling individuals how to live their lives ignores each person's uniqueness and that rules stifle individual expression. Rebelling and defying conventions might be important to you because you feel that rules are arbitrary and should be more carefully examined than dutifully observed. Another example might be someone who believes that cruelty to animals is absolutely wrong. This value, strongly held, probably has an impact on what that person eats, wears, or spends money on.

Something that is also worth thinking about is how publicly you express your values. Some people feel that their values are a deeply personal thing that they rarely talk about or debate with others. Yet other people are very public, constantly asking what you believe and inviting you to argue about the areas in which you disagree. It is up to you to determine how much you discuss your personal values. However, regardless of whether you choose to identify or talk about them, the values that you hold are a very important part of your identity and a strong influence on how you choose to act.

RELIGION

Religion is a very important part of many people's lives. What you choose to believe and how you worship can affect much more than just your faith—religious beliefs can impact things such as when you do not attend school, what you eat, what you wear, whom you can marry, what behaviors are acceptable, and many more. For many people, religion is determined by their family. What religious beliefs your parents hold get passed on to you. If they are observant Catholics, you grow up acting Catholic as well. Or if your parents aren't involved in organized religion, you probably won't attend regular religious services yourself, at least as a child. But during the teen years, when you are likely questioning your identity, the issue of your own personal religious beliefs may become very important. Adolescence is the time when religious conversion is most common.[4] And there are more religious faiths than you probably realized when you were younger—different types of Christianity, Judaism, Islam, Buddhism, Baha'i, Hinduism, Jainism, Scientology, pagan religions, Taoism, Sikhism, Zoroastrianism, Unitarian Universalism, and others.

What is religion? Religion is a system or code of ethics, values, beliefs, and philosophy of life, sometimes involving belief in a supernatural or divine power (sometimes not). It can be about worshiping a deity or god, performing rituals to honor sacred events or dates, praying to a higher power, or behaving according to a prescribed code of conduct. It's a pretty big thing, as you can tell. Because of this, religious faith is no small matter. About 60 percent of teens said religion is pretty or very important to them, and 80 percent of all teenagers pray.[5] In

fact, the United States is thought of as one of the most religious countries in the world, simply because of the number of citizens who feel that their faith is important in their lives.

While we called this section "Religion," we like to think that religion is also about spirituality—and while organized religion (e.g., Catholicism, Buddhism, Islam) is the most obvious and probably most common form of spirituality, there are many other ways you may find to express your personal faith. Some people are atheists and do not believe in a god or gods. Some atheists believe that their choice (to not believe in a god) is a

RELIGION IS BARBARA'S CORE IDENTITY

Barbara, who is 16, thinks of herself as someone who is introverted and likes to be that way because she feels more independent. However, she is very close to her parents and her older brother, and her dog Harold. She also spends a lot of time being social online, keeping in touch with both friends and relatives far and near. But for Barbara, the most important part of her identity is her religion.

Q: How would you describe yourself?

Barbara: I describe myself as a Christian first and foremost, because that explains a lot. More than just coming from a tradition of the Christian faith, I try to live out the lifestyle to which I was called. So, the most important thing people should know about me is that I'm Christian. If my being Christian makes people wonder why, then I can stand up for my faith, and (hopefully) show them the truth, with God's help.

Q: How do you think others see you?

Barbara: Other people see me as someone who is strong in her faith. They see me as a person who tries to do the right thing for a very specific reason, and that reason is Jesus.

rejection of faith, while others view it as a faith of its own that rejects the idea of a controlling force in the form of a deity. Agnostics, on the other hand, are sort of making up their minds about God or gods, and may not feel that they have enough information to decide. Some teens identify as Wiccan or

GREAT RESOURCE

What religion do your beliefs resemble? Check out Belief-O-Matic, www.beliefnet.com/story/76/story_7665_1.html. You answer twenty questions about your beliefs regarding God, the afterlife, human nature, and other things, and the site will tell you what religion your beliefs most closely match.

witches, and believe in a different set of rituals and deities than are found in traditional theistic religions. Or some may follow pagan religions, emphasizing nature and Earth more than gods or religious writings.

How do you make decisions about your religious identity? Well, remember the period of *rumspringa* that is observed within the Amish faith that we mentioned in the introduction to this book? In this period, Amish teens get to explore other ways of living and then consciously commit to the church if they so choose, with the new knowledge that this way of life is what they want for themselves. Because you probably know the most about the religion in which you were raised, you might not know much about other religions. You might be curious about other faiths, or you might feel comfortable with the beliefs that you learned from your family and church. Remember crisis and commitment? This is one area in which lots of people commit without a crisis—they believe they simply belong to one religion without the need to explore.

But because there are so many types of religious beliefs, you may want to be a little like the Amish and explore some. You may find that you need to get some additional information about why you are what you are, or whether you want to be what you think you are. For example, if you are Catholic, you might want to get more information about Catholicism—where it started, how it is governed, and why certain rituals and beliefs are central to the religion. You may wish to ask other people about their spiritual beliefs to learn more about what others believe. If you don't identify with any specific religion, you might want to explore a little bit by getting more information about different religions, talking to people who observe those faiths, and maybe even attending various religious centers or services.

Probably the most basic way to explore and decide on your religious identity is to think a lot. Try to answer questions like: How do you think the world was created or started? Is there such a thing as evil? Is there an afterlife? What is the purpose for human beings? Do you believe in angels? What kind of responsibilities do you think we have to one another as people?

Are you in control of your life and what happens to you, or is there a force greater than you that determines what goes on? The answers to these sorts of questions are pieces of your religious beliefs, and the more you discover what you truly believe and are most comfortable with, the more complete and vibrant your religious identity will be.

Committing to a religious faith can be a delicate issue, especially if you are interested in or choosing a religion that is different from your parents' or your friends'. A bit of advice we have for you is not to jump off the bridge right away—a sudden and overwhelming change to a new set of rituals or behavior can be really weird and make it hard for parents or friends to understand your new ideas. Also, just because you decide to follow a new religion, don't expect your life to change overnight. Deciding to follow a particular set of religious ideals is only part of the process; you also have to let those rules guide your life over time in order to truly understand them, appreciate them, and demonstrate how important they are to you. You may also want to talk about your interest in exploring different religious beliefs with your family, so that they understand what you are up to.

Something to consider in thinking about religious identity is also the amount of emphasis you want to give to your religion. There are very devout religious followers who adhere very strictly to the dictates of their religion, and who feel that their religion touches every aspect of their life—from diet and lifestyle choices, such as use of alcohol, to values and beliefs. And there are people who don't identify with any religion at all and who feel that it is not a part of who they are in any way. In the middle are lots of people who choose some aspects of a religion to follow and others to set aside. There are Jewish people who say that they will only marry someone who is Jewish, but who eat bacon. There are Catholics who send their children to Catholic school but who engaged in premarital sex. There are Buddhists who are vegetarians but wear leather. So you obviously have choices not only about what religious group you most closely identify with, but about how intensely you would like to use religious beliefs as a guiding principle for your behavior.

GOALS

While you are thinking about who you are, you are probably also finding yourself thinking about who you would like to be. Sometimes we recognize things about ourselves that we'd like to change, or we think of things that we'd really like to accomplish someday. When you know what you want and try to figure out how to get it, you are setting goals for yourself. Working toward goals is definitely something that adults think and talk about; but more and more, the popular media are recognizing that teens have goals too. Books like *What Do You Really Want? How to Set a Goal and Go For It: A Guide for Teens* and *The Seven Habits of Highly Effective Teens* have gotten published because of the importance for teens of setting and working toward goals. This might sound a little strange in a book on identity, to talk about goals and how to achieve them, but if you stop to think about it, you'll see that the goals people have for themselves can be a huge part of their identity. Think about someone who wants to be a doctor, a friend who wants to win the regional tennis tournament, someone who is trying to lose twenty pounds, a person who wants to stop gossiping about their friends. Each of these people has a goal, and chances are their emphasis on this goal helps determine how they spend their time and what they think is valuable.

Goals are important because they keep us moving forward. They guide our behavior by making clear what we are to do next, giving us direction. Teens who set and work toward goals generally have improved school performance, motivation, and self-esteem.[6] It's not that surprising that people who have a vision for where they want to go are more likely to get there than those who don't. People who don't have goals can be confused about what to spend their time and energy on, and can end up living a life filled with things that just happen to them rather than achievements that they created for themselves. And don't underestimate the feeling of satisfaction when you reach a goal—it's natural to feel pleased and proud to have accomplished something. Without setting goals, you miss out on this positive feeling.

So you know that having goals for yourself is good for you. How do you find your personal goals? Think about your life as it is right now. Is there anything that you are unhappy about or would like to change? Do you want to be more honest with your parents? Get in better shape physically? Bring your grades up? Quit smoking? Save money for a car? Then think about your life in the future. Where would you like to be a week, a month, a year, or ten or twenty-five years from now? Do you want to be a teacher? Earn a million dollars? Compete in the Olympics? Finish a college degree? Be a good parent? Learn to fly a plane? Setting goals for yourself is about identifying what you would like to become or achieve.

What kinds of goals should you set for yourself? Many coaches and advisors talk about setting "SMART" goals— which stands for Specific, Measurable, Attainable, Relevant, and Timely. Your goals should be *specific*—rather than saying "I want to get better grades," you might say that you want to get a B in biology or improve your grades on written essays in English. Or instead of saying "I want to be rich," you get specific and say that you want to have earned a million dollars by the time you turn 30. A *measurable* goal is a goal that you can measure so that you can tell when you are making progress and when you have achieved the goal. You will be clearer on your progress if you know how much, how many, or how far your goal is. You could do this by measuring weight loss in pounds, or academic improvement in grade point average, or other measurements. It is important to also set goals that are *attainable* and *relevant*. *Attainable* goals are ones that you can actually achieve and are realistic for you. If you are five feet tall, the goal of playing in the NBA Finals might not be realistic or attainable. Pick things that are just out of reach but that you believe you can actually do given your current situation, resources, and skills. *Relevant* goals are those that have personal meaning for you—that reflect who you are and what you think is important. You are more likely to stick to a plan and be motivated when your goals are things that you really truly want. Finally, *timely* goals are those that have a specific timeframe. People tend to be more successful in achieving their goals when they set a timeline for themselves. You might decide you want to finish your PhD by the time you are 30 years old, or run a marathon within the next twelve months. Putting your goal into a schedule will help you figure out how quickly or how hard you will have to work.

But setting goals for yourself is only the first part. Once you have identified some goals that you want to achieve, then you can start working toward them. You can start by writing your goals down, or letting other people know that you have them as goals. If other people know that you are working on something, they are likely to support you in your efforts and you will try harder so they can be proud of you. Figure out what it will take to reach each of your goals. Will you need training? Assistance? New skills? Try to break each of your goals down into smaller steps that you can work on right now. If you want to run a marathon, you probably won't go out and do it tomorrow—you probably can't! Instead, you make smaller goals—to run a certain distance this week, then more next week, and so on, until you get up closer to marathon distances. Say you want to get a B in biology. Then make your smaller goal to turn in assignments on time for the next two weeks or to spend an hour each day reviewing your homework. Perhaps your goal is becoming an astronaut. That's a pretty long-range goal—but you can certainly do things right now for that. Learn about astronomy, get good grades in science, keep yourself in shape physically, for example. Each of these smaller tasks is a short-term goal that leads you to your long-term goal.

Sometimes obstacles will come up that interfere with your ability to make progress toward your goals. For example, if your goal is to become a journalist, you may decide in your planning that you need to attend college and get a degree in English or journalism. However, you may discover that your parents are unable to afford to send you to college. So you may have to spend more time learning about how to finance higher education before you can continue with your short-term goals toward becoming a journalist. But as in this example, many obstacles are things that you can handle. You can deal with some of these when you start working toward your goal by anticipating them and working around them. You may need to spend more time learning something or getting to know different people. You may need to problem-solve in ways you hadn't expected. Or you may need to redefine your interpretation of the obstacle as a problem. In dealing with obstacles, you may also gain skills or experience that will help you achieve the goal itself.

While we definitely encourage you to find some goals for yourself and make working toward them an integral part of your identity, it is important to remember that there is more to you than where you are going. As you progress toward where you want to go, take some time to enjoy where you are. Sometimes it's good to put aside your goals for a minute. If you are constantly working toward something, you can fall into the trap

TRANG ON HOW VOLUNTEERING SHAPES HER GOALS

Trang is the 18-year-old daughter of parents who emigrated from Vietnam. She just graduated from high school and was accepted at her state university. Even though she sees herself as a "quiet and shy person" who is not "social around lots of people or big events," she spends a lot of her time volunteering at her local hospital, where she helps young children with severe learning disabilities. This experience, she says, has helped shape her goals and the way she carries herself.

Q: How does your volunteer work influence who you are?
Trang: My volunteer work helps me learn more about myself. Through volunteer work I realized that I changed into a more confident and outgoing person. I learned to ask more questions when I was confused and ask for help when I didn't understand something. I think that by getting involved in your community, you will learn to be more independent and helpful to both others and yourself.

Working at the hospital also helped me shape my goals. It showed me the part about the health-care field that you don't learn from a textbook. I get to see the reality of the health-care professions and had the chance to be involved in different settings and activities, so now I have a better sense of what I like about different health-care careers.

Q: How does your volunteer work influence how others see you?
Trang: I think that whenever you are doing good deeds, others see you in a positive way. People appreciate me more, I think. This is because teenagers more often than not are not seen in a positive way. By volunteering I think people base their judgment of what they have seen and hear about me before they judge my character based on how old I am.

of feeling like where or who you are right now isn't good enough—because you have to achieve your goals to really be worth something. But that's not true. We set goals and work toward them because we want to become better or different people, not because we are bad or inadequate to begin with. Even the most impressive people still set goals for themselves. So keep in mind that who you are right now is pretty cool, but that becoming something or achieving something in the future can motivate you and be an important part of your identity.

MAKING DECISIONS

Imagine that it's Friday night, and you and several friends are trying to make up your minds about how to spend the evening. How do you decide? Do you call other friends to see what they're doing? Do you check the paper to see what times movies are showing, or do you just take off for the theater without looking? Or do you take so long to decide that you end up spending the evening hanging out in your living room? Your decision-making style is a big part of who you are. After all, as you explore and commit to your identity, you are constantly making choices about what is and is not important to you. Understanding the process you use to make these decisions can help you make better decisions in the first place, but it can also give you a better sense of how other people see you. Are you rational? Impulsive? Hesitant? Wishy-washy?

There are many ways to make decisions—everyone is a little different in terms of how they evaluate their options and make choices. Consider these styles of making decisions:

- **Impulsive**—with little thought or planning, jumping at the first opportunity.
- **Fatalistic**—letting the universe decide, leaving it up to fate.
- **Compliant**—letting others decide or following someone else's plans.
- **Delaying**—avoiding choosing, postponing thought and action.
- **Agonizing**—getting lost in all the information, being overwhelmed by the number of choices and how to decide, often unable to decide.

- ⑨ Planning—using a rational approach, weighing options and results.

- ⑨ Intuitive—making choices based on whether they feel right.

- ⑨ Paralysis—unable to approach responsibilities.

- ⑨ Deviant—asking advice of others but then doing the opposite of what others suggest.

Which style sounds most like you? Do you take your time to think about what options are available to you, or do you just go for it? And if you just go for it, is it because someone told you not to or because someone recommended that you do so?

You might have different decision-making styles when you approach different sorts of choices, also. You may address your schoolwork or career planning one way, but your relationships and personal life another way. Additionally, your style will probably change somewhat over your lifetime. When you were younger, you were probably more content to leave decision making to your parents—they decided things like where you would go to school and what kinds of activities to sign you up for. But as you get older, you may want to take more responsibility for making your own choices.

Regardless of how you make decisions, you can learn ways to make decisions more deliberately and perhaps improve the quality of the choices you make. First, make sure that you get enough information about the options available to you. You will be a more informed decision maker if you understand what the choices are as well as the consequences of picking each of them. Second, consider as wide a range of options as possible— even find some new ones by asking people you respect or doing some research. The more choices you have, the easier it will be to compare them and the more likely you will decide on something that fits you. Next, evaluate each of these options. What are the pros and cons of each? What are the costs and benefits of different choices? Once you understand what each option is really about and how it compares to your other options, then you can make an informed choice.

Finally, you have to take the leap and make the decision. This can be the hardest step; for many people, it is hard to take the risk that you are passing up a choice that might have been better for you. Keep in mind that while over your life you will make lots of huge decisions, you will also have many opportunities to correct the things you would like to have done differently. You *do* get the chance to change your mind on lots of things—you can get out of relationships, give up habits or hobbies, change careers. While you should definitely consider the permanence of any choices you make at this stage in your life, remember that you will also be making many more choices in the future. It can be scary, but you can definitely make good decisions for yourself when you make them with your eyes open.

CAREER ASPIRATIONS

Your job or career is what you spend more time in your life doing than almost anything except sleeping. Therefore, it is pretty understandable that something you spend so much time doing will be a big part of who you think of yourself as. Even as little kids, we get really focused on thinking about the world of work. We played school or office or store (or even police officer!) and pretended to be doing work in each of those settings. Work seemed like a really grown-up thing to be doing, and it was fun to pretend to be grown-up. Then people would always ask you, "What do you want to be when you grow up?" You were expected to have an answer to that question—a firefighter, a ballerina, a poet, a truck driver, a veterinarian. You are still probably expected to have an answer to that question, but you are a lot closer to being asked to do something to make those wishes come true. What you choose to do for a career is a

The U.S. Department of Labor says that the average person will have 3.5 different careers in his or her lifetime and work for ten employers, keeping each job for 3.5 years.[7]

huge part of how you will think of yourself, how you will feel about your life, and how other people will see you.

Lots of teens agree that thinking about the future is one of the most stressful things they do, however. Worrying about getting good grades, getting into a good school, and then getting a lucrative job can really add up to stress you out. While it is certainly important to think about your future and take steps that lead you in positive directions, it shouldn't get in the way of enjoying where you are at right now. After all, you might change your mind. We know several people who busted their butts getting into competitive colleges and suffering through painfully difficult courses as preparation for medical school, only to find halfway through college that something else was far more intriguing. This is not only okay—it's expected! We write this section in the hopes that you will think carefully about what you want to do and be prepared to make reasoned decisions about it, but that you will also not get totally freaked out thinking that you need to decide *right now*, be totally right, and never change your mind. You're supposed to be learning, yes, but unless you are completely and utterly driven to do something, you definitely get to take some time to figure out what you want to do for a living.

First off, family and parents are a big influence on your career aspirations and plans. You will inherently be more familiar with the occupations performed by the people you know. For that reason, it might be easier to think about doing those things than doing jobs you have never heard of or know nothing about. It can also be easier to get into a particular business or field if you have connections. Some kids grow up in a family where there is a "family business"—a store, import company, woodworking shop, law firm. The expectation for teens in these families can be that they will enter the family business, because that is what people in their family do. And they might have a job waiting for them whenever they are ready. Or you might have better networking possibilities because of what your parents do. If your mom is a television producer and you're interested in screenwriting, she might be able to hook you up with people you can learn from.

So we learn about jobs from our family, and sometimes our families act as gateways to help us actually find positions. Parents can also put pressure on you to enter certain fields. There are definitely families in which you aren't considered a success unless you are a doctor or a lawyer, for example. If your parents are paying for your education, you might be even more pressured to follow their desires regarding your work. Or you might rebel and decide to pick something else. So your parents can be an influence on your career decisions, whether you want them to be or not.

There are lots of ways to find a career. Sometimes it is just a happy accident—you just happen to be in the right place at the right time and the right job comes along and finds you. But most

BRANDON CHOOSES A NON-STEREOTYPED CAREER PATH

Like many young people, Brandon has decided to pursue a career in medicine and is a premed student in his first year. What makes Brandon unique, however, is that he wants to be a nurse—a not-so-typical choice for a guy. But Brandon is dedicated to this career path; he's already got his nursing assistant license and has been working in nursing homes for two years. His motivation for getting this license came when he started visiting his grandmother in a nursing home. He felt that the place was understaffed, and he wanted to help.

Q: How do you describe yourself?
Brandon: Easy: outgoing and motivated.

Q: How do your career goals influence who you are?
Brandon: Being a certified nursing assistant has completely made me a more compassionate person. It has made me realize that getting older is not something to dread, but just to savor what you have now and having regrets will only slow you down. My job has also made me have to prioritize my work and other activities. As a result, I am a pretty organized person. This helps carry me through my day of work, school, and life in general.

Q: How do you think your career goals shape how others see you?
Brandon: With my goals being so focused and clear, people have different opinions of me. Some of their opinions are based on jealousy and envy and they therefore think that I only worry about myself. Others compliment me on my endeavors and see me as self-directed and motivated.

people aren't that lucky. When you are thinking about what to do for a living, you can consider three main areas: things you like to do, things you are good at, and situations you are comfortable in or enjoy. So as you think about what you might want to do for a living, you might want to consider what classes you enjoy in school. If you like English class, you might be meant for journalism or creative writing. If you enjoy foreign languages, you could teach that language to others or become a translator or even a diplomat specializing in a particular country. But there are lots of things you might like doing other than academic activities. Try things like drama, student government, woodworking, or taking care of younger relatives. An interest in almost any of these things could turn into a totally interesting career for you. Remember when we talked about hobbies in chapter 4? Things that you choose to do for fun often turn out to be great career choices. Some of the happiest people have made their hobbies into their jobs. As you think about what you enjoy, think also about what you're good at or know how to do. Most people want a job that they can succeed at, so choosing a field that you have strong skills in can be important.

There is a lot more to working than just the content of what you do every day, however. You also are in a workplace with other people under particular pressures. These factors might

also cause you to make specific career choices. For example, being a kindergarten teacher might not be the best choice for someone who doesn't enjoy kids and prefers to work alone, but a perfect match for someone very creative who needs lots of social contact. If you really enjoy working outside, that would limit the kinds of work you might want to take on, or even the locations in which you are willing to work. The work situations that various jobs put you in are definitely worth considering as you choose a career.

Another thing to consider in career planning is thinking about what you want to get out of your job—or how well certain types of jobs fulfill your values. Material values come up for people quite often. Some people are motivated by power, influence, advancement, and money, and they expect to get these things out of their job. If these things are important to you, then you'll pick different jobs than if you don't really mind making less money. For other people, their value of social contact is very important. They want a job that allows them to interact with lots of people or with a certain kind of person. If you love kids, you'll be attracted to different careers than people who would rather work with machinery. Some people are strongly motivated by spiritual values—they want to feel that their work contributes to the welfare of the world. For them, it is most important that they feel their work is valuable to others. But everyone defines "valuable" differently, and some people don't prioritize a feeling of contribution very highly in choosing a career.

Another factor in career decisions is what it takes to break into each field. Take professional sports, for example. Molly's sister would have loved to be a professional basketball player. But when she was growing up, there was no WNBA. Plus, she was only 5 feet, 6 inches. She probably would struggle to meet the minimum criteria to actually do the job. There are other less conspicuous examples—firefighters have to meet physical standards, and pilots must have good vision. The training necessary to do a particular job might influence your decisions about it. You might think that you would enjoy the work of an emergency-room doctor, but the idea of four years of college, followed by four years of medical school, four years of residency, and possible additional training might seem like too much for you. Sometimes the cost of receiving such training keeps people away from certain jobs. While you can often get loans and scholarships to attend school or training programs, the amount of money or debt required may be more than you're willing to take on. If it costs $15,000 per year to attend culinary school, but you can't work while you do it and you haven't saved the money, you might pause in thinking about whether you really want to be a chef. This doesn't just impact people starting out; it also affects people who want to change jobs.

It is important to keep in mind that sometimes career choices are either not choices at all or are affected by things beyond your control. Lots of people really don't like what they do, but they keep on doing it because they need to earn money. Or you might end up having to hold a job in a setting that you don't enjoy in order to progress to another position. More extreme is when choices are made for you—you are not hired, or you are let go. You may not have the qualifications to do a certain position and therefore not be admitted or allowed, or you may be a victim of discrimination, preventing you from succeeding in a particular field.

This whole section might sound pretty intimidating for you—and that's okay. As teenagers, everyone is at a different stage of what is known as career maturity. Career maturity is your readiness to make decisions about work and take on the tasks considered appropriate for your age. Some people reach this point very early—you probably know someone who chose a career field when he or she was really young and is sticking to it. These people can get a head start in their field, but they can also miss out on learning about other areas they might like just as much or more. Other folks take some time to get to the point where they are ready to begin making choices about their career through taking steps to get specific education or training. If you're not quite ready yet, don't worry. Remember that even if you had already made up your mind, you would be pretty likely to change it. Choosing to not yet follow any particular career path is just another stage of your personal career development. When you are ready to move, hopefully you'll do it.

CAREER RESOURCES ON THE WEB

Interested in doing some more research on career issues? Check out some of these websites for a start:

- ⊚ **Quintessential Careers (www.quintcareers.com/teen_jobs.html)** has a whole section of job and career information specifically for teens.
- ⊚ **Princeton Review (www.princetonreview.com/cte)** has a good resource list of career information.
- ⊚ **The Occupational Outlook Handbook (www.bls.gov/oco/home.htm)** produced by the U.S. Department of Labor provides information on virtually any career you could imagine, including the job outlook for number of jobs available.

If you would like more guidance in making decisions about your future career, there are lots of places to find help. There is lots of information available at your local library or on the Web for people who are exploring various career options. You can get information about specific occupations (e.g., salary statistics, areas of job growth), training programs, educational opportunities, and questionnaires to identify your areas of interest. Your school may have a college placement or planning office or vocational placement services offering guidance counselors who can help you put together a plan. There are also private career counselors who can provide you with career assessment and exploration tools, as well as support you in making decisions and following through on them.

YOUR TURN

Here are some questions for you to think about:

1. Name one moral value, one political value, and one personal value that you hold. Why are these important to you? How do these affect your behavior?

2. Where do you think you have learned most of your values (parents, church, media, etc.)?

3. What are your spiritual beliefs? Have they changed? How are they similar to or different from those of your friends and family?

4. How do your religious beliefs affect what you choose to do?

5. What short-term goals do you have for yourself? Long-term goals?

6. Where do you see yourself in five years?

7. What kind of career goals do you have for yourself?

8. What sorts of pressures do you feel regarding making career choices? Where does this pressure come from?

9. How do you make decisions?

NOTES

1. Free the Children, "About Craig Kielburger," accessed June 6, 2004, at www.freethechildren.com/aboutus/about_craig.htm.

2. Seeds of Peace, "Seeds of Peace History: A Decade of Peacemaking," accessed June 6, 2004, at http://seedsofpeace.org.

3. "The Power of Personal Values," accessed June 6, 2004, at www.gurusoftware.com/GuruNet/Personal/Topics/Values.htm.

4. C. Smith, R. Faris, M. L. Denton, and M. Regnerus, "Mapping American Adolescent Subjective Religiosity and Attitudes of Alienation toward Religion: A Research Report," *Sociology of Religion* (Spring 2003), accessed June 6, 2004, at www.findarticles.com/p/articles/mi_m0SOR/is_1_64/ai_99984520.

5. Smith et al., "Mapping American Adolescent Subjective Religiosity."

6. B. Bachel, *What Do You Really Want? How to Set a Goal and Go for It! A Guide for Teens* (Minneapolis, Minn.: Free Spirit, 2001).

7. U.S. Bureau of Labor Statistics, *Number of Jobs Held, Labor Market Activity, and Earnings Growth among Younger Baby Boomers: Results from More than Two Decades of a Longitudinal Survey*, USDL 02-497, 2002, accessed July 23, 2004, at www.bls.gov/nls.

The Influences around You

6

MEDIA

The media are everywhere. Just try to go for a day—an hour—without seeing any type of media and you're hard pressed to succeed. That's because the media basically are any type of communication that carries a message. The forms of media that usually come to mind first are movies, television, radio, print (newspapers, magazines), Web information, and music. But clothing labels, billboards, soda cans—anything with a brand name on it—can also be thought of as media because these things send a message. Try to think of anything that doesn't have a message behind it. It's trickier than you might think!

Media as Brainwasher

There are two basic ways that teens are influenced by media. The first way is how the media try to directly influence the behavior of teens (and pretty much everyone). Advertisers spend millions and millions of dollars trying to get your attention. And they often succeed. This is because teens are pretty serious consumers of the mass media. In fact, teens spend an average of 12.2 hours per week online, and 7.6 hours per week watching TV (over half of you have televisions in your bedroom). The average teen listens to music 3 to 4 hours a day.[2] So you are constantly getting

Four hours of television contain about one hundred ads.[1]

MARKETING TO TEENAGERS

Marketing firms, whose job it is to persuade consumers to buy their products, have a particular affinity for teenagers. Since teens spend a great deal of money every year, these organizations market directly to them, encouraging them to buy things. More than that, however, marketing firms seek to develop brand loyalty in teenagers—the idea is that if you learn to like Pepsi better than Coke as a teenager (or vice versa), then you will probably maintain that preference throughout your life. Because they hope this, even products that don't seem specific to teens develop marketing campaigns with a trendy, youthful feel to them. Some of the techniques that get used include "buzz marketing," where someone is paid to talk up a movie or TV show or musical artist, generally by being out in public and casually conversing with people about what he or she is paid to promote. Another technique, used by MTV, for example, is an "ethnography study." Researchers visit average teenagers in their homes and neighborhoods, asking them what they like, looking through their closets and music collections, and observing how they spend their time. "Cool hunters" use similar techniques—people who are generally considered cool head out to find teens identified as cool and spend time talking with them about what they like. They look for ground-breaking teens—those who have the influence to start trends through trying new things—in order to learn early about what might become popular in the coming months.[3]

---

information from the media—most notably advertisers—about what is cool, what you should wear, eat, drink, buy, and do.

Teens also have become a "target audience" for entertainment producers. Specifically meeting the needs and desires of teenagers has become very profitable for lots of adults in the media business. For example, in 2003, the popular women's magazine *Vogue* decided to launch a teen version, *Teen Vogue*. The editor-in-chief of *Vogue*, Anna Wintour, was quoted as saying: "I think of the *Teen Vogue* reader as a young version of the *Vogue* reader: someone who demands authoritative and practical fashion and beauty coverage, with a wide range of interests to be met. I'm pleased to say these girls appear to be out there."[4] According to Wintour, "Articles will

THINK ABOUT IT
Teen girls spend over $9 billion on makeup and skin products.[5] Who is it that is making them feel inadequate enough to spend so much money?

address the full range of teenage interests, from celebrities, movies, music, and shopping to peer pressure, body image, and self-identity. *Teen Vogue* will also feature current fashion items." (We leave it to you to decide if this list even begins to approach the "full range" of teenage interests.)

And it's not only girls who are the targets of advertising. Lately, soda companies have been targeting teens, particularly teen boys, associating drinking a certain beverage with a particular image. Sprite has latched predominately onto the hip-hop scene in order to promote its product, while Mountain Dew tries to appeal to younger people by associating itself with X-treme sports and activities such as skateboarding and snowboarding.

Media may also have an impact on your behavior more indirectly by influencing your attitudes about certain behaviors. For example, the media can influence your opinions about smoking and drinking. Research has shown that teens who

You see an average of 2,000 beer and wine commercials every year.[6]

viewed the most smoking in movies were more likely to start smoking.[7]

Young people who watch television ads about alcohol report more positive feelings about drinking and also are more likely to say that they intend to drink.[8]

The media can also influence your perceptions of yourself. The more time teens spend watching soap operas, movies, and music videos, the poorer their body image and the higher their desire to be thin—this is true for both boys and girls! In one study with fifth graders, girls and boys told researchers that they were more dissatisfied with their own bodies after watching *Friends* or a Britney Spears video, whereas before they were happier with what they looked like.[9] Playing violent video games can increase aggressive behavior, thoughts, and feelings, as well as decrease social behavior.[10] Finally, research has found that music with angry and depressing lyrics is associated with drug use, suicidal thoughts, and school problems.[11] Whether you realize it or not, the media can change what you think is acceptable, how you feel about yourself, and how you act in certain situations.

Four Ways to Be Smarter Than the Media

Don't like the way some of the media are trying to influence you? Fight back by being an active media watcher!

1. *Remember—media images are not reality.* It's sometimes hard to remember that what we see and hear in a movie, for example, is not real but is instead someone's interpretation of reality. But everything in a film is manipulated in some way to tell a story or make a point that will keep us interested. What is the point that your media are trying to make? How is it trying to influence you? Does drinking a particular beverage really make you a better person? Does wearing that brand of clothing make you more hip?

2. *Be aware of the strategies the media use to tell their stories.* These strategies are often hidden, but if you look carefully, you

can see them pretty easily. For example, music videos use lots of fast editing to get your blood rushing and your brain focused on the television. But in reality, people do not see the world in broken images. Also, think of how pictures in magazines use close-ups to make us think that people see every little detail of our appearance, like our pores and every little scar and blemish (not that models have any, of course). But in reality, we don't see people that close up. The media use techniques to trick us into feeling certain ways. Next time you are experiencing any form of media, ask yourself: How are these media trying to make me feel? What are they doing to influence my perceptions and emotions?

3. *Think about who and what the media consider important.* The media portray some groups of people more than others. It's easy to see that there are many more pretty people in the media than there are unattractive people. But what about other groups of people? African American? Native American? Disabled? Where are the images of these people in the media? A study of the diversity of characters shown during prime-time television in 2003–2004

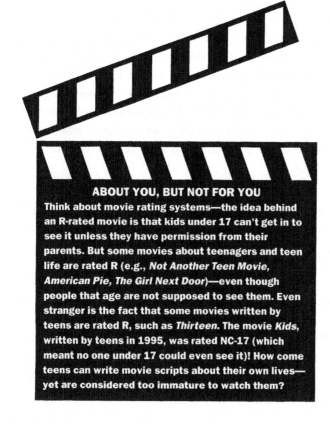

ABOUT YOU, BUT NOT FOR YOU
Think about movie rating systems—the idea behind an R-rated movie is that kids under 17 can't get in to see it unless they have permission from their parents. But some movies about teenagers and teen life are rated R (e.g., *Not Another Teen Movie, American Pie, The Girl Next Door*)—even though people that age are not supposed to see them. Even stranger is the fact that some movies written by teens are rated R, such as *Thirteen*. The movie *Kids*, written by teens in 1995, was rated NC-17 (which meant no one under 17 could even see it)! How come teens can write movie scripts about their own lives— yet are considered too immature to watch them?

found that only 6 percent of TV characters were Hispanic, 1 percent were Asian or Pacific Islander, and none were Native American. Women were most likely to be age 19 to 29, while men were more likely to be 30 to 39. Two-thirds of all TV characters were male, and 46 percent of Middle Eastern characters were portrayed as criminals.[12] And try to come up with a list of disabled people on television. There are a few (Timmy and Jimmy on *South Park*, Stevie on *Malcolm in the Middle*, Kerry Weaver on *ER*), but not enough to represent that population fairly. Video games aren't any better at representing people. In a survey of thirty-three popular Nintendo and Sega Genesis video games, there were no female characters in 41 percent of the games, and most of the characters were Caucasian.[13] What do the media say about people like you? Do the media even acknowledge that people of your race, class, gender, or sexual orientation exist? Similarly, the media show some values and beliefs more than others. For example, the media are more likely to portray sex as fun and exciting instead of risky. A survey of how males were presented in TV, movies, and music videos found that men were never shown crying.[14] How do the media portray your values and beliefs?

4. *All media are trying to sell you something.* Either directly or indirectly, the point of any media message is to get you to buy something. Commercials do this directly. But songs do too; songs try to get you to buy the CD, and the CD tries to get you to buy the next CD from that artist. Television shows try to sell you to their advertisers. A movie promotes its stars and type of film. Always ask yourself: What is being promoted here? Who is behind this production and what do they want me to buy?

By asking yourself these questions, and thinking of the media as commercial commodities, you are less likely to be influenced by media messages and more likely to become an independent thinker.

Teens in the Media

The other basic way that media can influence you is in the way media portray teens. These portrayals may not only influence how adults perceive you, but possibly how you perceive yourself. This is because when you look at representations of people who are supposed to be like you in some way (on TV, in videos, and in movies, for example), you get a sense of what the media think teens are supposed to be like. So your understanding of what the media image of teens is might have an effect on what you decide is important about you.

It has been argued that you are given a bum deal by the kinds of things said about teenagers in the news. Teens are often shown as the cause of many of society's major problems—stories about teen violence, pregnancies, and vandalism are all over television news programs as well as in newspapers. For example, teens get a bad rap from the media when it comes to crime—when a crime, particularly a violent one, is committed by a teenager, it gets more press than one committed by an adult.

> **Given the way the media portray teens in general, it's not surprising that you might question what the media tell you about who you are, who you can become, and who you are supposed to be.**

Talk shows also show teens as difficult creatures. Think of how teens are portrayed on shows like *Oprah* or *Jerry Springer*. If you thought all teens were like the teens on talk shows, you would think that everyone age 13 to 19 was drug addicted, violent, and having sex twenty-four hours a day. And we know that is not true. But shows like that emphasize the sensational, making it seem as though the teen years automatically mean troubled years.

YOU ARE WHAT THEY READ

Next time you are in a bookstore, take a look at the titles of books available to parents of adolescents: *I'm OK, You're a Brat; The Primal Teen; Unglued and Tattooed; Parenting Your Out-of-Control Teenager; Now I Know Why Tigers Eat Their Young: Surviving a New Generation of Teenagers; Yes, Your Teen Is Crazy.* Think about what these books imply—that teenagers are unruly, moody, miserable, and even crazy. These books also promote the idea that teens are a force that needs to be controlled. Not a pretty picture.

So what, you may ask? Turns out that the general public makes assumptions about what teens are like based on what the media show them. And since the news you hear about teens isn't usually about teens who are successful or doing really good things, the public ends up with a negative image of youth. Polls show that people think that teens in general are "rude, irresponsible, and wild." A Gallup poll in 1994 concluded that because of media coverage of crimes committed by young people, the average American greatly overestimates the number of crimes committed by teenagers.[15]

What is ironic about the image of teens in the news is that despite the negative portrayal, teen problems have actually tended to decline in recent years. Mike Males, a professor at the University of California at Santa Cruz, points out that all of the following have declined for teens: "suicide (now at its lowest level since 1958), homicide (lowest since 1964), felony arrests (lowest since 1959), drug abuse deaths (lowest since 1967), violent crime (lowest since 1967), births (lowest since 1949), HIV/AIDS infections (the fastest declining rates of any age group in the 1990s), accidental deaths (lowest of any time since statistics have been kept), and school dropout rates (lowest on record)."[16] In other words, while the media continue to show the dark side of teen life, the truth is that less "bad stuff" is going on than in the past twenty years. But thanks in part to the media, the public image of teens is much more negative than you might have thought.

So, the news and talk shows seem to show teens as dangerous and a problem to solve. But the rest of television and most movies show teens as cool. On television, teens are more trendy, unusual, and dynamic than adults and younger kids. The number of TV shows and movies that focus on teen issues or have teens as the main characters seems to have gone up recently, and many of them are commercially successful: *Dawson's Creek*, *Buffy the Vampire Slayer*, *The O.C.*, *8 Simple Rules*, and *American Idol*, just to name a few. The Olsen Twins have come out with movies and their own magazine.

In the movies, teens tend to be beautiful. They are always wearing the latest fashions and never seem to have any acne, wrinkled outfits, or a hair out of place. They also seem to spend

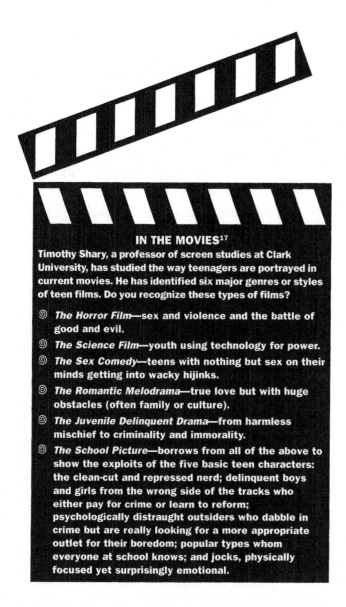

IN THE MOVIES[17]

Timothy Shary, a professor of screen studies at Clark University, has studied the way teenagers are portrayed in current movies. He has identified six major genres or styles of teen films. Do you recognize these types of films?

- *The Horror Film*—sex and violence and the battle of good and evil.
- *The Science Film*—youth using technology for power.
- *The Sex Comedy*—teens with nothing but sex on their minds getting into wacky hijinks.
- *The Romantic Melodrama*—true love but with huge obstacles (often family or culture).
- *The Juvenile Delinquent Drama*—from harmless mischief to criminality and immorality.
- *The School Picture*—borrows from all of the above to show the exploits of the five basic teen characters: the clean-cut and repressed nerd; delinquent boys and girls from the wrong side of the tracks who either pay for crime or learn to reform; psychologically distraught outsiders who dabble in crime but are really looking for a more appropriate outlet for their boredom; popular types whom everyone at school knows; and jocks, physically focused yet surprisingly emotional.

most of their time worried about getting a date (or having sex) instead of school, their friends, or their families. Think about it—how do movies like *Mean Girls*, *The Princess Diaries*, *Can't Hardly Wait*, *She's All That*, and *American Pie* portray teens? What do they look like? How do they act?

WHERE YOU LIVE

Less than one hundred years ago (to some extent, less than fifty years ago), different regions of the world were very separate and

Television has been a common feature in American households for only about sixty years. Commercial airline travel has been common for only about forty years.

fostered extremely different cultures. As the world seems to grow smaller, through airplane travel, communication technology, and simple exposure to one another, in many ways we are growing more similar. While two different geographical areas used to have completely different cultures, now they may share so many things

Source: Michelle DuBarry

that they are more alike than different. However, even though we seem to be sharing many things culturally, we are still separated by physical space, so where you grow up and live has a profound effect on who you become. Living in a rich neighborhood vs. a poor one, the city vs. the country, the north vs. the south—all of these differences carry with them different experiences and characteristics that become part of you. Your neighborhood and even the state you live in help shape the person you are as well. For example, research has established that the type of neighborhood you grow up in can have an impact on your social, psychological, and physical development. So thinking about where you live can provide some keys to understanding who you are becoming.

For example, the weather where you live can affect everything from fashion to hobbies. If you live somewhere where the weather is often warm, it might be pretty normal to see people wearing somewhat revealing clothing such as shorts

IN THE MOVIES

OT: Our Town (2002)—The Dominguez High School in Compton, California, with a multiracial student body of black and Hispanic youth and dismal outlook on school life, had not produced a play in twenty years. They had no school-supported theater program or budget and virtually no community support. Despite these challenges, they put together a production of Thornton Wilder's *Our Town* with the help of a dedicated teacher. This documentary takes you through the struggles of putting this play together and shows how drama became an important part of these teens' lives even though their community didn't value the arts.

and tank tops—after all, they might be doing it in order to keep cool. But if you live somewhere pretty cold and you see someone dressing in the same clothes, it might have a different meaning. The same holds for hobbies—we would be surprised to learn that someone from Hawaii was an avid snowboarder or someone from Colorado was an avid surfer, but we would think nothing of it if it were the other way around. So things that are important parts of your identity become that way in part based on where you live.

The size and location of the community you grow up in will also affect you. Much like your family influences you, what you see going on with the people around you in your community helps to determine what you expect to see in the rest of world. You may be more or less comfortable with diversity or you might be used to different kinds of families or professions, for example. Kids who grow up in rural communities or small towns might think it is normal to know virtually everyone in their neighborhood or high school; it might be a big priority to keep up on events in the area and the latest news about neighbors. On the other hand, teens who live in big cities might find it impossible to keep track of everyone they meet or everything going on around them. Then again, if a teen lives in the city and doesn't have a back yard, he or she might spend time hanging out on the front steps—and as a result might end up actually knowing his or her neighbors better than people in the suburbs who might choose to spend more time away from passersby.

The layout of a neighborhood also matters. If you live someplace where you can walk everywhere you need to go, you might end up being more active than someone who always drives because that's the only way to get anywhere. So you will probably spend your time differently depending on whether you live in a city, a rural area, or the suburbs. Access to different activities is also determined by where you live: kids in the city rarely learn much about raising sheep, but kids in the country might not have as many services or activities to choose from. Living on a farm may make you accustomed to a much different way of living—different chores, different lifestyle,

different things to do—than if you live in the heart of a large city. Even the type of music you listen to may depend on where you live; certain local bands may be very popular in your area, or the radio stations you get may play a particular type of music more often than

SAD, BUT TRUE
In New York City, 10 percent of teens said they did not go to school on one or more of the preceding thirty days because they felt unsafe at school or on their way to or from school. Only 3 percent of teens from Nebraska felt this way.[18]

stations on the other side of the country. In some places, you can't even get clear reception for any stations!

Different neighborhoods and regions also have different norms and customs for interacting with others. Lots of people talk about "Midwestern nice" or the graciousness of people in the South or notice that people walking down the street in Manhattan tend not to pay attention to others around them. Based on things like the weather and how crowded the space is, expectations evolve about how people are supposed to treat one another. If you grew up in a community that values being nice to strangers, you'll often act differently than if you grew up somewhere that prioritizes taking care of yourself amid strangers.

REGIONAL DIFFERENCES IN HOW YOU SPEAK AND WHAT YOU SAY

People talk differently depending on where they live. We have all probably noticed that people from some places (e.g., Boston, the deep South, Minnesota) have distinctive accents. But we also sometimes use different words for something. Take, for example, the word we use to describe a sandwich with deli meat and condiments on a long roll. In various places, this is called a hoagie, hero, grinder, submarine sandwich, poor boy, or torpedo. Do you stand "on line" or "in line"? Would you buy used clothing at a "flea market" or a "swap meet"?

Your school is another kind of community—and you probably know the kind of reputation your school has to kids from other schools. There are "jock" schools, where athletics is assumed to be very important, or schools where academics are emphasized, or schools thought of as "tough" or dangerous. For better or worse, because you are part of the community of your school, you carry some of your school's identity with you when you meet other people. You can decide to have that be important to you—some people have a lot of school pride and actively want others to know that they are part of a particular school—or you can emphasize other things about you. Or you can decide to change your school's reputation by fighting the stereotypes others have about the school.

On a more serious note, if you live in an environment where you feel safe and secure, that will influence your perceptions of life and its opportunities a lot differently than if you come from

HOW DO YOU FEEL ABOUT WHERE YOU LIVE?

If you were asked to describe your neighborhood to someone who has never been there, what would you say about it? What does your neighborhood look like? Sound like? What parts of your neighborhood do you love? What do you wish you could change? What do other people think about your neighborhood? How do your answers reflect the sort of person you are and how your neighborhood has influenced that?

a neighborhood full of violence, poverty, and feelings of hopelessness. If you worry about your own safety when you come home from school, you will feel very differently about participating in the community beyond your front door than those who feel safe.

> **Kris lived through the Loma Prieta earthquake of 1989 in the San Francisco Bay Area. To this day, people still ask her where she was when "the big one" hit (she was out jogging).**

Another way that where you live can affect your identity is through the experiences you share with other people who live there. Think about big events, such as the 1996 Olympics in Atlanta or the disaster of 9/11 in New York, or natural disasters such as hurricanes, floods, or earthquakes. People who have been through such events together have a shared experience and sometimes learn things that others who weren't present don't know as much about.

FAMILY AND FRIENDS

Though we have talked about family and friends in other sections of this book, we thought it was important to mention more specifically that the people you spend a lot of time with influence both who you are and how others see you. The people around you generally influence you in three different ways: by being role models and examples, by setting expectations for you, and by pressuring you to act in certain ways.

Role Models

Both your friends and family members can serve as your role models. In fact, while the media often talk about famous people (politicians, actors, athletes, etc.) as role

> ***Role model:*** **A person who serves as a model of behavior. Someone worthy of imitation.**

models, if you actually ask teens who their role models are, they are more likely to mention members of their family or even a friend. When you think about what you want to do and the sort of person you want to be, you sometimes look to the people around you for examples and insight. It only makes sense that this is the case—after all, you see these people all the time and in many different situations. It's no wonder their habits and characteristics rub off on you.

There are times when the people around you have a direct influence on your choices. You may choose to become a doctor because your mother is one and she has directly influenced your career goals. Or you may listen to a certain type of music because your best friend is really into a particular band. But modeling yourself after other people also can happen on a more subconscious level. For example, you might fight a lot with your girlfriend because you see your parents fighting all the time, and on some deep level you think that is how couples are supposed to act. How many times has someone told you that you are just like your mother or father because you are strong-willed, or always ready to lend a helping hand, or are great at seeing things from a unique perspective?

Sometimes, however, your friends and family can become "anti–role models." In other words, you can decide *not* to do something based on witnessing the consequences of someone else's decision. You might choose to make school a priority in your life because you see your friend, who is known as a partier, having a hard time getting into college. Or, if your parents are really strict with you, you may vow to be a more lenient parent when you have kids. Even though you are doing the opposite of what those around you are doing, they are still influencing your decisions about what you want out of your life. No matter the case, friends and family have a HUGE influence on a person.

Expectations

The people around you also have expectations of you. Your family may expect you to mirror their values and become a "successful" person (whatever that means to your family). Your friends may expect you to be like them, or at least be fun to hang around with. These expectations can shape your decisions about how you act, what you wear, and what your goals are.

Sometimes it's good when people have expectations of you. It means that they believe that you are capable of doing something. They have faith that you can get the job done. When people have expectations of you, it can help motivate you to do things that you know are good for you that you would not do on your own, such as study or send a thank-you card. We feel the need to meet the expectations of people we love because we don't want to disappoint them. But if the expectations are too high or too low, it may have a negative effect on you and your relationships. You may begin to resent people who demand too much from you, or you may feel bad about yourself if you fail to live up to what is expected of you. When people don't demand anything from you, you may feel that they don't really believe you can do anything—that they don't trust you or have faith in your abilities. This can also cause you to feel worthless or down. It's tricky, but this balance of expectations can really impact your sense of self-worth.

Pressures

Sometimes, as a result of the expectations people have of you, you may feel that they are pressuring you to do or be something that you don't feel comfortable doing or being. This is understandable—it's common to feel pressure to live up to the expectations of someone you care about. In the same way that family and friends can be role models on a direct or indirect level, the pressures they put on you can also be direct or indirect. Direct pressure is easy to point out. A parent may say, "If you don't get at least a C average on your report card, you are not allowed to join the basketball team." Or a friend may say, "Come on—why don't you want to go to the party? Everyone else is going to be there." The pressures you feel may force you to decide one way or another which action you take. And that action can have certain consequences that make a big impact on your life. Sometimes those consequences are negative—you miss out on hanging out with friends because you have to study all the time; by going to a party, you might end up lying to your parents and getting in trouble. Or the consequences can be positive—by studying hard and getting good grades, you get into the college of your choice; by going to the party, you get a chance to talk to that hottie from your math class. Many people feel that it is easy to resist this type of pressure, or at least recognize it and choose to go along with it based on the consequences. It's good to be able to see when people are pressuring you and understand that ultimately it is *your* decision to make—and your consequences to deal with afterwards.

But pressure can be indirect. When this happens, the pressure *exists in your own mind*, and sometimes this type of pressure is harder to manage. Here are a few examples of what we mean:

- ◎ **You want to watch the season finale of your favorite TV show but you also need to study for a major chemistry test. You are dying to know what happens on the show, but in the back of your mind, you see your mother's disappointment and feel her guilt when you come home with a bad grade on that test.**

- ◎ **You are in the locker room after a game. The rest of the gang is talking about who they have "done," and bragging about their sexual exploits. You and your girlfriend have talked about sex but have decided to wait until you have been dating longer, or that you want to wait until summer to have sex, when things are less stressful. You care about each other, and are happy with the decision. Yet you find yourself telling the team that you have had sex and are even giving a few details about things that have never happened.**

The two situations described above are a form of pressure, but they are examples of *internal* pressure. That is, no one is going directly up to you and saying that you should or should not do something. Instead, indirectly, the people around you make you act in a certain way so that you feel as though you are pleasing them or fitting into their expectations of you. It's natural to want to live up to the image your family and friends have of you. It's understandable that you would want them to see you in a positive way. When what you do does not match how other people see you, it's logical that you may worry— worry that you can never be the person that others think you ought to be.

The thing to remember is that, in the same way you experience direct pressure, indirect pressure can and will influence your decisions. However, you need to make a more conscious effort to recognize it and ask yourself, "Why am I feeling pressure to decide one way or another? Whose influence is in my head? What is it that I want to do that is best for me?" Hopefully, you will be able to make your own decisions in a way that makes you feel good and proud of who you are.

Sometimes the examples, expectations, and pressures you get from your friends and family contradict each other. Your father wants you to act one way, your best friend another. Your girlfriend wants you to get her name tattooed on your arm, which your grandfather would not approve of at all. What happens then?

We humans are very flexible and adaptable creatures. We are able to behave in different ways depending on the situation. We are quiet (sometimes) during school but noisy when cheering for our favorite team. We laugh a lot when with our friends but are very serious in front of our bosses. Does that

POSITIVE PEER PRESSURE

Although the words *peer pressure* often bring up images of a friend forcing another friend to do something that is harmful, sometimes peer pressure can be a good thing. Your friends may pressure you to try out for a sports team, or encourage you to ask someone out on a date that you would be too shy to ask otherwise. A friend may challenge you to see who can stick to a study plan the best. Or you may be pressured into *not* driving after you have had something to drink. As you probably already knew, your friends can be *good* for you.

mean we have no one true identity? In one situation are you more "yourself" than in another situation?

There are times when we feel that we have to act in a certain way that is not true to who we are. It can be difficult to do this, and we feel as if we are not being genuine—that we are being a fake—and that can be frustrating. But it is possible to act differently in different situations and still be yourself. Perhaps you are a serious student but a carefree sculptor in your spare time. You can be outspoken on the debate team but more of a listener when in a group of people. This does not mean you are being the "real you" in one situation and not in another. When you act one way in a particular situation and another way in a different situation, this might show that you are a complex person with many characteristics. It's not necessary to be the same person all the time—in fact, it may not be the best idea!

The trick, once again, is to act in a way that you can feel good about. Ultimately, it is you that you have to answer to, live with, and get along with. It will not always be easy to cope in situations in which different people want you to act in opposite ways, but when it comes right down to it, you need to do what you feel is best for you. That doesn't mean not thinking about other people—after all, what is best for you in the long run may require you to make sacrifices in the short term—but by living up to your own expectations of yourself, you will feel more consistent, whole, and secure in what you do and who you are.

MEMORABLE EXPERIENCES

One of the things that can have a huge impact on who you are and what you believe in is the events that happen to you. And stuff happens, unfortunately. Or fortunately, maybe. The experiences that you go through form who you are, as you develop new skills to deal with change and learn things about the world. Many people can pinpoint events that made them feel "I just wasn't the same afterward." These experiences can change the structure of your family, the way you lead your life, or your personal philosophy. What things might have had this impact on you?

A favorite essay question colleges use all the time in applications is "Tell us about a significant experience in your life and its effect on you." Some experiences seem small—like learning to ski or seeing the ocean for the first time. But others are really big—changes in your family, deaths of loved ones, accidents, and so on. A common big event is moving or changing schools. People move all the time—you may someday have to start over in a new school or a new state or even a new country. This could be a real bummer, as you leave behind people who have become important to you and have to "start all over" and make new friends. Or this could be a blessing, giving you a chance to be who you are outside of a

COURTNEY AND HER ALTERNATIVE SCHOOLING EXPERIENCE

Courtney is 19 years old and considers herself "short," not quite reaching five feet tall. She currently works full-time as a receptionist at a construction company. When she was 16, she spent some time at an alternative school for troubled teens that we will call "La Casa." Here, Courtney talks about how her experience there has influenced who she is today.

Q: How has your schooling at La Casa influenced who you are?

Courtney: My schooling at Casa has been a huge influence on the person that I have become. I learned several different tools and techniques that have assisted me in changing the way that I live. I would say without hesitation that La Casa has made me a better person, a happier person, and a healthier person. I have learned over the last few years the importance of being open-minded, of being willing to do some listening rather than all the talking, learning to obey the basic rules of life, some humility, and how desperately I need people in my life I can depend on . . . to a certain degree. In other words, I've learned that "no man is an island."

past reputation and develop a different image in an entirely new setting.

One of the experiences that can be most earthshaking (despite how common it is) is having your parents get divorced. When your parents get divorced, you might feel as if the most stable and consistent part of your life—your family, your home—has been ripped away. Nothing is the same. It can be disconcerting to see your parents not get along, not understand each other, or for you to realize that your family will never be the same. It can also be overwhelming—especially if you get caught in the middle of arguments or end up helping a parent go through this tough time. As children, we think that parents are supposed to be stable and supportive, so when the end of a marriage brings them to need the support and help of their children, it can be hard to adjust your relationship with them to accommodate this new role.

REMEMBER
Divorce is never your fault (even though sometimes it might feel like it). Make sure you have someone outside your family to talk to about how a divorce is affecting you.

Teens tend to respond to the stress of divorce in a couple of ways. Some kids feel that they need to grow up really quickly—as their parents are taking care of their own lives as individuals (rather than as a couple), teens can feel that they are not being attended to, and that they should learn how to take care of themselves. Teens might feel the other way as well; when your parents' relationship to one another ends, you could feel like your relationship with them is more important than ever, and you may not want to leave them on their own or move away. There can be a "sleeper" effect in terms of the impact of divorce on kids. While you might seem to be doing fine at the time of the divorce and cope very well with the huge changes, sometimes later on—a few years even—things catch up with you and it might be harder for you to deal with life issues than it was before.

After a divorce, there are often more changes. There are additional adjustments and stresses that come along with remarriage and new families. Sometimes these experiences are positive, but the amount of change that comes with the blending of families can still be difficult, especially in the beginning. Learning to share your home, suddenly being introduced to a whole new side of the family—it all takes getting used to. And the way you relate to these new family members can impact your role in the family and how you interact with others both inside and outside your relations.

Another way that divorce affects teens is by influencing their attitudes toward romantic relationships. A divorce can cause teens to doubt their own ability to be happily married or stay married. Or it can make a teen afraid of commitment. If there has been divorce in your family, think about how it has affected your feelings about relationships—both with your parents and significant others. By understanding how a family divorce has influenced you, you can get a better sense of who you are and how different types of relationships play a role in your life.

Even though divorce can result in what feels like the loss of a parent or other members of your family, the actual death of someone close to you—a family member or a friend—is another type of loss that can have a huge effect on you. When someone you love dies, you can feel lost or uncertain, even frustrated with the world or with a higher power for taking someone important away from you. The loss of a parent can be one of the most difficult things to face, because it is so difficult to no longer have someone in your life who took care of you and influenced you so enormously; some experts believe that the loss of a parent is the most stressful event that can happen to a teen.

If a friend dies, the experience can be equally traumatic, something you will never forget. You depend on your friends for support and companionship, and losing a friend is not something that you really think about (unless in a rare circumstance your friend is very sick). This is because most teen deaths are unexpected—through car accidents, firearm deaths, or other tragedies. What ends up happening is that they are here one day and gone the next. You may feel sadness, anger, confusion—everyone will grieve in their own way. And

STAGES OF GRIEF

You don't have to lose someone through death in order to feel grief. Moving, a divorce, even a breakup can all trigger grief in a person. So, what does grief look like? Although grief is expressed differently by everyone, here are some common phases of grief:

Denial: You refuse to believe what has happened. You carry on as if nothing is different, nothing happened.

Anger: You blame others (the other driver, Mom, God, this stupid world) for the loss. During this phase it is common to feel agitated, moody, and very emotional. You may become angry with yourself—though it is important to remember not to blame yourself for what happened. It is important to make sure that you let your anger out during this time. Keeping it in will only slow down your recovery process and make things worse in the long run.

Bargaining: You make a promise to yourself, or to a higher power, to become a better person if things can be the way they were before.

Depression: You may feel empty and hopeless. You might cry a lot or uncontrollably or even feel that there is no point to life. You may feel guilty for what has happened. If you feel like harming yourself or another person during this time, professional counseling is necessary. Although it's hard, it is important to realize that there is life after this loss.

Acceptance: You come to terms with the loss and realize that life goes on. This does not mean forgetting about the lost loved one, but it does mean becoming better able to cope with the memories and even have happy feelings associated with the person again. You carry the person in your heart while continuing with your life goals and the future.

coping with a friend's death may change the way you feel about the world. It might make you question your spiritual beliefs or the meaning of life. Losing someone may affect your sense of safety, your relationship with other friends and family members, the way you take care of your own health, or your personal goals.

Family changes, location changes, increases or decreases in income, job changes, illnesses and injuries—you are formed in large part by the things that you experience. We hope that as you think about who you are, you will make an attempt to understand how these experiences affect you, but also strive to see how who you are affects the way you deal with them.

YOUR TURN

Here are some questions for you to think about:

1. How do you think the media portray teenagers?
2. How do you think the media influence you? What you do? What you buy? Other things?
3. Where do you live? What kind of a community did you grow up in?
4. How does your community affect what you do? What you've learned?
5. Who are your role models? Why do you admire these people?
6. Who in your life puts the most pressure on you? What kind of pressure? How do you react to it?
7. What have the most important events in your life been? How have they affected you?
8. Have you ever experienced loss? How did you react? How did the loss change how you think about things?

NOTES

1. National Institute on Media and the Family, "Fact Sheet: Children and Advertising," MediaFamily.org, 2002.

2. A. Quart, *Branded: The Buying and Selling of Teenagers* (New York: Perseus, 2003).

3. "The Merchants of Cool," *Frontline*, WGBH, Boston, 2001.

4. "Conde Nast to Launch Teen Vogue in Spring 2003," accessed July 13, 2004, at www.writenews.com/2002/060702_teen_vogue.htm.

5. K. Kersting, "Driving Teen Egos—and Buying—through 'Branding,'" *Monitor on Psychology* 35, no. 6 (2004): 60–61.

6. National Institute on Media and the Family, "Fact Sheet: Alcohol Advertising and Youth," MediaFamily.org, 2002.

7. M. A. Dalton et al., "Effect of Viewing Smoking in Movies on Adolescent Smoking Initiation: A Cohort Study," *Lancet* 362, no. 9380 (2003): 281–285.

8. National Institute on Media and the Family, "Fact Sheet: Alcohol Advertising and Youth."

9. National Institute on Media and the Family, "Fact Sheet: Media's Effect on Girls: Body Image and Gender Identity," MediaFamily.org, 2002.

10. National Institute on Media and the Family, "Fact Sheet: Effects of Video Game Playing on Children," MediaFamily.org, 2001.

11. E. Benson, "You Are What You Listen To," *Monitor on Psychology* 34, no. 7 (2003): 33.

12. Children Now, "Fall Colors: Prime Time Diversity Report 2004," accessed June 24, 2004, at www.childrennow.org/assets/pdf/fc03/fall-colors-03-v5.pdf.

13. T. Dietz, "An Examination of Violence and Gender Role Portrayals in Video Games: Implications for Gender Socialization and Aggressive Behavior," *Sex Roles* 38 (1998): 425–442.

14. Children Now, "Boys to Men: Entertainment Media Messages about Masculinity," accessed June 24, 2004, at www.childrennow.org/media/boystomen/report-media.cfm.

15. M. Males, *Kids and Guns: How Politicians, Experts, and the Media Fabricate Fear of Youth* (Monroe, ME: Common Courage Press, 2001).

16. M. Males, "A Demography Defined by Its 'Crises,'" in *California Youth in Transition*, accessed July 9, 2004, at http://home.earthlink.net/~mmales/ch1-intr.doc.

17. T. Shary, *Generation Multiplex: The Image of Youth in Contemporary American Cinema* (Austin: University of Texas Press, 2002).

18. Customized analysis using the Youth Risk Behavior Surveillance System, 2002 data, accessed April 13, 2004, at www.cdc.gov/HealthyYouth/yrbs/index.htm.

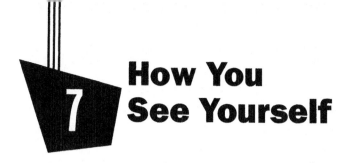

How You
See Yourself

7

PERSONALITY TRAITS

It's kind of weird that we waited until this late in the book to
talk about your personality, since we found that when we asked
teens who they were, they started out describing their personality.
Officially speaking, your personality is "the complex of all the
attributes—behavioral, temperamental, emotional and mental—
that characterize a unique individual."[1] From the inside out, it
seems that the first thing you think of when you define yourself is
how you act in the world—the way that you are and behave.

We are constantly responding to other people and situations.
Sometimes we make choices about how to do so, and other
times it is simply natural. We just do things without thinking too
much about them. Personality traits can be a lot like that—they
are really deeply ingrained ways of being that determine how
you act. Yet personality is one of the more fluid aspects of your
identity—your personality changes throughout your life. But
more interestingly, your personality, or what you express of it,
also changes across situations. You might be a really outgoing
person, but when you get around someone you really like, you
may feel shy and unable to talk. You might be unafraid to speak
up in class, taking the risk of stating your opinion or asking a
question, but when it comes to physical activity, you may be
completely afraid of risky activities where you might get hurt.
Does this mean you're not outgoing? Does this mean you're not
a risk-taker? You get to decide that, but it does illustrate that
even our personality is something that shifts around a little bit. It
also shows that we are much more complex than personality

labels—saying that you're an organized person still doesn't really capture what is true about you.

It should also be noted that what you think about yourself and what others see about your personality doesn't always match up. If you asked your friends and family to describe your personality, you might be surprised to hear what things they see as most obvious about you—but it might help you understand how others see you.

ASSESSMENT ON THE WEB

While the best psychological assessment is definitely done by a counselor or psychologist, there are some useful and fun tools on the Web that you can use by yourself. When you take these quizzes or tests, keep in mind that they are only working with data that you provide them, so they are only as good as the answers that you give. Also, remember that your best bet for official advice and assessment information is always a trained professional (especially regarding intelligence testing—be wary of online IQ tests).

Queendom: www.queendom.com/tests—Queendom has a huge assortment of psychological-type tests, many of which are free. Some of these are serious, like the Do You Need Therapy? test; others are for fun, like the Drama Queen test. Some of our favorites include the Emotional IQ test, the Values Profile, and the Type A Personality test.

Quincy Web: www.quincyweb.net/quincy/psychology.html— This website has links to a wide variety of psychological tests. The Humorous Personality Test is fun, as is the Official Nerdity Test.

Tickle: http://web.tickle.com/tests/teens.jsp—Tickle, run by eMode, provides a huge range of fun tests. The RealAge Test is interesting, providing some good health information. Some of the other tests can help you figure out your dog's or cat's personality, discover which car you're most like, or find the most appropriate TV family for you. But we picked it because it has a whole set of tests especially for teens (though they are aimed more at girls).

University of Life: http://universityoflife.com/default.htm— A good collection of tests, some serious, some fun. The Densa Test is great, and some of the personality tests listed are very similar to personality tests used by psychologists.

As you think about how your personality is part of your identity, it's important to remember that every trait has its benefits and costs. It might seem that being a kind and considerate person is nothing but good, but when you are so concerned with being there for others that you ignore your own needs, your strength has become a weakness. So don't judge your personality by good or bad—be open to thinking about how who you are makes your life both easier and harder.

There are many ways of thinking about personality, but we'll describe some basic ones to get you started thinking about which aspects describe you the best. Let's start with sociability. Are you an introvert or an extrovert, or a little of both? Lots of teens start to answer the question of who they are by saying, "I'm really outgoing." You might love interacting with other people, being the class clown, always ready to talk to someone. Some people aren't afraid to meet new people and enjoy adding to their circle of friends. They thrive on parties and large gatherings, feeling most at home and energized when they are spending time being social. Other people need a lot of time to themselves. They might prefer interacting with people one on one or in smaller groups. They might find it nerve-wracking to strike up a conversation with someone they don't already know or talk in front of a group of people. Or they simply might prefer to be alone more than with other people.

One of the authors of this book has a Scorpion tattooed on her ankle to represent her astrological sign (the other author is a Taurus).

When you think about it, this trait can influence a lot of other things about you, like the activities or hobbies you choose. If you are more introverted, you might spend less time partying or hanging out with lots of other people. Your sociability might lead you to be attracted to different kinds of occupations, too—shy people tend not to become stand-up comedians, and people who love crowds probably don't make up the majority of forest rangers.

Another trait to think about is how expressive you are emotionally. Do you cry at long-distance telephone commercials?

Or do you never show your feelings, no matter how angry or upset you are? Some people are unable to hide how they feel or the way they react. You might be the sort of person who jumps for joy when you hit all the green lights on your way home, or you may be someone who wouldn't even crack a smile if you won the lottery. Sometimes these traits are thought of as linked to gender—in general, men are expected to be more unemotional and rational, not letting others know how they feel, while women might feel more comfortable expressing their emotions. But there are expressive men and more reserved women.

Other people probably react to you differently based on how much emotion you express, also. How you communicate your

AILEEN IS FULL OF PERSONALITY

Aileen is 18. She grew up in a "wealthy, upper-class, Jewish family" with parents who worked in education and gave her and her three older siblings a lot of freedom to do what they wanted when they were growing up. Aileen considers herself to have been "trouble" as a younger teen, but she says that now you'd never know she was like that because she is doing very well in school and works on the side to earn extra money to help her afford college. When asked to answer questions about her identity, she focused most strongly on her personality and emphasized how she is with other people.

Q: How would you describe yourself?
Aileen: Extremely outgoing, energetic, confident, impulsive. I like to try new things and have met most of my best friends by flat-out approaching them out of nowhere and striking up a conversation. I'm very consistent, in that I never act like someone I am not to score points. I can also be extremely pragmatic (which is often misconstrued as cynicism), aloof, stubborn, and unyielding. I'm very bossy. I'm very "hyper," uninhibited, and energetic around friends. Some people equate this behavior with immaturity or naiveté, but really, I just know how to have a good time. Sorry if I scare you off.

Q: How do you think others see you?
Aileen: My friends whom I've known forever see me as a happy, secure person. I know I can be selfish and narcissistic sometimes, and I'm sure others see that too. I'm also viewed as very driven, ambitious, and flighty. I've switched schools three times in the last two years.

HEY, BABY—WHAT'S YOUR SIGN?

Some people believe that when they were born has a large influence on their personality and life experiences. The science (some say pseudoscience) of astrology states that by studying the alignment of the planets and stars at the exact time a person was born can help explain and determine one's basic life story, personality characteristics, strengths, and weaknesses. The individual "map" of a person's astrological configuration is called a horoscope.

In Western cultures, astrology involves twelve different signs under which one can fall, depending on one's birthdate. Here are the twelve signs and a basic personality description associated with each. Does your personality match your sign?

- Aries (March 21–April 19)—A born leader, assertive, and impulsive.
- Taurus (April 20–May 20)—Strong willed, dependable, but stubborn.
- Gemini (May 21–June 21)—Talkative, flexible, but manipulative.
- Cancer (June 22–July 22)—A homebody, nurturing, and traditional.
- Leo (July 23–August 22)—Proud, optimistic, but overbearing.
- Virgo (August 23–September 22)—Studious, critical, yet thorough.
- Libra (September 23–October 22)—Sociable, fair, but sometimes wishy-washy.
- Scorpio (October 23–November 21)—Passionate, motivated, but vengeful.
- Sagittarius (November 22–December 21)—An adventurer, idealistic, but pushy.
- Capricorn (December 22–January 19)—Responsible, materialistic, and serious.
- Aquarius (January 20–February 18)—Independent, progressive, and intellectual.
- Pisces (February 19–March 20)—Artistic, dreamy, but impractical.

After reading these, you may say to yourself: "Wow, my sign totally describes me perfectly," or "What the heck?!? I am nothing like that." Astrology is not for everyone, and the fact is, you are a lot more complex than a horoscope description. However, it's sometimes fun to see how well—or how poorly—you fit into your astrological description.

feelings may become an issue in romantic relationships or in your family. The people you have relationships with may need to learn how to interpret the way you act in order to understand what you are feeling.

How about your philosophy of the world? Would you describe yourself as an optimist or a pessimist? Do you think that the world and other people are fundamentally good and things happen for the best, or are you skeptical and expect that things will tend to go bad? What you expect things to be like definitely affects the way you act, and probably the way others react to you as well. You might be a worrier, or you might be more calm and satisfied. This probably will lead you to either be constantly thinking ahead and trying to control things so that they go well or to just sit back and let things happen the way they would naturally.

Another important personality trait is how well you get along with other people. Some people are courteous, kind, and easy to interact with—whether or not they are shy or outgoing. They're just easier to be around. Other people are more aggressive, suspicious of others, or less likely to notice the effect of their behaviors on others. Which are you? How other people treat you is often a result of the way you treat them.

Think about what your room at home looks like, or your handwriting. Are you a neat freak or a slob or something in between? Your level of conscientiousness—how careful or careless you are—is an important personality trait. Being an organized person can have real benefits—you don't lose things, you usually hand in assignments on time, things are clean when you need them to be. But organization has its drawbacks too; it can get tiring to try to keep your environment from descending into mess and chaos, and you may get frustrated by other people who aren't quite as careful as you are. The same goes for being a more carefree person—you might be able to avoid stressing out over small things, but you can tend to ignore details that need to be taken care of. It goes both ways.

How about the way you deal with difference or change? Some people like things to be done the same way every time— holiday dinners always need to have the same food, for example—and prefer things that are familiar. Other folks like trying new things and would rather find different or unusual ways to go about life. Your openness to change and difference, your sense of curiosity—that's a pretty important trait. It can have a strong effect on what you choose to do or try in the future and even the kind of lifestyle you want.

It goes without saying that your personality is an important part of who you are. So spending time thinking about what sort of personality you have—and reveal to others—can really help you understand yourself.

DEPRESSION

Everyone gets the blues. At some time or another, we all have bad days or have things happen to us that bring us down and make us feel low, sad, or even hopeless. This is so normal that it's practically universal. Some people even think that having a hard time in life now and then is necessary in order to enjoy and appreciate the better parts of life. Researchers used to think that "storm and stress" was a natural part of adolescence—that it was inevitable that teens would go through periods of being upset or angry or difficult. Teachers and parents got taught about this so that they could recognize and handle the "typical" teenager. But more recently, research has demonstrated that turmoil is *not* normal for teenagers. Sure, you'll have hard days and occasionally feel not so great about a certain event, yourself, or the world as a whole. But the level this rises to for the average teen is pretty minimal; so much for the idea of "storm and stress." In fact, the times you feel low usually aren't that different from what adults or younger children deal with, and they usually don't qualify you as having a mental disorder or illness of any kind.

But some teens can still find themselves getting so down that it feels much bigger than just a bad day. Or even a string of bad days. It's like a hole you can't climb out of—feeling awful and not knowing how to make it better. If you can think of ways that might help, you might not have the motivation or energy to do those things. You just feel empty, tired, and worthless. While you might occasionally feel sad, this is different.

Depression is different from sadness—it can be more intense, more frequent, and last a lot longer. Depression also takes many different forms. The symptoms of depression cover a lot of ground: irritability, losing or gaining weight, having trouble sleeping, crying frequently, feeling worthless, losing interest in things that were previously fun or pleasurable, having feelings of guilt, or fatigue. At times, depression can be obvious; you might feel like nothing is fun, not want to do anything, be really uncomfortable around people, tearful at the drop of a hat, and this can go on for a while. Sometimes, however, you don't even realize you're depressed until you notice it affecting people or things around you. You might pick more fights with your parents, talk less to your friends, stop doing activities that you like, have stomachaches every day, or sleep all the time. Realizing that those are signs of depression is kind of tricky. If you experience symptoms like these for more than two weeks continuously, you should consider talking to a professional to find out if you are depressed.

Unfortunately, people around you might not notice that you are struggling or feeling depressed, because sometimes parents and teachers expect teens to be moody or have trouble expressing their feelings. They might write off your feelings as something that is normal for this stage of life. But as we mentioned above, there is a limit to what is normal as far as feeling bad—and even though others may not completely understand the intensity of what you are feeling, it is not okay to suffer for a long period of time.

But what is even more difficult than recognizing that you might be depressed is asking for help when you are. It's easy to feel like you're some kind of failure when depression is bothering you—the illness itself can make you feel that you are not trying hard enough to be happy, or if you only put yourself to it, you could "snap out of it" and be happier or more productive. If you are struggling with a lack of motivation, it can be nearly impossible to imagine taking the steps to try to help yourself.

Being depressed is not a weakness; it's an illness. People who are usually cheerful, optimistic, or happy can have an especially difficult time when they wrestle with depression. When you are the person who regularly brings energy and joy to other people, it is really hard to admit when you don't feel that way anymore. When you are really depressed, though, usually just waiting for it to go away isn't enough. There are people who can help you. Psychologists, counselors, and other mental health providers can help you talk about how you feel and make some changes that may improve your mood and general outlook on the world. There are good treatments for depression (both medication and psychotherapy) and, with help, you *can* feel better about yourself and the world.

One of the reasons talking about depression is important is that people who are very depressed sometimes consider suicide. When the world is very dark and lonely and seems impossible to deal with, teens might think that the only way to cope is to give up—to kill themselves. They may feel that nothing matters, that things will never get better, or that they are nothing but a problem for others. These feelings are extreme and they are not normal. However, suicide is not a solution; it's just a new problem for other people to deal with. The solution to feeling hopeless, alone, or lost is to ask other people for help. That starts you on the path toward being your old self again.

HOW TO HELP A FRIEND WHO YOU THINK IS SUICIDAL

If you are concerned about a friend who you believe is suicidal, here are some things you can do to help your friend and yourself:

1. **Offer help and listen**—be there for someone who needs to talk about what hurts. It might be tempting to point out all the reasons your friend has to live, but it is usually more helpful to listen, try to understand, and reassure your friend that there is help available and they can feel better.
2. **Listen to your instincts**—if you think a situation is serious and you are really worried that a friend might hurt himself or herself, let someone know (like a parent or teacher)—it is better to break a confidence and save someone's life than keep the secret that someone is in danger.
3. **Take signs seriously**—pay attention when someone talks about suicide. Talk directly about it. Don't assume that it's just a phase or a whim—it could be serious.
4. **Get professional help**—you don't have to deal with concerns about a friend on your own. Talk to a teacher or counselor or religious leader to help you handle your own feelings as well as help your friend get the support he or she needs.

Why are we talking about depression in a book on image and identity? Some people get depressed for a little while and then manage to get over it. However, sometimes people fight depression for their entire lives. Just like coping with any other chronic illness, if you are someone who suffers from depression, you may end up considering that an important part of who you are. People who are prone to depression may have to pay close attention to how they feel over time, to figure out if they are sliding into another episode of depression. If you take medication to deal with your depression, you will have to be sure to follow the prescription accordingly—which could mean keeping a more regular schedule so that you do not miss doses, and not consuming alcohol. Some people think that the artistic temperament goes hand in hand with mental problems like depression, and that the often cynical viewpoint and intense emotions experienced by depressed people can make really good art and music. So depression, for these people, is an illness but also a viewpoint of sorts that colors how one sees the world. The danger for anyone who has depressive tendencies is when your moods significantly interfere with your

> **SAD, BUT TRUE**
> About 9 percent of teens attempt suicide every year.[2]

living the best possible life that you can have. Remember, you don't have to be miserable—you can choose to feel better by getting help.

TAKING CARE OF YOURSELF

How you choose to lead your life—your personal lifestyle—is an important part of who you are as well. We make choices all the time about how to spend our time. And sometimes how we take care of ourselves gets ignored. When we say "take care of yourself," we are not talking about how to avoid getting in trouble or having problems; we're talking about how to keep yourself up and running at your best. This sounds kind of basic, but you'd be surprised how many people ignore these sorts of ideas. We think of self-care as being built on six pillars that help any person be as healthy and happy as possible. These are:

1. Diet and nutrition.
2. Exercise and physical activity.
3. Sleep.
4. Stress management.
5. Social connections.
6. Fun and joy.

Although we have talked about some of these earlier in the book, let's think about these one at a time. First, you have heard about the food groups and a balanced diet and all that since elementary school. But what you eat can seriously impact how you feel and your long-term health. Even as a teenager, it's important to think about what's good for you. Eating food that regularly meets all your nutritional needs is important for keeping your body healthy. Keeping your body healthy helps contribute to having positive mental health as well. But remember that sometimes eating things that you like, even if they aren't all that good for you, is okay now and then. So French fries aren't the most nutritious items in the world, but if you absolutely love them, then once in a while, why not give in? If you're not eating them every day, and if your diet includes other healthy things, then you'll probably be fine. Moderation is the key—you don't have to give up everything that is bad for you; instead, use balance and restraint.

Second, exercise is very important (as mentioned in chapter 4) and the benefits are huge. You can participate in sports or in exercise classes with other people, which can improve your social life. You might lose or maintain a healthy weight or stay in shape, which is good for your health. Regular exercise helps keep many health problems away or under control. If you have trouble sleeping (either too much or too little), exercise is a good thing to try. Also, did you know that exercise is the best natural antidepressant there is? So by exercising you might even improve your mood, since sometimes things that get us out and moving are also incredibly fun: bike riding, hiking, walking around with friends, playing sports, and so on.

We often think that if we are going to start exercising, we have to do it really seriously—like go to aerobics classes every

day or run eight miles a day. But smaller changes are definitely enough. Try to walk more. Take the stairs. Start an active hobby. Experts emphasize the three most important aspects of physical fitness: strength, endurance, and flexibility. Think about how your physical activities help you stay in shape with regard to these three areas.

Then there's sleep. Teenagers are notorious for their sleep patterns. You might have to get up early for school or activities, then sleep in big time on weekends to compensate for how tired you got during the week. Some teens stay up late at night to do homework or talk with friends on the Internet until the wee hours. Or sometimes teens fall asleep at less than optimal times; you might find it difficult to stay awake in third-period algebra, for example. The National Sleep Foundation reports that 60 percent of people under 18 say that they are tired during the day, and some of them actually fall asleep in school.[3]

The average teen needs about nine hours of sleep every night.[4] But most teenagers don't get that much and end up being somewhat sleep deprived—they simply go to bed too late

---

TEEN SLEEP TIPS[5]

1. **Get enough sleep.** Learn how much sleep you need and try to make sure you get it.
2. **Keep a consistent sleep schedule**—try to go to bed and get up at the same time every day.
3. **Don't take naps.** Avoiding naps will help you be sleepy when it's time for bed.
4. **If you can't fall asleep within twenty minutes of going to bed, get up and do something boring until you're sleepy,** then try again.
5. **Take a hot bath about ninety minutes before bedtime.**
6. **Watch your caffeine intake,** and avoid caffeine after lunchtime.
7. **Relax before going to bed**—get yourself ready to shut down and go to sleep.
8. **Use your bed only for sleeping**—don't watch TV or read too much there. Think of your bed as the place where you are asleep, not awake.

and get up too early. Being sleep deprived has some serious consequences; it can make you tired, irritable, angry, depressed, or distracted. You might have difficulty concentrating or paying attention because you are so out of it from lack of sleep. Consequently, you might not do well in school or during a sporting event. So getting enough sleep is important. If you ever fully catch up on your sleep, you'll be surprised at how good you feel. In order to take good care of yourself, you need to make getting a good night's sleep on a regular basis a priority.

An often neglected area of teen life is *stress*. What is stress? Well, it's pretty much anything that takes your energy, attention, or time. Usually we think of stressful things as bad, such as studying for exams, moving away from your friends, being in a fight with a parent, or having an unpleasant boss. But sometimes good things can be stressful. The opening night for your show, getting ready for a big swim meet, the first day of a new job—all these things are events to look forward to, but they can still be pretty stressful. Managing all your different roles as student, family member, and friend can be stressful. These pressures add up, and we need to learn how to manage that.

Stress management takes a lot of different forms. Some people take up relaxing hobbies, like yoga or meditation. Some people cut back on the number of things that they are trying to do. Some people adjust the way they think about their priorities so they don't take things so seriously. Stress management can be thought of as having three parts. First, you have to manage the amount of stress that you experience in your life. You need to figure out how much pressure you can take personally. You may need to give up some activities or get help from others to manage some responsibilities. Second, you need to develop good skills for dealing with stress when you are faced with it. Some people just crack under pressure, while others seem to handle it gracefully. Learning how to cope with difficult or stressful situations is key to managing stress well. Third, you have to make time in your life to relieve stress—by getting away from stressful situations, relieving stress through activities, or counteracting stress by relaxing.

We could write a whole book on stress management, but this introduction will hopefully get you started thinking about your own strategies. You will have to find what works for you. Regardless of what you end up finding for yourself, it is important to remember that once in a while you have to slow down, listen to yourself, and reduce your stress level rather than add to it.

One way that people often find helps them relieve stress is talking about it with other people. This is only one example of the ways that having social connections helps keep you a healthy person. Human beings are meant to be connected to one another. We have relationships with family, friends, colleagues, co-workers—all sorts of different people. And we get a lot out of these relationships. The quality of your social connections is strongly related to how you feel about yourself. Think about what your relationships with others provide for you: entertainment, support, encouragement, information, approval, love, belonging. These things are incredibly important. So having and maintaining relationships with other people is another part of taking good care of yourself.

Finally, having fun and experiencing joy are essential parts of taking care of yourself. We spend a lot of time thinking about how to fix things that have gone wrong rather than find ways to keep them going right in the first place. It is all too easy to forget to enjoy yourself. Yes, this is sort of the "stop and smell the roses" idea, but more than that, it's a reminder that without pleasure, why do we keep going day to day? Make sure that you have things in your life that make you happy: friends who make you laugh, chocolate ice cream, sexy-looking shoes, a victory for your favorite team, a really cool song, TV shows that make you think—whatever works for you. Choosing to have a life that includes fun is good for you. And deciding that you deserve to have happiness in your life can be a big part of your identity as well.

SELF-ESTEEM—BELIEVING IN YOUR IDENTITY

Self-esteem has become a bit of a buzzword in the mental health field, as if all one needs to truly be happy is to have a little self-esteem—which, sadly, isn't available at your local mini-mart. So what exactly *is* self-esteem? Is it really the solution to all our problems?

Self-esteem is how much you like, accept, and respect yourself overall as a person. It's how you feel about yourself—the value you place on who you are. And self-esteem is definitely a part of your identity. Ideally, we would love it if every person who reads this book goes out and explores different things that could be important to them, consciously commits to various parts of themselves and things they find interesting and enjoy, and is proud of who they are. It would be really cool if you all liked yourself a lot.

But we know it's not that easy. When you aren't really sure who you are or what the impact is of being a particular kind of person, it can be hard to genuinely feel good about yourself. You might struggle with your feelings about how you look, the way you talk, the clothes you wear, who your family is, what you're good at, the things you like to do—everything, really. You are probably always aware that the world reacts to you. If you do certain things, people often notice and behave certain ways toward you as a result. And that, in turn, can affect the way you feel about yourself.

There seem to be three different components to self-esteem. The first is your sense of control—how much you feel that you can affect your own life. Feeling that you are in charge and responsible for your own experiences contributes to feeling good about yourself—you have a say in things, and life is more than just a series of accidents. The second part is a sense of belonging and acceptance. It always feels good to be connected to other people, to be approved of and included. This sense of acceptance and belonging can come from your family, your friends, and your community. And feeling you are appreciated definitely influences how you feel about yourself. The third piece of the self-esteem puzzle is your belief that you are capable and competent. When you believe that you have skills and are good at things, you are

Self-esteem is:

1. **Feeling in control of things.**
2. **Feeling accepted by others.**
3. **Feeling capable.**

more likely to try different things, seek out successful experiences, and be confident in taking on new tasks.[6]

Research has shown, time after time, that positive self-esteem is linked to things like achievement in school, lower levels of aggression and delinquency, lower teen pregnancy rates, more healthy attitudes toward drugs and alcohol, better moral decision making, and even better physical health.[7] So feeling good about who you are, as simple as it may seem, is related to many other things that are good for you and that you probably want for yourself.

However, the most important findings about self-esteem go deeper than just saying that high self-esteem is a good thing. Researchers have found that where your self-esteem comes from is almost as important as how positive it is. Teens who based their self-esteem on external sources such as the opinions of other people or one's appearance were more likely to have low self-esteem, while teens who emphasized more internal factors such as being a moral person or having family support tended to have more positive self-esteem.[8] It appears that being too concerned with having a "good image" can damage your sense of self-worth, which underlies your self-esteem. In other words, healthy self-esteem comes from your own feelings about yourself, not the opinions of others. And it is always important to keep in mind that feeling good about who you are is different from being arrogant, self-centered, or stuck up. You can be pleased about who you are without advertising it constantly or rubbing it in other people's faces.

So how can you improve your self-esteem? Think of good self-esteem as having two main parts. The first is a generally positive but realistic evaluation of yourself. You see yourself pretty clearly and feel like you know something about who you truly are, and you feel good about that. Basically, it's all about being honest with yourself but also liking who you are. The second part is a generally positive sense that you can handle life's problems.[9]

Your self-esteem comes from lots of things, such as what others tell you about yourself, whether you see people like yourself being accepted in the world, and your sense of success or accomplishment. So to feel good about who you are, try taking some of these steps:

1. Stop listening to people who tell you that you are worthless or bad. Instead, listen to people who give you positive feedback and help you see the valuable parts of yourself.

2. Focus on your strengths and abilities rather than things you feel are weaknesses. You are a complex person, and what you *can* do should be a bigger part of how you think about yourself than the things you struggle with.

3. Be realistic in your evaluation of yourself by holding yourself to achievable standards and goals; you may want to play like a star athlete or look like some celebrity, but it might be better to focus on making the team or being in the best shape you can. There are some things about yourself that you can't change. Set goals for yourself that you can achieve. You will feel better if your expectations for yourself are reasonable.

4. Look for role models whom you resemble or who inspire you; decide what you can learn from them and the things that you share with them. If people who are a lot like you are loved and admired, you can be too.

5. Take care of yourself—the better you feel physically and mentally, the more you will feel like there is something about yourself to like.

6. Have fun. The more you enjoy yourself, the easier it is to feel good about who you are.

YOUR TURN

Here are some questions for you to think about:

1. How would you describe your personality?
2. How would other people describe you?
3. What do you like about yourself?
4. What makes you feel good about yourself and who you are?
5. How do you deal with feeling bad or depressed?
6. How would you help a friend who was depressed?

7. **How do you take care of yourself? Physically? Mentally?**

8. **How do you manage stress?**

NOTES

1. Definition from www.dictionary.com.

2. Centers for Disease Control and Prevention, "Youth Risk Behavior Surveillance—United States, 1999," *MMWR* 49, no. SS-5 (2000): 10.

3. National Sleep Foundation, "Omnibus Sleep in America Poll" (1999), accessed May 23, 2004, at www.sleepfoundation.org/ publications/1999poll.cfm.

4. National Sleep Foundation, "Seven Sleep-Smart Tips for Teens," accessed May 23, 2004, at www.sleepfoundation.org/ PressArchives/seven.cfm.

5. National Sleep Foundation, "Seven Sleep-Smart Tips for Teens."

6. J. V. Schindler, "Creating a Psychology of Success in the Classroom: Enhancing Academic Achievement by Systematically Promoting Student Self-esteem," accessed February 14, 2004, at www.calstatela.edu/faculty/jshindl/cm/Self-Esteempercent20Article percent2011.htm.

7. R. W. Reasoner, *Self-esteem and Youth: What Research Has to Say about It* (e-book, 2004), accessed February 14, 2004, at www.self-esteem-international.org/content/8-orderbook.htm.

8. J. Crocker, "The Costs of Seeking Self-esteem," *Journal of Social Issues* 58, no. 3 (2002): 597–615.

9. C. E. Tucker-Ladd, "Methods for Changing Our Thoughts, Attitudes, Self-concept, Motivation, Values, and Expectations," in *Psychological Self-help* (chap. 14, e-book, 2002), accessed March 14, 2004, at www.mentalhelp.net/psyhelp/chap14.

Conclusion: Your Image, Yourself

By now, you have read all about how just about everything around you influences not only your sense of who you are but also how others see you. For our whole lives, from the moment we are born, we are surrounded by people and things that shape who we are. We continue to change over our lifetime as well, so you get to look forward to discovering new things about yourself as you continue to grow older. Ideally, in reading this book, you have learned to recognize how each part of yourself and your experiences can be important parts of who you are.

It's a pretty overwhelming thought, but hopefully you have come away with the idea that the choices you make and the way you present yourself to others are things that you can control. In other words, you have the ability to become the person that you want to become. It is easy to fall into the trap of thinking that who you really are is determined by things that you can't control like your gender, ethnicity, or economic status. But after reading this book, we hope that you realize that despite the fact that you can't change some things about you, you actually have quite a bit of control over deciding who you are going to be. This is because although there are some things about you that you can't really change, you can change how you react to those parts of you, and you can decide how much you want to make any characteristic a main part of yourself. You also get to determine the meaning of certain characteristics—you get to decide what it means to be female, or short, or outgoing, or interested in snowboarding. All of that is up to you.

And although you may sometimes face obstacles such as prejudice, media images, and biases when it comes to how others see you, there are many things you can do to show the world the type of person you are. Some people are quiet about their identity—you never really know what they like or think or how they spend their time. And they might like it that way. But others are more out there and demonstrate who they are and what they are about all the time. Then there are still others who show off some parts of their identity while hiding other parts, encouraging others to see them a certain way. You can decide to do any of these things when you choose what parts of you to show. In other words, you get to decide not only who it is you are going to be, but how you are going to show the world just who you are.

However, there is a reality that we all have to deal with. Although it is great to think that we can present any image of

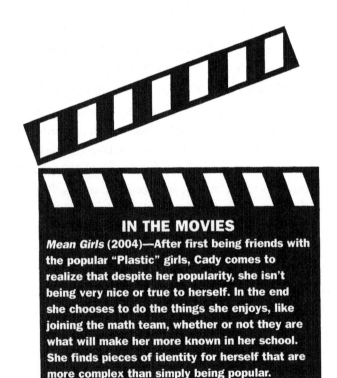

IN THE MOVIES

Mean Girls (2004)—After first being friends with the popular "Plastic" girls, Cady comes to realize that despite her popularity, she isn't being very nice or true to herself. In the end she chooses to do the things she enjoys, like joining the math team, whether or not they are what will make her more known in her school. She finds pieces of identity for herself that are more complex than simply being popular.

ourselves that we want, there are some limitations. While we believe that you have a lot of control over who you are and who you are becoming, you sometimes don't have much control over how other people react to you. You might be very sensitive to this and allow it to influence some of the choices you make. For example, even though the thought of joining the chess club is very exciting to you, you might not want to because it isn't the cool thing to do. It can be really difficult to feel like you're different from others.

But again there is a good side to all of this. You can also choose how to react to the way others treat you. You can let their opinions affect you and act differently as a result, or you can stand up for who you are and allow yourself to be different from others. People are often afraid of things that they don't understand, and perhaps they don't understand something about you. You may find that sometimes your decisions make

you temporarily lonely, disliked, or unappreciated. However, you have the power to be patient with people who don't relate to who you are yet, and you can have the strength to decide that their opinions don't matter. You can even help others learn how to be more accepting of you and others like you (because there are others out there who have similar interests and experiences, no matter how lonely you feel at times). Even though it can be hard sometimes, in the end you will feel better about yourself and likely be admired by others when you stay true to yourself.

The importance of expressing your genuine self—in the way you dress, how you act in relationships, or in standing up for what you want—cannot be overestimated. When you show your true self to the world, you learn that you *can* be accepted for who you really are, and you don't have to "pretend" just to get others to like you. Being real to yourself and everyone around you takes a lot of courage, and that can be hard to come by. But faking it or going along with the crowd is a dangerous game to play. That's because even if you are accepted by certain people while pretending to be someone you aren't, you will worry about exposing the parts of yourself that you are hiding. In other words, you will think to yourself, "If they really knew me, they wouldn't like me." And thinking that way isn't good for you.

But it's important to remember that no matter how much you know about yourself, or how comfortable you may be in your identity, there are things that are outside of your control that can influence you. Traumatic experiences such as death, divorce, abuse, violence, and natural disasters can become a part of your life. When these things happen, you are not to blame for them, and your actions could not have stopped them from happening. But with time and help from family, friends, and possibly counseling, these experiences can shape you in a way that makes you a stronger and more insightful person. The things that we learn from difficult experiences often become key pieces in our identity and help us change for the better, in ways we hadn't expected. Other, less painful (but just as meaningful) experiences may also have a profound and positive effect on you. Moving, traveling and experiencing different cultures, and going on retreats can also influence you by exposing you to new places and faces that many others do not get a chance to witness. In these ways, you can learn about who you are and grow as a person by interacting with others who are different from you.

In fact, every day something may happen that can change your perception of who you are—to yourself or to others. We are constantly changing and growing ever so slightly, adding to ourselves to create a complex and unique individual. The idea of a unified, true, finished product of self is somewhat of a myth—just when you think you know who you are, you'll probably change or learn something new. These changes don't have to be major ones, but even if you have a new experience, or meet a new person, you become just a little bit different than you were before. It's a deep thought, but sort of neat, if you think about it.

Ultimately, when we say "just be yourself," we don't mean that there is some correct concept of who you are that you must discover and display to the world. Your identity is made up of many parts, some of which you like, and some of which you wish you could change. What we encourage you to do is to accept all parts of yourself—good, bad, ambiguous—and learn about how they each help make up who you are. That way, you can explore the different parts of yourself, and believe that whatever you choose to be, you are still a whole, admirable, and decent person. If you are able to accept yourself even if there are parts you don't like, you will have an easier time working on those things that you can change to make you into a better person.

So, be true, sincere, and have the courage to be and to change. Learn who you are and who you may become.

Index

About the Authors

Kris Gowen, PhD, EdM, holds a doctorate in adolescent velopment from Stanford University. Gowen has facilitated line message boards and advice columns where teens ask estions about sex and relationships and has helped develop veral health curricula for high school students. She currently aches in the Department of Community Health at Portland tate University.

Molly C. McKenna, PhD, is a psychologist in private practice in Portland, Oregon, specializing in assessment and treatment of adults and adolescents. She received her doctorate in counseling psychology from the University of Illinois at Urbana–Champaign. McKenna has authored articles on health psychology and vocational assessment and has served as a consulting expert on stress management, wellness, and general mental health for other writers.

CPSIA information can be obtained at www.ICGtesting.com
Printed in the USA
BVOW09*0956081215

429571BV00013B/23/P